THE BOYS' BOOK OF

EBURY
PRESS

For Ellie and Alice. Remember girls: 'To the moon and back.'

I would like to thank everyone at Hornby and all those associated with Airfix and Humbrol who helped me while I was working on this book. I would particularly like to thank Frank Martin, Trevor Snowden, Darrell Burge, Carl Hart, Hedda Falk, Dale Luckhurst, Martyn Weaver, Josep Pastor, Paul Chandler, Chris Morgan, Roy Cross, Jeremy Brook, Peter Allen, Carol Allen, Ralph Ehrmann, Stanley Lerner, Ken Askwith, Jo May-Prussak and Alison Gale. I would also like to thank the designer of the book, Tony Lyons.

10 9 8 7 6 5 4 3

Published in 2009 by Ebury Press, an imprint of Ebury Publishing

A Random House Group Company

Text © Arthur Ward 2009

Photographs © Arthur Ward 2009, except photographs on p11, p12, p15, p17 © Jo May-Prussak 2009

Arthur Ward has asserted his right to be identified as the author of this Work in accordance with the Copyright, Designs and Patents Act 1988

The Random House Group Limited Reg. No. 954009

Addresses for companies within the Random House Group can be found at www.randomhouse.co.uk

A CIP catalogue record for this book is available from the British Library

The Random House Group Limited supports The Forest Stewardship Council® (FSC®), the leading international forest certification organisation. Our books carrying the FSC label are printed on FSC® certified paper. FSC is the only forest certification scheme endorsed by the leading environmental organisations, including Greenpeace. Our paper procurement policy can be found at www.randomhouse.co.uk/environment

MIX
Paper from responsible sources
FSC® C008047

To buy books by your favourite authors and register for offers visit www.randomhouse.co.uk

Printed and bound in China by C & C Offset Printing Co., Ltd

ISBN 978-0-09-192898-8

THE BOYS' BOOK OF

WHO SAYS YOU EVER HAVE TO GROW UP?

ARTHUR WARD

EBURY
PRESS

The Airfix collection
photographed for the company's
catalogue in April 1976

CONTENTS

INTRODUCTION

Airfix wasn't the first manufacturer of plastic construction kits. Established four years earlier to make flying model aircraft, by 1936 British company FROG had introduced a range of constant scale replicas, non-flying aircraft appropriately branded Penguin, a flightless bird. The same year, North American Gorden Varney began producing HO scale locomotive kits.

However, neither manufacturer employed the modern plastic polystyrene – FROG Penguins were made of cellulose acetate, and Varney replicas were made from a plastic called Tenite.

Immediately following the Second World War, Revell and Monogram, two other US companies, did produce injection-moulded polystyrene construction kits. These sold very well and a large number made their way into British shops to be eagerly purchased.

Airfix was founded in 1939 and by the mid-1940s was manufacturing a wide range of injection-moulded items. Indeed, Airfix was the largest manufacturer of injection-moulded plastic combs in Britain.

Founder Nicholas Kove fed his hungry moulding machines with polystyrene from a wide variety of sources. He even stripped obsolete cabling of its plastic sheathing on the occasions when supplies of raw polystyrene granules dried up amid the austere conditions of a post-war Britain, still subject to rationing.

Betta Builder Modern
Truck Teeny Truck (1969)

Airfix Building Set No. 1 Starter Set

In 1949 Airfix released a scale model of the then brand new Ferguson Model TE20 tractor. Although this was a ready-assembled replica and intended as a sales promotion piece to be used by Ferguson reps, it is considered Airfix's first model. It was eventually released as a kit of parts, but not until the early 1950s following the commercial success of Airfix's first real construction kit in 1952, a tiny replica of Francis Drake's flagship *Golden Hind*.

Determined to grab a significant slice of the domestic market for model kits, which up until then was dominated by US imports, Kove quickly increased the size and variety of his kit range, and in no time at all Airfix was the premier British manufacturer of such products.

The 1960s and 1970s were the high points of worldwide kit production, and Airfix enjoyed an enormous share of this market, towering over its domestic competitors and also selling significant volumes for export. Each year Airfix sold some 350,000 Spitfires, about 80,000 Hurricanes and almost as many Lancaster bombers.

Since its peak Airfix has had its ups and downs, going bust in 1981 and again in 2006. Fortunately, the famous brand is currently stabled with other iconic names, such as Scalextric and Corgi, at its new home, Hornby plc. I'm delighted to say that Airfix appears to be riding high once more and at the time of writing plans to release its largest ever kit, a gigantic 1/24th scale Superkit of the DH Mosquito, the laminated timber 'wooden wonder' of wartime RAF fame!

Why is Airfix important to me?

Well, in common with lots of other baby-boomers I suspect, I enjoy the comfort and warm familiarity of things remembered with fondness from my youth.

I also get a real kick out of the enormous range of simply fantastic artwork decorating kit boxes, and I enjoy seeing how successive artworks chart changes in design and fashion across half a century. Alterations in the look of cars, aircraft and ships not only reflect developments in technology, their styles are sometimes a reflection of the surrounding zeitgeist – the Airfix Bond Bug and VW Beach Buggy could have only been spawned in the late 1960s.

Without, I hope, sounding too pretentious, I also believe Airfix is important because it is one of Britain's all too few manufacturers. It makes things. Many of those employed at Airfix are directly linked to a disappearing engineering tradition in which careers started with apprenticeships and progressed through a variety of highly skilled phases until multi-skilled professionals were trained and ready to join industry.

Finally, I believe construction kits are important because they encourage manual dexterity – you have to use your fingers carefully to prepare, assemble and paint myriad tiny components. This must be done slowly in order to achieve a properly finished scale replica of a full-sized object. Surely, encouraging kids to take their time to follow instructions and stick lots of different pieces together in a measured, unhurried way is a good thing in a world full of high-speed action, extreme activities and instant gratification? Don't get me wrong – computer games and MP3 downloads are great – but isn't there also a place for file, tweezers, polystyrene cement and enamel paints?

Arthur Ward Sussex, October 2008

Left: Although the details are somewhat indistinct, Bernard Prussak's 1942 ID card, classifying his occupation as electrician, is the earliest surviving 'Airfix document' I've ever seen

Below: Smell that burning rubber! Vintage Airfix slot racing catalogue from the 1960s

Top: By the 1950s FROG was the only serious British competitor to Airfix

Above: Overseas there was some well established competition. Revell was probably the biggest kit company stateside.

Below: Chicago's Monogram started out in the 1940s by combining Balsa wood and plastic components. Monogram, Revell and another US company, Aurora, conspired to capture the British market.

CHAPTER 1

ASSEMBLING AIRFIX

🛩 **Anyone embarking on** a career in corporate design or brand management will soon encounter the do's and don'ts of trademark protection.

'Trademark owners should never use their brand name as a verb or noun, implying the word is generic,' students are told. Such misuse apparently encourages the trademark to 'become synonymous with a particular type of product or service, to the extent that it often replaces the formal term for the product or service in colloquial usage.' So, don't dilute brand equity! Which is why professional brand managers are employed to ensure that such alleged sloppiness never happens.

Nevertheless, I'm sure that Nicholas Kove, the founder of Airfix, a brand name that has certainly become everyday shorthand for 'plastic construction kit', would be quite chuffed. He chose the name because it would naturally appear at the beginning of trade directories. The fact that it evolved into a byword for an entire toy genre would have certainly appealed to his entrepreneurial spirit.

Above: A rather benign-looking Nicholas Kove relaxing in his armchair

Top: Nicholas Kove and family (1940s)

Above: This clockwork chick is another novelty toy from Airfix's earliest years when it was based at 24–26 Hampstead Road, London NW1

Kove did not live long enough to see the Airfix name so fully assimilated into modern English usage, but even by 1958, when he died, his creation was well on its way to massive commercial success.

I also think the irony of the fact that Airfix is at the head of references listing international brand names that have also evolved into household terms would have delighted Mr Kove. His baby turns up in front of Aqua-Lung, BAND-AID, Bic, Coke, Formica, Hoover, Jeep, Lycra, Perspex, Sellotape, Tannoy, Velcro and Xerox. A pretty impressive epithet indeed.

So who was Nicholas Kove, and what drove him to establish such a famous firm?

Koves the Hungarian

Just like the famous war machines – the Spitfire and Messerschmitt fighter planes or the Sherman and Tiger tanks – with which Airfix models are most commonly associated, Nicholas Kove was tough and resilient. He had many faults and undoubtedly made lots of enemies, but the life he led before he even established Airfix clearly defined his later character and perhaps explains his irascibility and his stubbornness. His early life also encouraged a vigour that seems contrary to his more obstinate characteristics and at odds with his pugnacious appearance and stocky build.

Kove had tasted battle, held political office in a revolutionary government and, within a short space of time, gained intimate knowledge of Hungarian, Russian, North African, Spanish, Italian and German realpolitik and popular culture.

Born Miklos Klein, he uttered his first outburst – the encouraging cry of a healthy newborn – in the village of Anarcs in Carpathian Ruthenia, a rugged area of north-eastern Hungary bordering the Ukraine. Later, as a member of the well-integrated Jewish community, which made up around five per cent of Hungary's population, Miklos changed his surname from Klein to Koves (pronounced Kurvesh).

In August 1914, at the outbreak of the First World War, young Miklos Koves was serving as a junior cavalry officer in the army of Austro-Hungarian Emperor Franz Josef. Whilst the world's attention was focused on the Western Front, Russian forces launched two major offensives in the east, threatening Prussia in the north and Galicia in the south. Hungarian forces stood as a vital bulwark against Russian invasion.

Although they were trounced at the Battle of Tannenberg

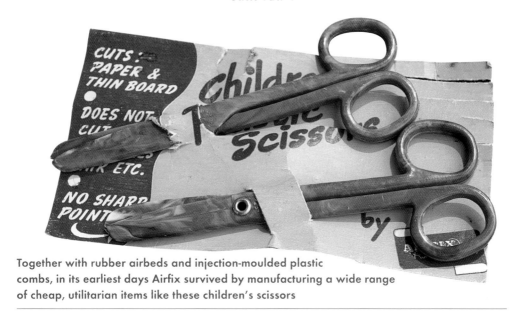

Together with rubber airbeds and injection-moulded plastic combs, in its earliest days Airfix survived by manufacturing a wide range of cheap, utilitarian items like these children's scissors

in September, Russian forces were enjoying some success against Austro-Hungarian forces further south. From November 1914 they besieged the powerful Hungarian fortress of Przemysl, finally capturing it in March 1915. The fall of this defensive position on the northern side of the Carpathian mountain range left the Hungarian plain open to inundation.

Allegedly, Koves was captured during the first cavalry charge made by his regiment, and it is likely that this occurred in this general area of the threatened Galician front. In May 1915, an Austro-Hungarian counter-attack succeeded in ousting Russian forces from this region and Przemysl was returned to the central powers.

Unfortunately, this reversal in Austro-Hungarian fortunes came too late for Koves, and he and his batman were shipped off to a desolate Siberian prisoner of war camp not far from the Korean border. As we shall see, this wasn't the only forced internment he would experience.

Fortune shone kindly on the resourceful and energetic Koves and, perhaps because he was a non-practising Jew, and certainly not orthodox, he enjoyed the help and support of some Catholic priests who helped him escape from imprisonment. Their assistance was almost certainly due to the fact that although of Jewish origins, Koves had been a student at Hungary's premier boys' school, which was administered by the Catholic Church (he was later to tell Ralph Ehrmann how difficult it was for him to actually gain entrance to this institution). With Soviet Russia repudiating any links with the almighty, the Catholic Church was even keener to support the well-being of citizens from the mainly Catholic Austro-Hungarian empire. Amazingly, Koves and his benefactors trekked from Siberia to Hungary on foot. The journey back to Carpathia took them four months.

At the war's end, with Hungary on the losing side, Koves's homeland was in turmoil. In October 1918, a month before the armistice, Hungary had dissolved its union with Austria and the ethnic divisions within its borders resulted in the creation of Czechoslovakia later in the same year.

Hungary was further dismembered at the Treaty of Trianon in 1920, when the Allies drew new borders for the country and carved off two-thirds of its territory, most of which was ceded to Czechoslovakia and Romania.

Politics Calls

At war's end Koves left the defeated Hungarian army, and with no job and no money the prospects facing him in this bankrupt country were to say the least bleak. This situation had been exacerbated by his father having patriotically invested the family's fortunes in Austro-Hungarian war bonds – they lost not just their savings but also ownership of a pretty impressive property.

As ever, fate seemed to favour Koves and, just in the nick of time, opportunity presented itself. An old school-friend of his had been awarded a position in the revolutionary government of Béla Kun, and via this connection Koves was appointed an assistant minister.

A journalist before the war, Béla Kun was also of Jewish origins. However, like Koves, he was a largely secular Jew and had also Magyarised his birth surname, previously Kohn. He had also been a prisoner of the Russians but here the similarities to Koves's epic experiences end. Rather than being exiled to the icy wastes of the east, Kun was held in captivity near Moscow and in 1917 enjoyed a ringside view of the Bolshevik revolution.

He had been enormously impressed by communism in action. Once back from the war Béla Kun managed to persuade the Russian Soviets to sponsor his political ambitions in Hungary and to help him establish a regime modelled on their experimental administration.

However, opposition to Kun's fledgeling government was intense, and in August 1919 it collapsed. He escaped to Austria, becoming an active supporter of the communists there and in Germany. As in Hungary, however, communism failed to build a firm foundation in either of these countries and Kun was encouraged to return to the Soviet Union. It was there that he died, ironically, executed on the orders of his hero Josef Stalin in 1939.

In 1920 Miklós Horthy was declared Hungary's head of state. A right-wing conservative, Horthy, who had been an admiral in the Austro-Hungarian navy during the First World War, was head of the counter-revolutionary National Army. Once he was in power the so-called White Terror ensued, leading to reprisals against all those sympathetic to the previous communist regime and especially towards Jews, long suspected of complicity with Béla Kun's endeavours.

The First Fix

Being Jewish and a part of Béla Kun's overthrown regime, albeit of relatively junior rank, Miklos Koves decided to emigrate. So, with his wife Clothilde and newborn baby daughter Margaret, in 1922 he moved from Budapest to Algiers.

Apparently always on the move, by 1934 Koves and his family were living in Barcelona. In Spain he at last entered the plastic business. This was a high-tech enterprise in the early 1930s, employing a series of raw materials based on cellulose, very difficult to use, but it was all there was until the advent of polystyrene transformed the industry and factory owners' profits.

It appears that the outbreak of the Spanish Civil War in August 1936 encouraged Koves to move his family once again, but this time in rather a hurry. Koves had likely become quite comfortable whilst in Barcelona.

He wasn't running from the fascist Franco but rather from the conflict that was beginning to overwhelm Spain. With communists and anarchists creating death and outrage all about, Barcelona was certainly not a safe enough place for a prosperous manufacturer and his family.

Koves next pops up in Milan – Mussolini's regime being based on a fairly stable centre-left government. Anyway, he felt secure enough in Italy to continue in the field of plastics production and it is the name of the new operation he began at this time that gives us the first hint of what was to come.

There is a difference of opinion about whether Koves patented Interfix, a process for stiffening shirt collars, whilst in Spain or later when he moved to Italy. Regardless, his grandson Jo May-Prussak tells me that this was probably his first big breakthrough. Jo says that his mother Margaret recalled the excitement surrounding the formulation of the Interfix collar treatment: 'During their time in Milan she said her father had his first invention called "Interfix", designed to give the soft collars on men's shirts a stiff appearance whilst retaining their softness,' he told me. Jo also said that his mother remembered 'big excitement' one day when her mother, Clothilde, ironed together two linen pieces of material each impregnated with a special liquid with the result that they stuck firmly together. 'This was the beginning of a world patent which Father sold to various countries,' she told her son. Interfix is an early example of Nicholas Kove's predilection for trademarks ending in 'ix'.

Ralph Ehrmann, who worked with Kove between 1950 and Kove's death in 1958, was an intimate confidant of his. Ehrmann is of the opinion that Kove most likely picked up the process on which Interfix was based during one of his regular trawls of lapsed patents and possibly even helped improve the process for this invention whilst running a factory in Spain.

Top: Nicholas Kove and his wife Clothilde enjoying an evening out

Above: Jo May-Prussak with his grandfather, Nicholas Kove

Airfix of London

In the autumn of 1938 the travelling came to an end when Nicholas Kove and his family arrived in London. As the base for developing a Jewish-run business, however secular the owner, Italy had ceased to be a viable prospect since Mussolini had sidled up closer and closer to Hitler. In England Koves changed his name to Kove and in late 1938, or more probably early 1939, he founded Airfix Products Ltd.

The name Airfix was chosen not only because it would appear early in any alphabetical index of company names, but also because it was suggestive of the type of product produced by Kove's new company. I'm sorry to disappoint any enthusiasts who might naturally assume the brand name has anything to do with fixing or assembling model aircraft, but it relates to a line of 'air-filled' items and is nothing to do with building planes! When the business began, Airfix's products included little rubber bricks of the sort fitted with a vent enabling them to be squeezed and then left to pop back to shape, and babies' rattles made from off-cuts of whatever material was available. It wasn't long before they were making an air mattress of the type best known as a lilo. Jo May-Prussak says that his mother claimed that her father had indeed taken out a worldwide patent for such an airbed design, though whether he is actually the inventor of the lilo per se is open to dispute.

> The name Airfix was chosen not only because it would appear early in any alphabetical index of company names, but also because it was suggestive of the type of product produced by Kove's new company.

For a short while before they arrived in England, the family lived in Berlin. I have been told that whilst he was based in the Reich's capital Kove was in the habit of virtually haunting the city's patent office, snapping up lapsed or unused patents if they took his fancy and he felt he could develop them commercially.

It is perfectly possible he came across the idea for the newfangled pneumatic mattresses during one of his forays in Berlin. He didn't stop here, though, for during this time Kove also registered a process for manufacturing artificial suede.

Airfix didn't start with the somewhat elaborate airbeds. Their first air-filled items were cheap novelties, as Kove's daughter told her son. These were most often of the squeaking block type, marketed to pre-school infants. I understand that London's famous Selfridges department store was a valuable early customer for these items.

Most of Airfix's early products were pliable, a quality derived from a key ingredient – rubber. Indeed, Ralph Ehrmann told me that Airfix Products Ltd was actually formed from an existing Ceylon and India rubber company that had been incorporated in the 1920s.

Margaret Brings in Money

Margaret Kove was only 16 when she joined her father at work in the autumn of 1938. 'I first started working for Father in the office,' she told her son years later. 'As I had my father's business head, we clashed, so I told him we had better not work so closely together and please could I go out and sell instead. Father agreed and I finished off by selling singlehanded the entire factory's production.' In those days Airfix's premises were based in London's Edgware Road.

By 1940 Margaret had begun a relationship with one Bernard Prussak, a Latvian Jew she met at the Linguist's Club in London, an association founded in 1937 with the aim of promoting a better knowledge of languages by organising meetings, discussions and events.

'Nicholas and his wife thought Bernard was an unsuitable partner for my mother because he wasn't rich enough and was also 17 years her senior,' Jo May-Prussak told me. 'On the other hand, my father says in his 1945 letter to his sister, that it was he who "put them in business" because they didn't have a penny before,' Jo continued.

Bernard might not have ticked all the right boxes for Nicholas Kove, but his bank balance clearly appealed and he was soon invited to join Airfix.

Margaret Elliott, Nicholas Kove's daughter

An interesting aside here: It appears that Bernard's father, Joseph, died around the same time as the Bolsheviks took over Latvia, seizing all of Prussak senior's property to boot. 'It occurs to me that since Nicholas worked for Béla Kun's government, he would have been on the opposite side of the political fence to my father, who always described his family as White Russian. So there may have been lurking political differences as well as emotional ones,' Jo reflected.

Anyway, apparently crucial to Kove's new operation, Bernard Prussak stumped up £200 in 1940 to help finance Airfix's north London factory and facilitated the manufacture of Airfix airbeds or 'blow-up rubber mattresses' as Bernard called them. The loaned sum was a considerable investment in 1940.

For six months during 1940 Bernard Prussak was employed as Airfix works manager at Kove's new premises. It appears that it wasn't exactly a happy time for Airfix's young benefactor. He was sidelined by Kove and left the company, losing his stake in the new business and without receiving any compensation, financial or otherwise, for all his valuable input.

In 1941 Bernard and Margaret wed, although without receiving the blessing of either Nicholas or Clothide Kove. Nicholas and Clothide Kove were present at the wedding but they didn't approve, Nicholas effectively disowning his daughter and refusing to speak to Bernard. After the marriage Margaret stopped working at Airfix.

Interned Again

If the unsanctioned marriage of his daughter to a former business partner caused Nicholas Kove's blood pressure to reach dangerous levels, he was soon about to encounter even more stressful times. At the outbreak of the Second World War, along with more than 60,000 British citizens of mainly German and Austrian descent, Kove fell foul of Rule 18B of the Emergency Powers Act (1939) and faced internment as a potential undesirable.

When war began 500 or so individuals, those who were considered a high security risk and who fell into Class A category, were interned in camps on the Isle of Man. Like most of the others earmarked for internment, Nicholas Kove fell into a low-risk category and, given that he was present at Margaret's wedding in May, it looks as if he wasn't sent to the Isle of Man until the second half of 1941.

Many in power thought internment a very clumsy instrument of state, especially unfair to those of Jewish descent who had fled Nazi persecution on the Continent. However, in June 1940, Italy's entry on the side of Nazi Germany naturally exacerbated fears of a hidden fifth column of foreigners who couldn't be trusted. Kove was considered trustworthy, though, and along with the majority of internees was released, probably in 1942, once the fear of invasion had passed.

Wartime Opportunities

In a May 1990 interview with Percy Reboul, the then chairman of the Plastics Historical Society, the late John Dolan, Airfix's works manager in the 1940s, recalled that Nicholas Kove 'came out of internment on the Isle of Man with £25 in his pocket and a suit of clothes on his back'. Following his unwarranted absence Nicholas Kove returned to his London home, a large six-bedroom house on the Finchley Road in Hampstead. Jo May-Prussak told me it was far from 'poky' having living and dining rooms, a study and even a billiard room.

Whilst Kove had been away it appears that Airfix lay largely dormant. Newly-weds Margaret and Bernard were making a living elsewhere. For three months Margaret worked as an assistant in Gallerie Lafayette, the London branch of the Paris fashion store, located in Regent Street. Meanwhile her husband established a jewellery workshop. A skilled draughtsman and trained electrical and mechanical engineer, Bernard made what his wife later described as 'gold-plated artificial jewellery' (presumably costume jewellery). He would later establish a business, Alumartic, and manufactured innovative items such as coloured anodised aluminium tea trolleys (this new process was state-of-the-art in the 1930s). A photograph from the period shows Bernard with nine other craftsmen amongst workbenches, coils of wire and an assortment of precision drills and presses.

Margaret actually went to work with Bernard, helping him with office administration, but according to her son they often rowed and when Nicholas Kove came home, intent on resurrecting Airfix, she opted to rejoin him.

'He [Kove] punted around for something to do and he settled on combs,' recalled John Dolan in his 1990 interview. 'He then found someone to make a mould and someone to give him a machine. That was R.H. Windsor.' Dolan went on to say that Windsor's provided the machine and a four-inch, four-impression comb mould on easy credit terms. 'He then found himself a mug as an engineer – me,' recalled Dolan. A new factory was required, and premises were secured in a vacant building in Hampstead Road, London NW1.

John Dolan recalled that when the first of the Windsor machines arrived it was so large that drastic surgery had to be done on the building to get it inside Airfix's new premises. 'I cut a hole in the floor of the shop and lowered in the machine – which was waiting outside – through that hole, after going to borrow the lifting equipment in a taxi to do this; and I had to pay the taxi fare myself.' Mr Dolan went on to say that

> 'He [Kove] punted around for something to do and he settled on combs,' recalled John Dolan in his 1990 interview. 'He then found someone to make a mould and someone to give him a machine. That was R.H. Windsor.' Dolan went on to say that Windsor's provided the machine and a four-inch, four-impression comb mould on easy credit terms. 'He then found himself a mug as an engineer – me,' recalled Dolan. A new factory was required, and premises were secured in a vacant building in Hampstead Road, London NW1.

after securing the new machine he immediately marched out into the street and recruited the first man to show interest in the shop-floor vacancy Kove had tasked him to advertise.

Despite cold-shouldering his son-in-law following his daughter's wedding, Nicholas Kove once again turned to him for assistance. Bernard agreed to help Kove pick up Airfix where he had left off, but this time would not be providing finance. Despite the timely offer of help when he most needed it, Kove made it clear that he didn't want Bernard Prussak as a business partner, rather as an employee.

This was all well and good, and Bernard Prussak evidently went to work as product designer for Airfix, perhaps utilising some of the skills developed whilst working in the jewellery trade. Regardless of his efforts, however, it appears that he worked for weeks without being paid by Kove, who claimed to be penniless.

Airfix's first success had undoubtedly been with the manufacture of pliable rubber toys and airbeds, or lilos, but following Japan's entry into the war in 1941 and its rapid capture of British plantations in the Far East, imports to Britain of this precious raw material all but dried up. With Kove home from internment and Airfix back in action, a range of new products was required. Popular utilitarian items were required – especially those which could be mass-produced by a small factory such as Airfix. A cheap cigarette lighter seemed a good bet, and Bernard set about designing the pattern for one.

The war effort required manufacturers of non-essentials to apply for permission to use raw materials for the manufacture of any commercial items. This was secured, and Airfix set about manufacturing another big seller. In a short time, with its workforce of 35, Airfix was churning out 1,200 lighters each and every day. They were also soon to corner the market in plastic injection moulded combs, their competitors relying on the cruder, less satisfactory saw-cut variety.

At this time Airfix also manufactured cheap babies' rattles and fulfilled a variety of official contracts in support of the armed forces. In fact Airfix was one of the largest suppliers of die-stamped metal belt buckles. Wily old Kove never missed a trick, and whilst fulfilling government contracts he became adept at making something marketable from any leftover scraps and off-cuts.

Although it would become famous in the 1960s for its cheap and ubiquitous HO-OO toy soldiers, as early as the immediate post-war years Airfix included warriors, such as these plastic cavalrymen, in its range of products

Airfix was now thriving, and despite the wartime conditions things were looking good for Kove. Allegedly, although Kove and his daughter frequently clashed because she had inherited some of his business acumen, she was intimately involved in selling the Airfix utility lighters. To the delight of her father, Margaret proved a natural salesperson.

Sadly, however, these buoyant circumstances conspired against Bernard. Now that Kove was doing well, he had little more use for his son-in-law. Bernard told his son that it didn't take long for Kove to 'learn how to do things' and rather bluntly made his displeasure apparent. Consequently, in 1943 Bernard walked out. It is not known if Margaret accompanied her husband at the same time or left a little later because of her pregnancy. She gave birth to a son, Jo, on 11 May 1944.

Nicholas Kove and his daughter were naturally reconciled by the birth of his grandson, and Kove even offered Bernard another position at Airfix. Although he certainly didn't feel any great benevolence towards his father-in-law, given the new circumstances he had no choice but to behave in a civil manner. Anyway, following the birth Margaret took her baby to the relative safety of Penrith in Wales. Ironically she returned to London just as the first of Hitler's so-called 'vengeance weapons', the V-1 flying bomb, fell on London.

Jo May-Prussak told me that his father felt slighted by Kove, especially given his early financial and production support. 'He doesn't say how much money he put in – it couldn't have been a lot because he was not wealthy and was an immigrant himself'. He was naturally bitter about not being repaid or compensated for the six months he initially worked with Nicholas Kove – all the more so after he helped set up another factory following the latter's internment.

Injection Moulding

There's no doubt that a significant contributory factor to Airfix's early success, and indeed the basis for its later hegemony in the field of plastic kits, was the injection moulding machine.

Ever the opportunist, Kove appreciated the significance of this innovative power tool from its earliest incarnation. Just as the process of die stamping, surprisingly an offshoot of the fledgeling 'hot-metal' typesetting business, had revolutionised the production of cheap utility items and toys, injection moulding offered huge potential. However, unlike a new metal alloy, Mazak, the basis for millions and millions of die-cast toy cars in the 1930s and beyond, injection moulding largely depended on a new synthetic, plastic. Initially plastics were manufactured from rather unstable cellulose acetates or phenol-formaldehydes like the famous Bakelite. Now the exigencies of total war urgently required the development of more reliable plastic materials. There was a huge demand for synthetic components on weapons and for the numerous switches, knobs and dials in war machines.

Now the exigencies of total war urgently required the development of more reliable plastic materials.

Polyvinyl chloride (PVC), polymethyl methacrylate (Perspex) and polystyrene were developed to satisfy the new demand. The more flexible materials were used for the production of oxygen masks, gas masks (respirators) and hoses for flying helmets, and the more brittle materials for items such as pistol grips, radar fairings and even badges and buttons.

Although the chemicals giant ICI played a vital part in the development of polystyrene when

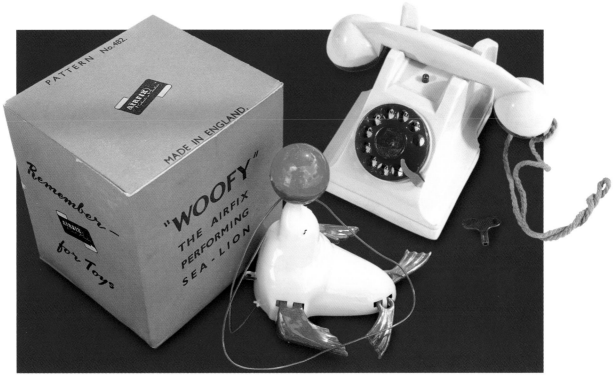

Above: 'Woofy' the Performing Sea-Lion – 'Novelty toy which tosses ball into the air and flaps its flippers when pulled along' said the entry in the 1949 price list. Woofy cost 2/3d

Top right: Although not every home had a real one, in the late 1940s it was possible to own a toy telephone. It rang when wound up with the provided key. Not cheap – the 1949 price list said it cost 11/2d

in 1937 they patented a method for stabilising the material so that it could be safely stored, the previous cellulose-based materials having a nasty habit of spontaneously catching fire, the origination of this new wonder plastic was largely a German invention. One chemist, Simon, had discovered its potential as long ago as 1839.

There are stories, probably apocryphal, about Airfix's first injection moulding machines being copies, or even originals, of German machines encountered by colleagues or acquaintances of Kove's during the Second World War. Having donned khaki for the duration, these individuals are said to have discovered examples of the new technology in the deserted factories of the shattered Reich as the Allies swept through Germany in 1945 and then arranged for their transport back to England. However, it is more likely the early machines were obtained legitimately. Certainly Kove was familiar with the commercial developments of this new science and acquainted with Dr Islyn Thomas, the Welsh-born pioneer of plastics manufacture whose family had emigrated to the US in the early 1920s and who by the 1940s was one of the leading international experts on the subject.

Thomas joined the Ideal Novelty & Toy Company in 1942 in the position of general manager. However, his skills were applied to the US war effort, being used in the manufacture of proximity fuses rather than children's playthings.

In 1944 Dr Thomas formed the Thomas Engineering Company, the Plastics Parts Development Corporation, and then the Thomas Manufacturers Corporation. For the next ten years he was one of the largest producers of plastic toys and household goods in the US. With the war's end in 1945 he helped establish a number of plastics companies in England and Wales, and he was also instrumental in helping several US companies establish divisions there. During this period he came into contact with the entrepreneurial Kove and as a consultant to R.H. Windsor (the manufacturer previously mentioned by Airfix's first foreman John Dolan) it is likely that Thomas was active in helping Airfix secure its first injection moulding machines.

> **So, by hook or by crook, Airfix secured some of the latest technology and managed to keep the majority of their kit serviceable and well ahead of any domestic competition.**

'When I arrived at Airfix [in 1950] there were six three-ounce Windsor moulding machines and one eight-ounce Watson Stillman machine,' recalls Airfix's financial guru Ralph Ehrmann. 'Only three of the Windsor machines were still working, the others having been stripped for spare parts.' He also thinks it likely that Islyn Thomas was responsible for procuring the mould tools for the very first Airfix toy soldiers.

So, by hook or by crook, Airfix secured some of the latest technology and managed to keep the majority of their kit serviceable and well ahead of any domestic competition.

In 1947 Dr Thomas wrote *Injection Molding of Plastics*, for a long time the standard work on the subject. He was also closely associated with the US retailer F.W. Woolworth – who stocked lots of his products, especially larger items such as outdoor toys, whilst other US toy companies like Renwall concentrated on smaller playthings. It is likely that his relationship with the store helped Airfix cement (no pun intended) their relationship with the emporium on British high streets. In 1975, Dr Thomas was awarded an OBE for his contribution to the advancement of plastics. He died in 2002.

During the immediate post-war years Airfix consolidated its reputation as the premier supplier of plastic combs in Britain. Its enviable relationship with Woolworth was put to good use, the store shifting enormous quantities of these and dozens of other cheap and useful items made from plastic. Scissors safe for children were another popular item. In his interview, the late John Dolan had something to say about Airfix's children's scissors. 'I remember once, I was running out of eyelets for toy scissors,' he recalled. Although Dolan's job was looking after the manufacturing plant and he was not responsible for purchasing, Airfix

Before the advent of large catalogues in the 1960s, Airfix made do with flimsier publications. This one (top) dates from Summer 1959 and (above) Airfix's February 1960 price list adorned with an illustration of the new Fairey Rotodyne, a kit of which had recently joined the Airfix range

Above: Airfix's famous association with construction kits really began in 1949 when it released its famous replica of the new Ferguson Tractor. When first available, however, the tractor came ready assembled

Below: Only after Airfix had reached agreement with FW Woolworth in 1953 and supplied kits in plastic bags with printed headers which opened out into instructions was the Tractor made available in this format

having a dedicated buyer, he felt that this critical situation called for action.

Consequently, Dolan left the factory floor and went to the management office. 'Mr Dolan, what are you doing here?' his boss exclaimed. Trying to explain that he had an appointment with Mr Crossley, the buyer, but not wanting to get a fellow employee into trouble, Dolan was understandably nervous. Nevertheless, Dolan was forced to explain the nature of his mission and the fact that production of the popular plastic scissors had halted.

'You will buy them. You will buy the eyelets,' stormed Kove.

'Why should I buy them?' Dolan asked. 'Mr Crossley knows the suppliers. Why should I be able to buy them any better than the man you employ for the job?'

'Mr Dolan,' Kove replied calmly, 'out there is a city of eight million people. Somewhere in that city are the eyelets that we want. You go and buy them!'

Dolan was also quick to point out Nicholas Kove's benevolent side, however, and recalled how following periods when Airfix were operating double shifts and working around the clock, the firm's owner often showed

Toy soldiers were another popular Airfix line from the 1940s. Mounted 54mm cavalrymen, though crude by contemporary standards, predated the company's world-famous HO-OO sets by 20 years.

his gratitude to his staff. 'He was paying me so much money,' Dolan recalled. 'He would say, "Mr Dolan, get yourself a present", and he would give me a blank cheque, saying, "Give me bills [receipts], please".'

Cheap plastic toys of the kind purchased from seaside novelty shops in an effort to keep children amused on rainy days were another staple. Cheap and easy to produce, they could be purchased for pennies. Toy soldiers were another popular Airfix line from the 1940s. Mounted 54mm cavalrymen, though crude by contemporary standards, predated the company's world-famous HO-OO sets by 20 years.

In 1949, to satisfy a commercial commission, Airfix produced a miniature replica of the latest Ferguson Tractor. The new TE range of Ferguson tractors had been introduced in England in 1946 and followed 30 years of continuous development of the Ferguson System since 1916. It was big news, and owner Harry Ferguson even established a production line for his new model across the Atlantic in Detroit, giving Ford a run for their money in their own backyard.

Airfix's model of the new tractor came ready assembled and was used as a sales promotion premium by Ferguson reps as they visited prospective purchasers across Britain. The miniature was manufactured from a quite brittle acetate-based material and was allegedly a devil of a job for Airfix's production staff to assemble. Furthermore, it was so delicate that numerous replicas were returned for repair because small pieces had snapped off. Nevertheless, it was very popular and extremely accurate, the original pattern maker having excelled himself.

Opposite page: John Gray, with Ralph Ehrmann below him. Above: John Gray (centre in light suit) and Ralph Ehrmann (immediately to his right) at a trade show in 1960

New Blood: Gray, Ehrmann...

The same year that the Ferguson tractor appeared Kove began to relinquish some control of Airfix. In 1949 John Gray, a former Lines Bros executive, was given responsibility for buying. Soon afterwards Gray was promoted to general manager. In fact, whilst Kove had been in hospital suffering from a serious stomach ailment, the aforementioned John Dolan, who was actually works foreman, had assumed the role of general manager. Dolan left in 1948 upon his boss's return.

In 1950, at the insistence of his bankers Warburgs, Kove employed another key executive when the 25-year-old Ralph Ehrmann, a graduate in industrial administration, joined Airfix after being on secondment to the British division of the famous German toy train manufacturer Bing. Ehrmann was appointed assistant manager to Kove who, with his health failing and his famously volatile temperament exposing the cash-rich Airfix to a host of potential risks, was viewed as a potential liability by the firm's creditors.

'When I met Nicholas Kove he was almost incapable of running a business single-handedly because of his violent outbursts,' Ralph Ehrmann told me. 'I spent a great deal of my time dissuading many of those at Airfix from leaving, so fed up were they with his violent outbursts and temper. The noise level coming from "meetings" in his office can only been

imagined by anyone who wasn't there to experience it. However, it has to be said that despite his unbridled temper the man was a powerhouse. He had a very good brain and in the early days Airfix and those who worked for the company would have been out of a job if it had not been for Kove's brute strength and courage.'

> **The tractor is erroneously considered Airfix's first kit. Indeed 1949 is still considered the birthday of its construction kit activities. Whilst it did indeed appear in 1949, that year marked its introduction only as a fully assembled model.**

The Ferguson Tractor is erroneously considered Airfix's first kit. Indeed 1949 is still considered the birthday of its construction kit activities. Whilst it did indeed appear in 1949, that year marked its introduction only as a fully assembled model. It has to be admitted that it wasn't long before the merits of producing it as a kit of unassembled parts and letting the purchaser put it back together, suddenly dawned on the management of Airfix. However, this almost certainly wasn't before Ralph Ehrmann joined in 1950. 'Turning the tractor into a kit was decided upon following a meeting between Nicholas Kove, John Gray and myself,' he recalls. 'It was decided that because the assembled tractor was so fiddly and regularly fell to bits it was perhaps a good idea to actually sell it as a kit of parts and let someone else have the headache of assembling it!' Naturally the Ferguson Company were delighted that their new vehicle would receive such further free promotion.

Classic Ships

With new blood like John Gray and Ralph Ehrmann on board, Kove's Airfix was at last equipped for great things. Both Gray and Ehrmann knew the international toy industry well. Both of them could see how American companies like Revell, Aurora and Monogram had a virtual monopoly on the polystyrene construction kit industry. Both realised that the manufacture of plastic kits admirably suited the new technology of injection moulding. Rather than having to employ dozens of production line staff or outworkers to assemble moulded pieces into a

The original header for Airfix's first 'real' kit, the *Golden Hind* , released in 1952

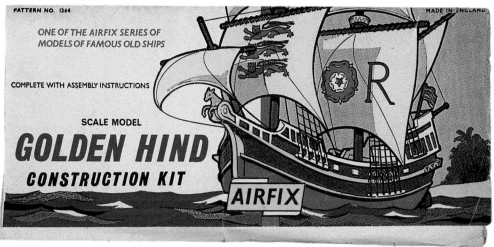

Top: Before Airfix established a regular system of packaging design, created by TV artist Charles Oates, the *Golden Hind*, the first of the successful Classic Ships range, was available with a variety of header designs. Below: This is the famous graphic design Charles Oates introduced on all Airfix bagged kit headers and box tops and which was prevalent well into the early 1960s

saleable finished product and also, perhaps, additional staff to paint or decorate particular objects, all that was required before a kit reached the point of sale was to insert the ejected moulded frames directly into a box with the addition of a cheap one-colour instruction sheet and some crude decals to boot.

The only problem facing Airfix at this time was getting F.W. Woolworth, their largest customer, to agree a purchase price. At the time the retailer was shifting vast quantities of an Airfix plastic toy Ice-cream Tricycle. They wanted another inexpensive Airfix product that would be snapped up by youngsters or their parents in similar abandon. Whilst they were prepared to stock a boxed version of an assembled tractor, which justifiably sold for more than a kit, they couldn't accept Airfix's asking price for a box of unassembled bits and pieces. And Airfix had had enough of accepting the responsibility for assembly.

A selection of early Airfix items including the Ukelele and Harbour Master toys from the very early 1950s, through to items like the Attack Force Jeep and Trailer and even Fred, the Homepride mascot from the 1960s

Allegedly it was the late Jim Russon, Woolworth's buyer and Ralph Ehrmann's direct contact at the retailer, who suggested that Airfix consider producing kits of miniature sailing ships. Sir Francis Drake's flagship, the *Golden Hind*, was doing good business in Woolworth's US stores, albeit as a ship-in-a-bottle version, and Russon thought Airfix should have a stab at a construction kit version of the same subject. After much horse-trading between Woolworth and Ehrmann, who was fast assuming the financial stewardship of the Airfix company, a price point was agreed. However, so low was the amount Woolworth were prepared to pay that packaging the item in a box was out of the question. The only way Airfix could achieve the target purchase price was by packaging the new kit, not in a box as originally intended, but in a far cheaper transparent polythene bag. The illustration of the subject and any branding were to be printed on a single sheet, a folded header which was stapled to the bag and which could be suspended from a suitable shop display. Unfolded, the header featured the all-important kit instructions. Consequently, the first true Airfix construction kit and the first of the firm's products to appear in the iconic 'poly bag' was number one in the new Classic Ships series, the *Golden Hind*. The year was 1952.

Shortly thereafter Airfix also cut an acceptable deal for Woolworth to retail the Ferguson Tractor as a construction kit. But, as with the new Classic Ships range, the tractor was packaged in a simple plastic bag attached to an illustrated header. The delicate and complicated tractor wasn't an ideal candidate for such retail presentation – there were too many fiddly bits, and pieces frequently became detached from the runners (often wrongly called 'sprue', which in fact refers to the tiny connection between each part and the thicker runner frame). Because

The *Golden Hind* and HMS *Shannon* in assembled and painted form, the latter being first available in 1954

of these shortcomings, Ralph Ehrmann called it a 'bugger' to run, and the tractor was soon removed from the range. It didn't even feature in Airfix's first construction kit catalogue.

Classic Ships, however, proved a real success. Popular with consumers and a retailer's dream, these tiny miniatures were also ideal for the smaller injection moulding machines then equipping Airfix's factory floor. In fact, all the required pieces fitted easily into a single tool and complete kits spewed from the presses like spent machine-gun cartridges.

Ralph Ehrmann – from the RAF to Airfix

Whilst the very fact of Airfix's existence and the speed with which it had carved itself such a well-defined niche in the marketplace were both undoubtedly attributable to Nicholas Kove's dogged tenacity and nose for a mutually agreeable deal, it was Ralph Ehrmann who took the company to its greatest heights. When Ehrmann joined, Kove was a very sick man and past his best. In fact he had almost become a liability. Although he was surprised and impressed by the success of the Classic Kits range (initially he had even attempted to get Ehrmann to personally underwrite the cost of the *Golden Hind*'s mould!), Kove didn't really have the foresight to see how Airfix could exploit this new market.

It was Ehrmann's market intelligence that forced Kove's hand and led to Airfix extending its range of kits to include aircraft, cars, figures and tanks. His job was doubtless made all the easier when the *Golden Hind* was soon joined by the *Santa Maria*, HMS *Shannon*, HMS *Victory* and other galleons in the same scale comprising the Airfix Collectors Fleet of Classic Ships series, and production batches quickly increased from 10,000 to as much as 100,000 units.

Above: How Airfix kits were delivered to retailers in the 1950s. The Darracq and Bentley date from 1956 and the Morris Cowley from 1959

Below: A design classic – Charles Oates' Stukas from 1957

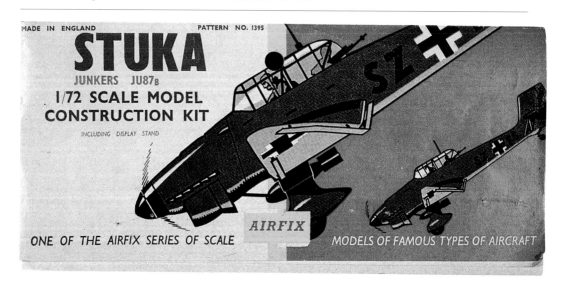

By the time Ralph Ehrmann joined Airfix at the age of 25 he, like many of his contemporaries, had already experienced so much. These days, individuals of a similar age join corporations with perhaps only a university course, a gap year and the occasional stint of internship behind them. Not so the wartime generation.

Ralph Ehrmann was born in Leipzig in 1925, and his family moved to London in 1931. When he left school he was intent on taking a degree in agriculture, but his studies at Reading University were cut short by the war and he enlisted in the RAF.

'I flew Wellingtons until some time very early in 1945, when my crew was meant go to an Operational Conversion Unit to join a Lancaster squadron. Unfortunately on our last flight from the Operational Training Unit we crashed at St Mawes due to the complete failure of the hydraulic system and we were all sent on leave whilst a court of enquiry sat. We were all given a commendation in our log books for saving the aircraft, but when we returned to our unit, we found that the Australian crew had been sent home as the European war was coming to an end. The navigator and I were meant to join Tiger Force in Singapore, but the powers that be decided that Bomber Command was too big for 1945 requirements and we were classified as Obsolescent Air Crew...'

One of Airfix's first HO-OO sets, Civilians

SAUNDERS-ROE

S-R 53

MADE IN ENGLAND

PATTERN No. 1407

¹/₇₂nd SCALE MODEL
CONSTRUCTION KIT
INCLUDING DISPLAY STAND

AIRFIX

ONE OF THE AIRFIX SERIES OF SCALE MODELS OF FAMOUS TYPES OF AIRCRAFT

Rare 1st issue Airfix Saunders Roe SR53 from 1958. Fifty years later Airfix continued with classic British test aircraft with the release of their TSR-2 replicas

Upon leaving the RAF in 1947, Ralph Ehrmann initially occupied himself with a variety of writing jobs – he was even *Town & Country* magazine's Scandinavian correspondent for a while. His family urged him to get 'a proper job' and after a succession of well-meaning uncles descended on his London abode he was encouraged to see Sigmund Warburg, who had founded UK investment bank S.G. Warburg & Co. in 1946 and was the bank's managing director until the 1970s.

Ehrmann spent a 'fascinating' hour with Warburg and was captivated by the banker's erudition and charm. Despite the wide-ranging nature of their conversation – they discussed history, poetry and literature – Ehrmann was brought back to earth with a bump when Warburg recommended joining the burgeoning plastics manufacturing industry.

Following evening classes to complete

An iconic favourite of mine, this Detached House dates from 1957

Airfix were quick to supplement their HO-OO civilian, station accessories and farm animal ranges, all originally designed for use with model railway layouts, with toy soldiers. The soldiers in this British Infantry Combat set are resplendent in their new Cold War period 1949 pattern battle dress

his business diploma and stints at various firms, including manufacturers and toy companies such as the German firm Bing, who had established a partnership in Northamptonshire with the equally famous British toy train manufacturer Bassett Lowke, in 1950 Ehrmann was encouraged by Warburgs to join Airfix.

'I was sent to Airfix because Nicholas Kove needed somebody to help him and, also, because Warburgs were frightened that he might go bankrupt because the business was no longer profitable due to the loss of the comb trade,' Ralph Ehrmann told me. He also revealed that Nicholas Kove still owed Warburgs £32,000 owing to the asset-stripping they had indulged in.

Meanwhile Warburgs were becoming increasingly concerned about Kove's wellbeing. It appears he had often 'cried wolf', claiming ill health at times when he felt the bank was pressurising him. As Ralph Ehrmann said: 'He appeared to be a health risk, as he often used this as a protection when they pressed him. Warburgs were no angels at this time, interest was limited by government regulations, but they charged Airfix percentages for interest, book keeping, advice etc, which meant that we were liable for something like 20 per cent for the debt,

Surviving Airfix Toy Catalogue from the late 1950s

and £6,500 at that time must have been the equivalent of £130,000 today.' It was in Warburgs's interest to have an executive of their own choice manning Airfix's helm alongside Kove.

Pressures and Problems

In 1951 the marriage of his daughter Margaret to Bernard Prussak hit the rocks and the two parted company. Margaret opened an upmarket beauty clinic in Central London. There she saw a wide range of clients from the upper echelons of society, including Barbara Cartland, numerous European aristocrats and minor members of the Royal Family.

After his marriage to Margaret broke up, Bernard Prussak returned to Italy where he worked for Fiat in Turin until the 1960s. In 1971 he emigrated to Israel, to be joined a year later by his only surviving brother on his release from Russia. Bernard died in Tel Aviv in 1974.

Kove's own poor health and concerns over his daughter's happiness naturally poured fuel on his often fiery temper. Ralph Ehrmann provides a pretty colourful impression of these times: 'Nicholas Kove was highly intelligent but probably knew that he was unable to really talk to his employees and, though he was respected by the workers, they were unable to work to his instructions because he was inconsistent and flying off the handle in different directions all the time. One of my first jobs was to keep the various professionals in the company by keeping him from venting his fury on them.'

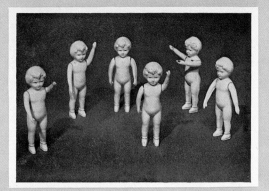

4¼" DOLL

PATTERN No. 703F

Flesh coloured 4¼" Doll with articulated arms, ideal for dressing as Christmas Fairy Dolls, etc.

AIRFIX PRODUCTS LTD., Haldane Place, Garratt Lane London, S.W.18

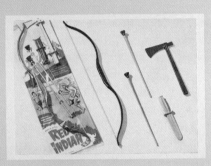

RED INDIAN SET

PATTERN No. 1378

Comprises Bow and two rubber suction tipped safety Arrows, realistic Tomahawk and Knife in safe polythene material. Brightly coloured card (size 24½" x 7½"). Packed in polythene bag.

AIRFIX PRODUCTS LTD., Haldane Place, Garratt Lane, London, S.W.18

REMOVAL VAN

PATTERN No. 8500

20" long polythene articulated Removal Van, fitted with metal axles. Bright dual colours. Packed in polythene bag. Companion to Oil Tanker. (Patt. No. 0101.)

AIRFIX PRODUCTS LTD., Haldane Place, Garratt Lane, London, S.W.18

Top: Cheap plastic toy dolls had been a staple of Airfix since its earliest days. Above left: The term Native American was rarely used when this Red Indian Bow and Arrow Set was released. Above right: When this toy removal van was released the ingenious three-wheeled Scammel Scarab, upon which it was based, was selling very well. Below: Airfix's Toy Ukelele could be strummed. Youngsters could also make music with the Airfix Playable Plastic Toy Violin & Bow, which was available around the same time. The Ukelele cost 8/4d in 1949

UKELELE

PATTERN No. 1621

A very attractive musical instrument, nylon strung with plectrum. Plain bright colours. Packed in bright 3-colour box (size 15½" x 5" x 1½").

AIRFIX PRODUCTS LTD., Haldane Place, Garratt Lane London, S.W.18

Apparently one of Ehrmann's other duties was to ensure that Kove's wife Clothilde didn't enter the factory, because when together the two were a very volatile combination! However, Ehrmann's intercessions were obviously the tonic Kove required. 'He frequently said that I was the best thing that Warburgs had ever done for him,' he told me. 'At other times he was not so polite!'

During the early 1950s Airfix was thriving once more and the company's profits increased year on year. Management reorganisation and modern administrative processes were having the desired positive effect, and the Airfix brand was firmly established as a leading manufacturer of polystyrene construction kits.

It wasn't all nose to the grindstone for those involved with Airfix – especially not for Nicholas Kove. Ralph Ehrmann told me that his boss was a favourite of the bookies. 'Nicholas Kove's betting was sufficiently large for his bookmaker to regularly present him with expensive gifts such as items of furniture. However, he made money rather than lost it.' During the period from 1950, when Ehrmann was involved with Kove, it appears the great man rarely needed to spend much more than a couple of hours each day in the Airfix factory. Ralph Ehrmann was keen to point out that he didn't consider Kove's penchant for the turf a weakness. Rather he felt that his success, especially with complex bets such as accumulators, was an example of his boss's numeracy. 'I admired his mathematical ability – he organised lots of complex combination and sequential bets.'

John Gray was an increasing asset to Airfix. In 1954 Gray was promoted from chief buyer to general manager and not withstanding frequent clashes with Kove, he built his career with Airfix. Ralph Ehrmann frequently interceded in their clashes, however, and spent a considerable

Top: Airfix Harbour Master Toy
Right: Airfix Ferguson Tractor 1949

The Bristol 192 helicopter, soon to be re-branded Belvedere (1959)

amount of time and effort dissuading Gray from resigning each time he had had enough.

In 1956 Kove's daughter Margaret remarried, this time to Bob Elliott who, following a promising career as a professional footballer (he had been Walsall FC's goalkeeper), was then enjoying a profitable career in the building industry, being one of three partners of F.E.B., a company making chemical additives designed to harden concrete.

The following year Ehrmann was instrumental in making John Gray his fellow joint managing director of Airfix Products. Everything was in place for a successful flotation and, also in 1957, Airfix went public.

At least Nicholas Kove had the satisfaction of seeing the business he had created and nurtured become a public company. His good fortune was short-lived, however, for on 17 March 1958, only three weeks after the death of his wife, he died at his home at 252 Finchley Road, London.

Margaret Splashes Out

Margaret Elliott inherited her father's estate and immediately became a very wealthy woman. She held some 52 per cent of the company. As the company's shares rocketed more than predicted, she started selling some shares and naturally began enjoying her increasing wealth.

To support Margaret Elliott in her endeavours, her husband joined Airfix, becoming non-executive chairman of the holding company, Airfix Industries. Airfix Industries' board consisted of Margaret and Bob Elliott and Ralph Ehrmann.

In the hope that the shares might reach even higher values Margaret Elliott asked Ralph Ehrmann to make some over-optimistic forecasts, something he was unwilling to do. At least Margaret's beauty salon in Welbeck Street, London W1 (which she ran until 1960) proved that she could in fact run a successful business and had definitely inherited her father's head for business.

For a while Margaret even entertained the notion of running the Airfix company herself, but with Ehrmann refusing to 'push' the shares (he was supported by Warburgs as well as Airfix's other financial associates and banks), she realised that a senior management role was untenable and decided to divest herself of her remaining shares.

MADE IN ENGLAND PATTERN No. 1316

SCALE MODEL

SPITFIRE

CONSTRUCTION

KIT

IN HIGH IMPACT PLASTIC

INCLUDING DISPLAY STAND

ONE OF THE AIRFIX SERIES OF SCALE MODELS OF FAMOUS TYPES OF AIRCRAFT

MADE IN ENGLAND   PATTERN NO M3C

RENAULT
DAUPHINE

1/32 SCALE MODEL CONSTRUCTION KIT

ONE OF THE AIRFIX SERIES OF SCALE
MODELS OF MODERN CARS

AIRFIX

COMPLETE WITH ASSEMBLY INSTRUCTIONS

Opposite top: Spitfire BTK. Dating from 1953, this was Airfix's first in a huge range of Spitfires, new versions of which are still being produced today. The serial BTK was never used by RAF Spitfire Squadrons, in fact the kit, a copy of an unreliable 1/48th, or quarter scale one released by US manufacturer Aurora was full of inaccuracies

Opposite below: Renault Dauphine (1961). Below: SS *Southern Cross*, an ultra rare kit dating from 1955

'She therefore decided to turn many of her shares into cash,' Ralph Ehrmann told me. 'We created A & B shares to make this possible and restructured the board.' Class A shares have greater voting rights than Class B shares or any other class of shares. One reason for creating this disparity in voting rights between classes of stock is to insulate company management from interference by non-executive investors.

Having to sell the shares in the company her father started was not easy for Margaret. It was, as Ralph Ehrmann remembers, quite a 'shock' to her. However, after this abrupt change in her position in the Airfix hierarchy, Margaret could at least enjoy the proceeds of the sale of stock, which amounted to a significant fortune then. Ralph Ehrmann and the Elliotts quickly resumed their normal friendly relations, he and his family occasionally staying with the Elliotts in their new home in Spain. Margaret Elliott enjoyed a good life as an artist and prominent socialite, throwing lavish parties from her cliff-top villa. She kept three yachts, one of which was even skippered by an Italian prince. She mixed easily with the highest echelons of Majorcan society. 'Nothing was too much trouble in her desire to entertain her guests,' read *The Times* obituary. 'On one occasion she hired a troupe of tightrope walkers from Madrid to perform over her swimming pool, which she had filled with sharks.'

In the 1980s Margaret Elliott returned to London to be closer to her grandchildren. In 1992 she made her first visit to Budapest since she had left as an infant some 70 years earlier. The *Times* again: 'Although she recognised none of the modern city, to the astonishment of her family she immediately broke into fluent Hungarian, the language that had been spoken at home when she was a child.' Perhaps this linguistic skill shouldn't come as such a surprise. She was known to count only in French! Margaret Elliott died in 2002. She is survived by her daughter Judy Boden, an interior designer, and her son Jo May-Prussak, an author and retired psychologist.

Airfix Industries was reversed into the old Ceylon Cocoa and Rubber Company, a convenient shell that had itself gone public in 1926, Airfix Products being an operating subsidiary. After Airfix went public in 1957 and the Elliotts relinquished their holding, Ralph Ehrmann succeeded Bob Elliott as chairman.

The company was now ready to enter its busiest and most profitable period.

S.S. SOUTHERN CROSS
CONSTRUCTION KIT

AIRFIX

1/72nd SCALE
CONSTRUCTION KIT

OVER
75
PARTS

AVRO
LANCASTER
BI

AIRFIX

1/72nd Scale
CONSTRUCTION KIT
OVER 70 PARTS

VICKERS-ARMSTRONG
WELLINGTON B III

VICKERS-ARMSTRONG
WELLINGTON B III
AN AIRFIX 1/72nd SCALE KIT

MOVEABLE CONTROL SURFACES
ROTATING TURRETS
FULLY-DETAILED COCKPIT
RETRACTABLE UNDERCARRIAGE
TRANSPARENT PLASTIC CANOPIES & DISPLAY STAND

4

AIRFIX
HALIFAX B.MK.III

HANDLEY PAGE
AIRFIX
1/72 SCALE CONSTRUCTION KIT
42" WING SPAN
INCLUDING ADHESIVE

AIRFIX
BRISTOL 192
AIRFIX SERIES
BRISTOL 192
TWIN ROTOR TRANSPORT
1/72 SCALE MODEL
CONSTRUCTION KIT

AIRFIX
1/72 SCALE CONSTRUCTION KIT
14" WING SPAN
INCLUDING ADHESIVE

DOUGLAS C-47
DAKOTA

AIRFIX
1/72 SCALE CONSTRUCTION KIT
14" WING SPAN

AIRFIX
1/72 SCALE CONSTRUCTION KIT
DORNIER 217 E.2.

AIRFIX
SCALE CONSTRUCTION KIT
14" WING SPAN

AIRFIX
1/72 SCALE MODEL CONSTRUCTION KIT
12 kg in WING SPAN

INCLUDING ADHESIVE
HEINKEL HE.III H-2

AIRFIX
1/72 SCALE MODEL CONSTRUCTION KIT
INCLUDING ADHESIVE

OVERALL LENGTH 10½ ins.

BLACKBURN
N.A.39

AIRFIX
1/72 SCALE MODEL CONSTRUCTION KIT
18" WING SPAN

DORNIER 217 E.2.
DORNIER 217 E.2.
1/72 SCALE CONSTRUCTION KIT

DE HAVILLAND
COMET 4B
1/144 SCALE MODEL CONSTRUCTION
INCLUDING ADHESIVE
COMET

CHAPTER 2

BOXING CLEVER

By the time it became a public company in 1957, Airfix was well on the way to establishing its core brand values of quality and value for money. Following the success of the Classic Ships range in the early 1950s, the company's kit range was greatly augmented by scale replicas of lots of other subjects, especially model cars and aircraft, for which the company was achieving international acclaim. Furthermore, commercial success had enabled Airfix to move from their initial premises in north London to larger and more suitable factory and warehouse space in Garrett Lane in the Wandsworth area of south-west London.

Post-war Britain was rather drab. Numerous residential areas bore scars from the Blitz, and bombsites abounded. In 1951, after almost bankrupting the country in its attempt to prosecute the war from the top table alongside its US and Soviet allies, the government was determined to advertise Britain's reconstruction and modernism. In May 1951 it heralded the nation's achievements with the Festival of Britain on London's South Bank.

Opposite page top: Two very rare examples of Airfix's first large kits, 1958's 1/72nd scale Wellington BIII and Avro Lancaster BI. Below: Within a very short space of time Airfix expanded their range to include more complex kits

This page: Workhorse of the allied forces in WWII, the Douglas Dakota

HMS *Endeavour*, the first of the larger Classic Ships (1963)

Despite this morale-boosting display, British citizens continued to suffer an austere regime. To the consternation of many, rationing, an understandable consequence of British imports of food and materiel being greatly restricted by enemy U-boats, continued well after the end of the war. In one way things were worse: bread, which was not rationed at all during the war, was supplied on a strictly limited basis from 1946! Youngsters couldn't buy sweets freely until February 1953, or liberally sprinkle sugar on their Cornflakes until sugar rationing ended in September of that year. Rationing didn't actually end until 1954, its demise signalled by the return of an exotic fruit no children under the age of 14 had ever tasted: the humble banana.

However, as is always the case when the British are looking for solace, there were always past glories to revel in. Fortunately, amongst the horrors and tragedies of the recent world war, there was abundant satisfaction and pride to be had in British military prowess. What's more, the British had punched far above their weight as far as their technological contribution was concerned. Along with the Spitfire, radar had helped win the Battle of Britain; British proximity fuses helped defeat the V1 menace, while ASDIC, or sonar, helped thwart the U-boat; and Frank Whittle's turbo-jets propelled the first modern airliners. The nation even had the atomic bomb and was planning a fleet of futuristic 'V-bombers' to deliver it.

Although much of what the nation had executed was still top secret, such as the key success of reading the enemy's Enigma codes and the developments in computers that were a consequence of such critical code-breaking, there were numerous inspiring tales of daring-do about which schoolboys enthused during their breaktimes.

The sinking of the German pocket battleship *Bismarck*, the Dam Busters and their bouncing bomb, the Desert Rats at El Alamein, the epic seaborne assault on D-Day, paratroops at Arnhem and US Marines at Guadalcanal fuelled myriad childish fantasies. Each one of these epics naturally depended on the bravery, stoicism and fighting spirit of soldiers, sailors or airmen, but most juniors were more interested in the aircraft, ships and tanks with which

Before the Channel Tunnel the fastest way to take your car to the Continent was aboard a Bristol Superfreighter

> **Airfix was becoming increasingly famous for its growing assortment of highly detailed 1/72nd scale fighter aircraft.**

these fighting men were equipped.

Toy companies – especially manufacturers of plastic construction kits like Airfix – were in an ideal position to satisfy the enormous demand for replicas of the weaponry and war machines produced in such profusion during the Second World War.

Airfix was becoming increasingly famous for its growing assortment of highly detailed 1/72nd scale fighter aircraft and similarly compact HO-OO soldiers and tanks from almost every wartime theatre. Not just from the most recent conflict. There was a big demand for subjects from the 1914–18 period too. Airfix would be forever associated with little plastic Spitfires, Messerschmitts, Sopwith Camels and Fokker Tri-Planes as well as Sherman, Tiger and Churchill tanks. In fact until the late 1950s, when Airfix revenues had grown sufficiently for it to afford machines with increased injection moulding capacity and capable of accommodating larger mould tools, most of the firm's miniatures were pretty compact. The first Airfix Avro Lancaster and Vickers Wellington bombers were not available until 1958 and Airfix's *Bismarck* didn't feature until 1962, the wingspans and hull length of each of these kits being too large for the firm's early injection moulding machines. These larger kits not only required larger boxes and of course cost more, they dramatically enhanced Airfix's presence on the shelves. The company was fast becoming a major player in toy and hobby shops and with the ubiquitous high street retailer F.W. Woolworth.

The two principal architects of Airfix's ascendancy during this period, Ralph Ehrmann and John Gray, had both scored rather well in the field of aircraft recognition whilst in the services

Left: First issue box of Airfix HO-OO Indians. Right: 1st issue box of Airfix HO-OO 8th Army soldiers

Inexpensive enough to be purchased with only a week's pocket money, Airfix Series One kits were enormously popular purchases.

during the war, so it's not surprising that the kits their company produced achieved accuracy of silhouette. Ehrmann and Gray's tutelage encouraged rapid improvements in the design and manufacture of successive new kits. Nowhere is this more evident than in the component design of the kits with which Airfix will forever be associated – model aircraft. The first fighter replicas can be identified by the crude representation of the pilot beneath the cockpit transparency – the so-called 'flying heads'. Before long kits were including complete pilot figures, despite the fact that they were affixed to a rather unrealistic internal protrusion, and by the end of the decade pilots came complete with basic representations of a proper flying seat.

Inexpensive enough to be purchased with only a week's pocket money, Airfix Series One kits were enormously popular purchases. Their rapid, often

Originally designed as an accessory for model railway layouts, Airfix HO-OO figures sold like hot cakes

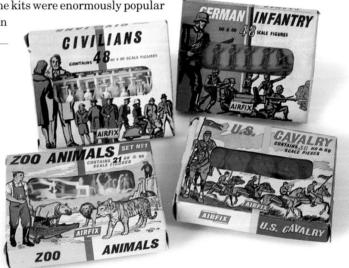

Designed by Alexander Issigonis in 1959, Airfix's Morris Mini-Minor was first available in 1961

messy assembly and their destruction by air rifle or in the flames of an acrid funeral pyre was an important right of passage for most boys of the baby-boomer generation.

It wasn't long before there were enough kits in the Airfix range to warrant the production of eye-catching brochures and eventually a series of annual catalogues entirely dedicated to them. Airfix's traditional annual Toy Catalogue, resplendent with photos of the firm's top-selling plastic Pull Along Train, Ice Cream Trolley and Parking Meter Money Box, faced being usurped by a more successful range.

Before the first bound Airfix Catalogue appeared in 1962 (it has been published annually ever since), new kit releases were heralded in a series of printed sales leaflets – often little more than two-colour flyers. Despite their relative lack of impact, these publications have since become highly collectable and display an excellent procession of the company's earliest kits. Unlike the annual catalogues that were subject to a year's potential price fluctuations, because they were destined for a shorter shelf life these leaflets generally displayed actual retail prices. Although comparing prices across half a century is pretty pointless, discovering the prices of Airfix kits in 'old money' is tantalisingly frustrating. Oh for a time machine …

By careful study of successive sales leaflets from the late 1950s, many of which were printed

AVRO ANSON I

AIRFIX-72 SCALE

AVRO ANSON 1

DERWYN'S
3/8
SIDLEY

AMERICAN CIVIL WAR CONFEDERATE INFANTRY

HO & OO **48** SCALE FIGURES

CONFEDERATE

AIRFIX

AIRFIX

1/72nd SCALE CONSTRUCTION KIT · 17" WING SPAN

AVRO

LANCASTER

with Dutch or German translations, the importance of Airfix's export trade to continental Europe can be gauged.

By the end of the 1950s Airfix kit production was proceeding at a frantic pace. New kits appeared almost every month and the company's published leaflets to promote the new releases on an equally regular basis. Airfix's dramatic rise at this time was doubtless due to several factors. There was the obvious demand of a public keen to relive recent wartime achievements and ready to devour books and comics or collect models of soldiers and war machines from the recent conflict. It helped that Airfix was a British company and Britain was one of the victors. Ehrmann and Gray's innate understanding of wartime technology, about which both had learned at the sharp end, was another important contributory factor. Ralph Ehrmann's astute business sense being a pre-requisite to Airfix making the right commercial decisions.

Another critical factor is perhaps less well known. Airfix ascendancy was also down to the accuracy and innovation inherent in the new kits. Airfix kits were accurate. As they were built around a constant scale, purchasers could display or play with finished models, all of which looked harmonious when arranged side by side. During this period, model kits coming from North America, the biggest market and the home of the most successful and well-established construction kit manufacturers, were all produced to a variety of scales. Although 1/48th, or what Americans call quarter scale, was the most common, it seemed that US kits were scaled to fit a box and a budget – some were huge, others small, cheap and nasty. In fact US manufacturers often omitted to signify a scale on the box or instruction leaflet. This was something that serious enthusiasts found enormously frustrating.

Airfix played a significant part in standardising not just the scale, but the assembly sequence and component breakdown of plastic construction kits. As soon as youngsters became familiar with the assembly process and learnt how to decipher instruction leaflets and their exploded diagrams at speed, any confusion or resistance to the often laborious kit making process would be removed. Making models would become easier and more acceptable.

> **Airfix ascendancy was also down to the accuracy and innovation inherent in the new kits.**

John Edwards, Designer

Achieving more sophistication in each model was obviously a design function. Fortunately Airfix had employed a chief designer who was a doyen of this very complicated and precise art. His name was John Edwards. Following the 1953 release of Airfix's first model of the RAF's legendary Supermarine Spitfire, a rather ropy miniature of dubious provenance and accuracy, John Edwards wrote to Airfix, highlighting the kit's errors and suggesting he could design a better version.

John Edwards's short life – he died in 1970 aged only 38 – was nothing if not eventful. After

Opposite page top: This Airfix Avro Anson dates from 1962 and is of particular interest because it depicts an example of the work Howard Jarvis, a member of the Royal Society of Marine Artists who, before Roy Cross took over, painted many of Airfix's earliest full-colour box-top illustrations

Middle: Early box HO-OO Confederate Infantryman. Bottom: The second version of Airfix's 1/72nd scale Lancaster bomber box

doing well at school in Essex, John was apprenticed to an uncle who owned a photographic studio in France. He learnt the tricks of the darkroom and salon and became fluent in French, but decided to return to England, where he joined the Crittal Metal Window Company as an engineering draughtsman. Called up for national service, John joined the Royal Artillery and used his technical abilities as an aid to gunlaying, meaning the setting of sights. It was his language skills, however, which most interested the army. With the Cold War at its frostiest, John was asked if he would learn German. He agreed, already having a facility for French, and was posted to Berlin to join the Intelligence Corps.

John had long been a passionate modeller. Like his language skills and technical ability, his spare time barrack-block model making had also come to the attention of his superiors, and they decided to put this skill to good use.

So prolific was John's clandestine model making that he had soon amassed a considerable collection.

Amazingly, each night, John and some of his colleagues would cross into the Soviet sector – construction of the Berlin Wall still being some time off – and whilst there note and sketch state-of-the-art Russian equipment. A Soviet missile battery was a particular favourite and it could be readily studied, the crew often vacating their post to nip into local beer cellars.

Once back in his billet, John would apply all of his skills as a scale modeller to create accurate scale replicas of the new kit he had been asked to observe.

So prolific was John's clandestine model making that he had soon amassed a considerable collection. The army decided to combine all of this important reconnaissance evidence into a trailer, which toured the Allied sectors of Berlin and was put to good use to educate servicemen about the equipment possessed by their Soviet adversaries.

Before he was demobbed the army offered John a commission, which he declined, returning to his previous job at Crittal in the early 1950s. He was there when Airfix released their first ever Spitfire kit – the infamous BTK.

This aircraft is especially remembered by its serial code because this, as John and many other enthusiasts noticed, was one of the model's classic errors. The code BTK belonged to a wartime RAF Supermarine Walrus squadron. The Walrus was an amphibious seaplane – about as far away from a high-speed monoplane as it was possible to be.

In fact Airfix's first Spitfire featured numerous errors in profile, in wing shape and around the cockpit. It seems that this 1/72nd scale miniature was a direct copy of a larger, quarter scale Spitfire model manufactured in the US by Aurora. Certainly Aurora's kit features precisely the same mistakes as the Airfix one – down to the erroneous markings. In the 1990s the late John Gray, managing director of Airfix's kit division for so long, told me that he recollected stories of Aurora's kit being used as the larger pattern for the new British kit. He told me that such plagiarism was not uncommon in the 1940s and 50s. Rival manufacturers regularly copied the hard work of competitors by simply reducing each other's kits in size (scale) and cutting a mould tool for a smaller, though identical model.

Like lots of other modellers, John purchased an example of Airfix's new Spitfire and hoped for the best. At around the same time he had just finished another model aircraft, an import from US manufacturer Monogram. Monogram's Mitchell bomber was constructed of composite

AROUND THE WORLD IN 3 HRS.
NUCLEAR AIRLINER

NUCLEAR WORLD AIRLINES N900

AURORA

HOBBY AURORA KITS

SCALE MODEL PLASTIC ASSEMBLY KIT

BRITISH MADE

Sky "GIVJOY" Birds

SERIES Nº 7

PLANES OF ALL NATIONS

GET OUR COLLECTION

"GIVJOY" Registered
1/72 Scale Model

STRONG, EASY TO BUILD

Price **2/-**

THE
FOKKER. D VII.

Contents :
Fuselage fitted with
    2 Machine Guns and
    Exhaust Pipe
2 Main Planes
    Tail Plane and Rudder
2 Under Carriage V Struts
    Axle with Fairing
2 Wheels
2 N Wing Struts
4 Centre Section Struts
    Airscrew
    Brass Spinner and Pin
    Tail Skid
Rivet Pins

CONSTRUCTIONAL

MODEL AEROPLANE

Top: In the US plastic model construction kits were well established by 1950. Aurora was one of the big three American manufacturers

Above: James Hay Stevens' famous Sky Birds range from the 1930s really established the universally adopted scale of 1/72nd or 1" to 1'. However, Sky Birds kits weren't manufactured from plastic but a variety of media including partly shaped wooden components and metal castings and turnings

Left: Another British manufacturer, FROG, famous for their flying model aircraft, are the real originators of the British plastic model construction kit business

materials – injection-moulded polystyrene and partially shaped balsa wood. This was a traditional method of construction. Indeed kits from the British manufacturer Sky Birds, the originator of the classic 1/72nd scale, were fashioned from a combination of balsa wood and metal components, some of which, such as wheels and engine cowlings, were quite sophisticated and turned from solid brass. Nevertheless, the Monogram Mitchell bomber was a revelation.

Released in October 1953, Monogram Speedee Bilt Kit No. H-1 set new standards for kit production. John Edwards could see that the Brits lagged far behind. Indeed, nearly 40 years later, co-founder of Monogram Robert Reder recalled the impact of this new kit: 'The wing panels had the airfoil, finished tapered trailing edges and spars machined in from solid balsa sheets. Plastic moulded wing tips ensured accuracy. Fuselage sides and formers were accurately cut with razor dies. Balsa blocks were used for the top and bottom of the fuselage and were contoured and cut to the exact size. All of the plastic parts – cowls and props, turrets and windows, engine nacelles, landing gear and other "hard to make" parts – were included.'

Edwards Comes Aboard

As luck would have it, at the time of his disappointment about Airfix's latest efforts, John Edwards saw an advertisement in which the London kit manufacturer was advertising a vacancy for a design draughtsman. Armed with a list of the inherent errors in the new Airfix

These rare boxes are surviving examples of the original test shots and associated packaging. These were kept at Airfix HQ in order to monitor the quality of subsequent editions

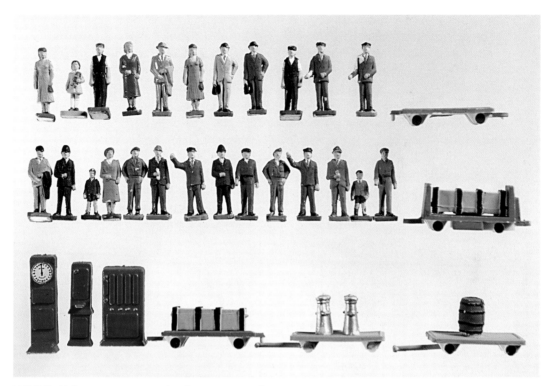

HO-OO Airfix passengers and railway accessories

Spitfire and taking an example of Monogram's groundbreaking Mitchell bomber along for good measure, John turned up for interview.

Brandishing the Monogram kit, John pointed out the numerous special features and highlighted the sophisticated packaging, instructions and assembly sequence. He obviously impressed his inquisitors, because immediately the job interview ended, they went into a huddle and without hesitation asked him when he could start. 'Tomorrow, first thing' was the answer.

One of John's first tasks when he joined Airfix was to right the wrongs inherent in the firm's current inaccurate Spitfire kit. In 1955 Airfix's classic Spitfire MkIX was released. Accurate throughout, it quickly became a bestseller. Airfix did, in fact, improve the tool for this kit in 1960, but only with minor amendments. Airfix's exquisite replica of the famous machine of RAF Fighter Command ace Johnny Johnson, with its distinctive JEJ code, remained in their range for nearly 50 years. In fact it outlived its creator.

Airfix's exquisite replica of the famous machine of RAF Fighter Command ace Johnny Johnson, with its distinctive JEJ code, remained in their range for nearly 50 years.

Following his untimely death, praise was heaped on John Edwards. The prestigious British aviation magazine *Aircraft Illustrated* said of him: 'John had been at Airfix for 15 years, almost from the beginning of the company, and was personally responsible for directing the design of all Airfix construction kits. It is only necessary to compare the early kits with such models as the Boeing B-29, HP 0/400, He 177, Bristol Bulldog or Sikorsky Sea King to see what vast improvements were made. John's latest venture was the introduction of the new range of 1/24th scale kits, but he has sadly only lived long enough to see the first, the magnificent Spitfire Mk1, put on to the market.'

John's obituary in *Airfix Magazine* – the hugely popular magazine published in conjunction with the kit manufacturer – appeared in May 1971 and perhaps best summed up the designer's contribution. 'Mr Edwards leaves behind a fine memorial in the big range of kits he has designed and which continue to give pleasure to millions of modellers throughout the world.'

> **John's real legacy can be found in the sophistication of Airfix's kits produced from the late 1960s onwards.**

It is true that John's real legacy can be found in the sophistication of Airfix's kits produced from the late 1960s onwards and can especially be seen in the aforementioned 1/24th scale Spitfire, released just prior to his death. This, the first of Airfix's groundbreaking large-scale Superkits, set the modelling world alight. As a series they were big on features and small on gadgets and novelties.

However, it has to be admitted that throughout most of the 1950s and early 60s Airfix kits were designed to appeal to the enthusiast but mostly the casual modeller – the schoolboy. Youngsters were by far the largest market, and to grab their attention even John was obliged to design features that were not strictly true to scale. Consequently, such early kits featured numerous compromises to enable gun turrets to rotate, flying surfaces to operate and bomb-bay doors to open and close.

A glance at the sales promotion literature distributed to toy and model shops during this exciting period, illustrates how confident Airfix were becoming. Tackling an increasing variety of often complex topics, they nevertheless demonstrated a real facility for mould design, cutting tools which moulded more and more sophisticated kits.

Left: The enthusiast will notice that the proprietor of this Trackside General Store is none other than Airfix managing director John Gray! Right: Airfix HO-OO Detached House (1957)

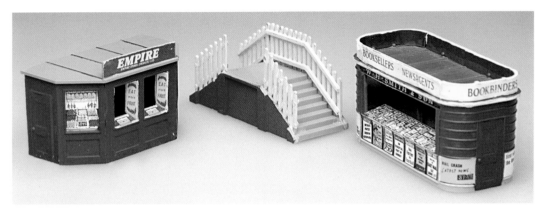

Kiosk and Platform Steps (1958)

Previously, when construction kits were simply a sideline and company fortunes depended on items like a Playable Plastic Toy Violin & Bow, or 'Woofy' the Performing Sea-Lion, Airfix packaging was emblazoned with the strapline: 'Remember Airfix for Toys'. Things were beginning to change, as the profusion of new construction kits depicted in Airfix sales leaflets confirmed.

Promoting Sales

The earliest plastic kit sales leaflets also testify to Airfix's growing independence when deciding which kits to produce. Prior to the 1960s several kits, certainly the most elaborate ones, were often produced in conjunction with companies who had developed the original subject – as Ferguson had with their new tractor – or who operated an air or shipping line they were keen to promote.

> **The Autumn 1958 Construction Kits flyer was the last catalogue to list the Ferguson Tractor.**

The Autumn 1958 Construction Kits flyer was the last catalogue to list the Ferguson Tractor and the *Southern Cross*, another legendary kit released in tandem with a third party and intended as a promotional item. The *Southern Cross* was built in Belfast by Harland and Wolff in 1955 for a new round-the-world passenger service of the Shaw Savill Line. It took no commercial freight, carried 1,100 one-class passengers and was one of the pioneers of the engines' aft layout. Escalating costs and competition from the air caused its withdrawal in 1971, when it was sold to a Greek shipping line.

The following year, 1959, saw the inclusion into the Airfix range of two more relatively large kits: the Bristol Superfreighter and the Short Sunderland. The Superfreighter was a capacious twin-engined freight aircraft equipped with clam-shell doors at the nose and capable of admitting motor cars to be stored in the hold whilst each vehicle's passengers took their seats in the aircraft's passenger cabin. The kit was once again the product of a commercial agreement, and this time the business partner was Silver City Airways. Formed in 1947, this new airline had equipped itself with designs which, like the Avro Lancastrian, were pretty simple developments of wartime machines, enabling the massively expanded British aircraft industry to find markets in peacetime. One such machine, the Bristol Freighter, was significant in the development of the airline, and the fleet soon expanded to four aircraft, three of which were used in the Berlin Airlift in 1948.

The first managing director of Silver City was Wing Commander 'Taffy' Grimth James Powell, who quickly realised he could adapt the Bristol Freighter to fly passengers and cars from Britain to Continental Europe via an 'air ferry'. Thus the Bristol Superfreighter was born. Silver City's service from Lympne in Kent to Le Touquet was a success, for a while, but it soon became apparent that the grass runway at Lympne was not suitable for the increased volume of traffic and other airfields were sought. Nevertheless, at the time of Airfix's 1/72nd scale kit of the Bristol Superfreighter, Silver City's exciting new concept was a huge success.

Like those on the *Southern Cross*, passengers aboard the Superfreighter were encouraged to purchase a souvenir and, after travelling in the real thing, settle down to make a scale replica to keep at home.

Woolies Steps Up

As has been mentioned earlier, it was the critical commercial relationship with F.W. Woolworth, their biggest customer, which forced Airfix to reluctantly package their kits in plastic bags rather than more robust but expensive cardboard boxes. Ironically, of course, Woolworth's intervention meant that Airfix more or less stumbled across a method of packaging that was to become an iconic component of their famous brand and, helpfully, enabled youngsters to see what they were buying without opening boxes and damaging the contents.

However, F.W. Woolworth's market position and commercial clout was also helpful in more immediately apparent ways. One of these was the retailers' useful co-operation with the distribution of promotional items advertising the Airfix range – Woolworth printed their own in-store sales leaflet. For some reason F.W. Woolworth's 1958 leaflet only featured aircraft and some trackside models – cars and miniature sailing ships are noticeable by their absence. However, perhaps the most striking aspect of this publication is the price of kits. There are

The HO-OO Newsagents and adjacent toy shop, admirably stocked with Airfix kits, was managed by someone with the same surname as chief designer John Edwards!

only two variations: two shillings for Series One models and three shillings for the larger Series Three items.

Most of the trackside models were available for two shillings (10p in decimal currency!). These ranged from No.1, a Country Inn, a marvellous half-timbered construction and now one of the most collectable of Airfix's early models, to my favourite, No.11 Kiosks & Platform Steps, redolent to me of arriving at Ramsgate railway station at the beginning of seaside holidays in the 1960s. The most expensive trackside kit in the list was No.201, Footbridge, a kit necessarily large enough to span a couple of Hornby Dublo ('OO') model railway tracks.

There were 20 different Series One aircraft depicted – each a real bargain at a couple of shillings. Airfix's rather dubious Spitfire MkI (BTK) was illustrated on the leaflet's cover and shown inside as model No.81. This was to be the infamous replica's swansong, as it would shortly be replaced by John Edwards's much more accurate MkIX version. Amazingly, some of these construction kits would remain in the Airfix range for nearly half a century.

Airfix's growing design and production confidence, not to mention the increased capacity of its larger moulding machines, was evident in the depiction of the Series Two aircraft ('Larger types of aircraft in the same 1/72nd scale'). Five were shown, all Allied types of the Second World War – the RAF's Mosquito and Beaufighter, the Fleet Air Arm's Swordfish and Walrus and the token Yank, Republic's powerful twin-engined Lightning fighter-bomber.

Featuring a photograph of the new 1/72nd scale Lancaster B1 bomber on the cover, the spring 1959 edition sales leaflet reinforced Airfix's commitment to larger and more involved kits. The company would begin the new decade with a range of new kits destined to raise the bar as far as design and production standards within the construction kit industry were concerned.

Fifties Foundations

Throughout the 1950s plastic kits had quickly eclipsed all other Airfix products as far as their commercial significance to the company's future was concerned. Indeed, the summer 1959 sales leaflet saw the first promotional use of the classic phrase 'constant scale'. These definitive words spelt out Airfix's determination to become a major player in the burgeoning plastic kit industry and signalled to enthusiasts that Airfix kits were accurate and could be trusted. It was clear that the company was preparing to enter the new decade with a product line that could rival the best from the US – still the largest manufacturer of polystyrene kits. Because they were generally inexpensive – compared with Dinky toys and Hornby trains, which were usually reserved for gift purchases, restricted to birthday or Christmas presents – Airfix kits were bought on a regular basis. Indeed the design of the catalogues conspired to encourage youngsters to build a collection consisting of lots of kits. Consequently, Airfix kits became almost a pocket-money purchase. Indeed, so frequently were they purchased and from so many sources, not just F.W. Woolworth but also from newsagents, post offices, convenience stores and even sweet shops, that Airfix's share of the toy and hobby market increased with prodigious speed.

Throughout the 1950s plastic kits had quickly eclipsed all other Airfix products.

Whilst it is true that Airfix came into its own in the 1960s, turning into Britain's largest and most profitable toy and consumer products group by the 1970s, the most crucial decade for the company was the 1950s. That was when all the pioneering hard work of first Nicholas

Kove and then his young protégé Ralph Ehrmann, especially the business brains of the latter, established the foundations on to which the company's future success could be firmly built.

Having dipped their toe into the plastic kit market in 1952 with the release of the first in the Classic Ships range, the *Golden Hind*, by 1955 Airfix had manufactured only eight construction kits (I'm not including the legendary Ferguson Tractor, which wasn't originally designed as a construction kit when it first appeared in 1949). The other seven kits were the dodgy Spitfire MkI (BTK), the additional Classic Ships *Santa Maria*, HMS *Shannon* and *Cutty Sark*, the *Southern Cross* (which like the tractor really started life as a promotional item and didn't remain in the kit range for long anyway), the 1/32nd scale 1911 Rolls-Royce – Airfix's first venture into the profitable area of automotive construction kits, which was then almost exclusively the preserve of US kit firms Gowland & Gowland and Revell – and John Edwards's 1/72nd scale Spitfire MkIX, which corrected the calamitous errors of the earlier Spitfire BTK.

By the end of the decade, however, Airfix's kit production had increased to the extent that in only four years, between 1956 and 1959, they had produced an amazing 88 more kits.

By the end of the decade, however, Airfix's kit production had increased to the extent that in only four years, between 1956 and 1959, they had produced an amazing 88 more kits. Some of these, such as the *Golden Hind*, the 1911 Rolls-Royce, the *Santa Maria*, *Cutty Sark* and HMS *Shannon*,were modified versions of existing kits, re-tooled after Airfix's staff had become more adept at mastering all aspects of the injection moulding process. Improvements were practicable because, now with more money in its coffers, Airfix could revisit the design and development stages, more confidently applying new skills learnt the hard way in what was still a very new industry. Consequently a variety of things were done, such as perhaps redrawing crucial General Arrangement (GA) engineering drawings, making an improved wooden pattern and then cutting a new tool or modifying individual kit components so that they were better than before. Only a handful of its kits needed such modifying, and these naturally were the ones manufactured when the firm was learning the hard way and money was tight, as it often is where new ventures are concerned.

The prodigious rate of production that produced nearly 100 kits in only a few years gives us some idea of what a gold mine Airfix had stumbled into. Although they weren't quite printing money, it was a highly streamlined process. As the injection moulding presses opened and closed they spewed moulded parts, and these were popped into a polythene bag to which an integral header and instruction sheet was folded and stapled, then packed into cartons and quickly distributed to retailers. Enthusiastic modellers snapped them up. In fact they were so inexpensive, they were eagerly purchased by youngsters and their parents as a cheap and fun activity toy which required only the additional purchase of a tube of polystyrene cement to construct a plaything that was both enjoyable and, to some degree, educational. Modellers were happy, and parents were delighted. Airfix won all round.

It's no exaggeration to say that although few of the larger kits for which Airfix would later receive justifiable plaudits were manufactured prior to the 1960s, the kits released during the 1950s remain the core of the Airfix brand. They are the kits that people of a certain age remember with fondness. Not that you have to be a senior citizen to have enjoyed them. Most of these kits were available for decades after they were first released, and at the time of writing (Summer 2008) the Gladiator MkI from 1956 has just been moulded by Airfix's manufacturer in India, producing a kit that's been warmly received by 21st-century modellers.

All-in-one starter kit compendiums aren't a new thing. In the 1950s Airfix regularly packaged a selection of Series One models complete with paints and brushes

Desert Island Kits

The following selection includes some of my favourites from these early years. I can still see Airfix poly bags including Bristol Fighters, Me 109s, Hurricane IV's, Westland Lysanders, 1904 Darracqs, S.E. 6B floatplanes, Great Western paddle steamers and Walrus flying boats swinging beneath the carousel from which they were suspended as I rotated the display looking for a new kit to rush home with on Saturday morning. If a relative had visited I might have a bit more to spend (perhaps as much as three shillings – a whole 15p in today's money) and then I could afford a boxed Series Two aircraft model of perhaps an American twin-boom P38-J Lightning fighter or a Bristol Belvedere helicopter with its box-top illustration showing British troops jumping from it into a jungle clearing during the Malayan emergency. If I fancied making a figure model, Airfix had a super range of 1/12th scale figures from which I could choose, so I might pick a model of the Black Prince in his armour (if you were careful you could get his helmet visor to open and close). If I fancied a different figure I might change the guard with a busby-wearing Coldstream Guardsman. Or I might invest in an HO-OO scale Signal Gantry to go with my model railway layout. Of course if it was my birthday or I had managed to save some pocket money – very unlikely – I could splash out and for a few more shillings acquire a 1/72nd scale Wellington BIII (6/-) or even larger Avro Lancaster BI (7/6d). The largest Airfix kit, the massive 1/72nd scale Short Sunderland, first appeared in 1959 and cost only ten shillings and sixpence, so even this monster wasn't out of reach. There was a dazzling choice, and modellers embraced almost the entire range with gusto.

CHAPTER 3

BOOM TIMES

Airfix began its momentous journey into the 1960s by laying down a marker – a firm signal of its intended endurance – when it confidently began its own monthly magazine.

Airfix Magazine No.1 appeared in June 1960 at a retail price of one shilling (5p). Its first editor was John Webb, the proprietor of Airfix's PR company, John Webb Press Services, who were based close to Harrods in London's Knightsbridge.

Airfix Magazine was destined to grow very quickly, both in physical dimensions and in circulation, and within a decade would become one of Britain's most successful affinity publications. To its credit, however, *Airfix Magazine* was never a typical example of contract publishing, in fact it often criticised the products of its parent, a habit that began to engender resentment at Airfix HQ and ultimately led to the publication's demise. But that was a long way in the future – in the early days *Airfix Magazine* was clearly one of the kit manufacturer's shrewdest marketing developments.

Left: The late great Brian Knight joined Airfix in 1967 and one of his first jobs was to revise the box art of the large scale Classic Ships. This is Brian's original painting for *Revenge*, first released by Airfix in 1964, originally treated in Charles Oates' graphic 'half-and-half' style

Above: Airfix B-17G Flying Fortress in 2nd edition box featuring artwork by the legendary Roy Cross

A Talented Line-up

Although originally a clever exercise in loyalty marketing, from its inception *Airfix Magazine* was much more than a PR puff for its owner and namesake. Indeed, an early edict from Airfix management stipulated that no more than four consecutive pages should focus on 'own brand' products. A pretty savvy policy, this treatment engendered a feeling of editorial independence which appealed to readers who enjoyed the publication's unbiased approach. Commercially of course, it also meant that the *Airfix Magazine* attracted the widest variety of advertising matter. Rival kit manufacturers such as Revell and Aurora were happy to advertise in it, as were manufacturers of other toys and products, such as Corgi die-cast cars, Coronet cameras and Wrenn Formula 152 slot racers. Consequently, *Airfix Magazine* went down equally well with both readers and advertisers.

Airfix Magazine first appeared in June 1960. Despite the odd up and down this august publication provided modellers with their monthly fix until the last edition was published in November 1993. A thirty-three year life isn't bad for an affinity publication...

> From its inception *Airfix Magazine* was much more than a PR puff for its owner and namesake.

Key ingredients of *Airfix Magazine*'s success were the quality of the editorial staff and the detail and value of the articles between its covers. Although Airfix's PR consultant John Webb assumed the role of editor at the time of the inaugural publication, within a few months this position was filled by Webb's deputy, Alan Hall, an aviation buff and specialist writer well known to hobbyists and transport enthusiasts. A brief glance of some of the editorial staff and contributors associated with *Airfix Magazine* down the years reveals a veritable who's who of talent familiar to the enthusiast. Following on from Alan Hall, subsequent editors included such luminaries as John Blunsden, Chris Ellis, Darryl Reach and Bruce Quarrie.

Many long-running features became familiar and trusted repositories of ideas and advice. Readers devoured articles such as Michael J.F. Bowyer's 'RAF Fighting Colours' and 'RAF Bombing Colours', A.J. Day's 'Shipping Notes' and Alan Hall's legendary 'In the Air'. Famous names (well, famous to us enthusiasts, and that's what counts) such as Bruce Robertson, Sid Horton, Gerald Scarborough, Roy Dilley and Derek Whiting told readers how to convert or cannibalise a variety of kits so that every conceivable aircraft type, armoured vehicle or military costume could be fashioned to create unique models. For *Airfix Magazine* a new plastic construction kit was merely the beginning of a creative enterprise. Rarely were readers encouraged to build a kit straight from the box. Instead it was a veritable handbook for inventive conversion, a guide to ingenious surgery, necessitating numerous scalpel or razor-saw cuts in order to transform wing-tip profiles or reconfigure engine nacelles.

The initial success of *Airfix Magazine* was largely due to the efforts of the advertising

Above: Roy Cross art for Renault Dauphine. Below: Hawker Hart (1957)

manager of John Webb Press Services, one Patrick Stephens. Later he would become full-time advertising director of the magazine, and when in 1968 he formed his own company, Patrick Stephens Ltd (PSL), he assumed the role of publisher with overall responsibility for monthly sales. At their height in the early 1970s these reached a dazzling 100,000 copies each month. PSL published the magazine until 1978.

A closer look at some classic *Airfix Magazine* articles from the 1960s provides a flavour of the decade of the company's fastest growth spurt.

Although it only had 32–48 pages, from cover to cover the earliest issues of *Airfix Magazine* were jam-packed with features of interest to modellers whatever their bent, be that cars, ships, aircraft or miniature railways. In a nod to the competition it faced from *Meccano Magazine*, famous for its wide variety of topics – and in a shrewd move intended to encourage some of Frank Hornby's readers to jump ship – in the early days *Airfix Magazine* even included some articles totally unrelated to modelling. Berry Woods's regular feature on stamps springs to mind. Appreciating the dichotomy of combining philately and scale modelling, Mr Woods dealt with any suggestions of a mismatch with particular flair: 'Collecting old-time models and comparing them with present-day developments is fascinating, and you can have an interesting time with stamps showing locomotives, ships, cars and other means of transport in bygone days.' Genius. Fortunately the majority of articles were perfectly suited to the core market purchasing models of tanks and fighter planes.

Issue One, published in June 1960, kicked off in style. Apart from the aforementioned stamps feature, virtually everything was directly related to plastic models and more specifically to encouraging readers to purchase the latest Airfix kits and use them as the basis for super-detailing.

Airfix 1/600th scale warships – small but perfectly put together

Consequently, an article such as 'Realistic Victorious', in which Stephen Jones told readers 'how to make the most of a clever piece of miniaturisation', not only explained how to achieve the scale accuracy of features like the lattice-work communications pylons and cargo davits of Britain's latest aircraft-carrier, it also helped shift quantities of Airfix's brand new kit of the vessel. Similarly, two other pieces in the same issue, 'Motorise your Zero – Motorising a 1:72 A6M Zero' and 'Make it Authentic – Detailing the Airfix Bristol Superfreighter', were intended to encourage the purchase of Airfix's new 1/72nd Second World War Japanese fighter and cross-channel car transporter respectively.

From the beginning *Airfix Magazine* made great efforts to involve its readers and build a loyal community.

But it wasn't just about marketing. From the beginning *Airfix Magazine* made great efforts to involve its readers and build a loyal community. A prominent panel headed 'Write for *Airfix Magazine*' invited contributions from enthusiasts: 'The editor will be pleased to consider for publication articles and photographs of interest to readers of *Airfix Magazine*. Of particular interest will be descriptions of readers' own layouts in which plastic kits, of any make, have played a significant part. An early decision will be given on all material submitted and original copy will be quickly returned. Payment for contributions used will be made at the end of the month of publication.'

Buccaneers

'News from Airfix' in *Airfix Magazine* No.3 (published in August 1960) featured a neat link to the article about the aircraft-carrier HMS *Victorious* that appeared in the first issue. Readers were encouraged excitedly to purchase a Model Atom Bomber, the new Blackburn NA-39, available as Series 3 kit for only four shillings and sixpence (22.5p!): 'The NA-39 is the world's first aircraft designed to attack beneath the cover of radar and guided missiles. In September 1959 the Royal Navy ordered a large number of NA-39s following successful trials aboard the carrier HMS *Victorious* – the subject of another Airfix model. The NA-39 has a rotary bomb bay which can hold either conventional or nuclear weapons and these can be placed with unprecedented accuracy. The extensive electronic equipment carried ensures that the pilot knows precisely where he is, and is capable of avoiding obstacles ahead, despite his low level 600–700 mph high-speed flight. Airfix's splendid new model will be generally available at the end of August.'

Keen-eyed aviation enthusiasts will doubtless know that the NA-39 was soon to be christened the Blackburn Buccaneer. Amazingly, from June 1952, when the original specifications for NA-39 were published, the Buccaneer remained in front-line service in one form or another until March 1994, when the aircraft was fully replaced by the Tornado. Airfix kept pace with the numerous developments of this redoubtable machine from its first 1/72nd scale kit of the prototype right up to the release of a much larger and more sophisticated 1/48th scale replica of the final S2B/S2-CD S Mk50 in 2005 and, most recently, a 1/72nd scale version of the same variant in 2008.

The Buccaneer popped up again in *Airfix Magazine* No.6, but this time as part of a full-page advertisement. This ad is noteworthy for being one of the earliest occasions Airfix used their famous 'Just Like the Real Thing!' headline. Above this exclamation are two Buccaneers photographed climbing high above a maritime scene showing HMS *Victorious* afloat on the high seas. 'Believe it or not, the nearer one is the Airfix

Above: Wild West Playset. A variety of such items were available and each provided a neat method of combining the existing HO-OO figures with the new forts, gun emplacements and castles designed to add play value to these hugely popular toys

Below: Although not as accurate as later offerings, there is a certain charm about this early 1960s D-Day diorama

All Hell is let loose below the battlements of Sherwood Castle as Robin Hood and his merry men battle the Sheriff of Nottingham's knights

model of the Blackburn Buccaneer. Behind it is a picture of the real thing.' Fortunately the coarseness of 1960s lithographic printing conspired to create the illusion of two strikingly similar images.

Remarkable Figures

In 'News from Airfix' in the January 1961 edition of *Airfix Magazine* attention was focused on the firm's expanding range of tiny HO-OO scale polythene figures. Like their 1/72nd scale aircraft, the success of these cheap and plentiful characters was crucial to Airfix's prosperity. The fact that they were so inexpensive was made plain by the article's heading: 'German Soldiers for a Halfpenny Each'. 'Just 20 years after the expected Nazi invasion of Britain millions of German infantrymen are spreading across the country. They have "landed" in answer to the appeal of thousands of British model makers to Airfix and are, of course, made in plastic. Costing only 2s.0d. for a colourful box of 48 figures, Airfix's German infantry set is wonderful value. It is to the same OO scale as Airfix's other 2s.0d. figure sets of British Infantry, Guards Band, Guards Colour Party and also Farm Animals; the soldiers are therefore suitable for use, not only in battle scenes with other Airfix figures, but also with any 1/72nd scale model aircraft, tank or gun or any piece of OO scale railway accessories.'

As all serious modellers know, this last point isn't strictly true, and in fact OO scale corresponds to 1/76th scale and HO scale to 1/87th, both ratios originally developed

1/72nd scale Hawker Harrier (1969). Airfix had released the prototype P1127 Kestrel as long ago as 1962.

Assembled and painted Harrier

to work with the enormously popular Hornby Dublo ('OO') scale miniature railway sets. Nevertheless, to the naked eye there's not much in it, and when you consider the variations in height amongst full-size human beings, any discrepancies can be discounted.

Actually the fact that Airfix toy soldiers were originally produced to accompany model railway layouts was made clear in another piece in the same issue's 'News from Airfix'. In a passage entitled 'Even a Policeman', much was made of the firm's new HO-OO Civilians set.

'Modellers are going to jump for joy when they see the new 2s.0d. 48-piece set of OO-scale plastic civilians. Finished in white plastic, ready for painting, they are just what modellers have needed to give really human realism to railway layouts and model aircraft settings. Airfix plastic people are far from looking starched or stereotyped – they are just like real life humans. For instance, there are two old men with sticks, and two fat men; six men are sitting down (two cross-legged, two with overcoats and two in suits); two more are walking and two running and, of eleven standing still, two have caps, two greatcoats, three duffle coats, two short jackets and two are in shirts and holding their hats. Others include a postman, newsboy, policeman and scooterist, together with a separate scooter. There are women and children too – three schoolboys and three toddlers, two sitting women with babies and two more without. There are also eight standing women.'

Today, especially if in a 1960 first edition box, surviving examples of this very evocative and retro figure set command high values amongst collectors.

I have been told that Airfix employees frequently joked that the enormous popularity and regular repeat sales of HO-OO figures was largely attributable to the fact that soldiers dropped on the living-room floor by youngsters were frequently hoovered up by their mothers!

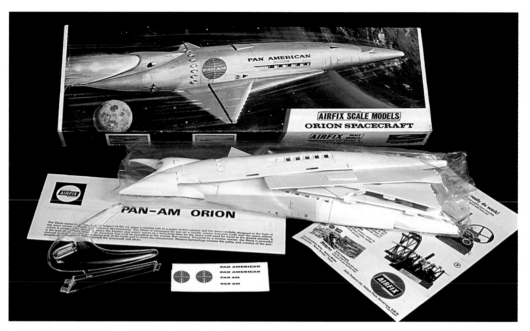

The Orion Spacecraft from Stanley Kubrick's *2001: A Space Odyssey*

Issues of Scale

At the tail end of 1961, Airfix management braced themselves for the fury of modellers who had been told to expect aircraft only in the established 1/72nd scale. Entitled 'A Quart into a Pint Pot', the editorial of *Airfix Magazine* Volume 2, number 5 published that October went on to explain:

> 'Now that Airfix have introduced their new Skyking series of aircraft model construction kits we are prepared for a great outcry from the enthusiasts who have come to expect the constant scale of 1/72 from the manufacturers. But let's think for a minute. Why have they done this? The obvious answer can be judged from the tremendous number of readers' letters asking for models of airliners and the larger bombers of the post-war era. These could be produced in the present scale, but what would the modeller's wife or mother say to having a 1/72nd scale TU-114 in the house with a wing span of over three feet?... and what would the retail price be? The introduction of the Caravelle and Comet 4B in 1/144th scale by Airfix is a very bold decision. They are, however, convinced that the two new models and the others yet to come, lacking nothing in the detail with which Airfix models are associated, will very quickly start the collectors on a new and equally interesting time.'

Although there was a rationale behind Airfix's decision to limit the size of airliners to the smaller 1/144th scale, another significant factor was that even the largest injection moulding machines owned by the company were incapable of moulding wingspans for a Strato Cruiser,

Top: Ton-Up-Tony, one of the Airfix Weird-Ohs from the mid-1960s

Left: Tollway Daddy, an equally whacky 1960s Weird-Oh kit

Below: Selection of rare and original 007 kits manufactured under licence to Eon Productions in the 1960s

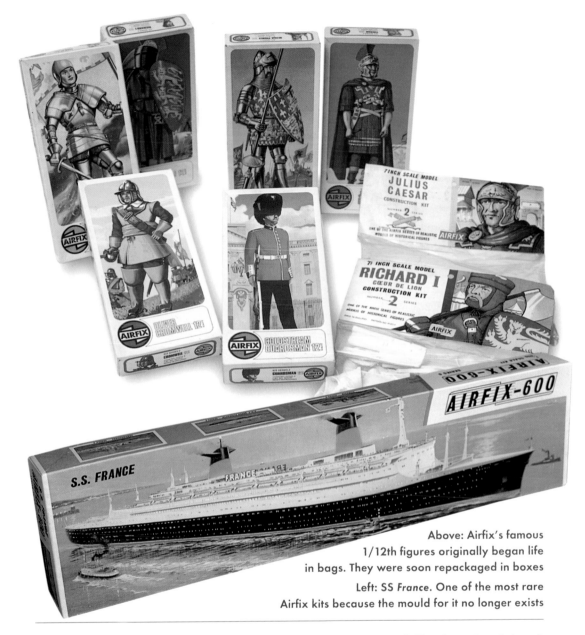

Above: Airfix's famous
1/12th figures originally began life
in bags. They were soon repackaged in boxes

Left: SS *France*. One of the most rare
Airfix kits because the mould for it no longer exists

or Boeing 707, for example, in the favoured constant scale of 1/72nd. This disparity of aircraft sizes was always frustrating to the serious modeller, preventing him or her from adding any super detail or interior details. At the time British modellers had to turn to the products of US kit companies such as Revell or Monogram, both of whom seemed to have no trouble manufacturing or retailing aircraft models with monster wingspans.

In reality the kit designers at Airfix knew that the limitations of 1/144th scale, precisely half that of 1/72nd scale, restricted the potential of Skyking kits. It would be nearly 50 years before Airfix reversed its decision and released 1/72nd scale kits of really large aircraft. Their first was the Rockwell B1-B, the first of the so-called stealth bombers released in 1984, and the most recent is their marvellous 1/72 Nimrod MR.1/MR.2/MR.2P/R.1 kit. Ironically, the latter aircraft is a development of the ill-fated De Havilland Comet, the Mk4B version of which was, with the French Caravelle, one of the pioneers of the small-scale debate and kick-started Airfix's 1/144th scale range in 1961.

Peter Allen told me that he agreed the deal with MPC, Airfix's US partner, which led to the release of the B1-B at the same time as the new Airfix Avro Vulcan. 'If they backed us for the Vulcan we would back them with the B1-B. The Vulcan would sell well in the UK, but the B1-B would only be around 5,000 units. We did the design and tooling of both.'

Building Better

In February 1962 *Airfix Magazine* announced the launch of Betta Bilda. 'An entirely new plastic building set,' crowed the editorial. 'Costing only 10s [50p!] and strongly boxed, Betta Bilda contains 360 rigid interlocking polystyrene parts conforming to 24 different designs of bases, bricks, doors, windows and roofing tiles.'

Betta Bilda wasn't entirely new. An earlier British construction toy, Bayko, was patented as long ago as 1934 (it survived until 1967), and another famous British toy company, Tri-ang,

Rare *High Chaparral* figures (1967)

Above: Roy Cross's first commission for Airfix, his 1964 painting of the Dornier Do-217, a revision of Charles Oates' 1959 artwork. Below: 1/72nd scale RAF trainers. Beagle Bassett 1968 (left) and DH Chipmunk (1970)

were selling a not dissimilar product called Arkitex. In fact, even before Betta Builda, Airfix had their own Building Set construction toy on the market. The Number One Starter Set is illustrated in this book on page 70. There was also Minibrix, from the Premo Rubber Company, and Chad Valley's Girder and Panel set, an American invention made under licence in the UK, to contend with. However, as all Airfix fans know, Betta Bilda most closely imitated, I never said copied, the famous Danish construction toy LEGO, which like Bayko was invented in the 1930s.

It was, of course, the striking similarities with LEGO which finally put paid to Betta Bilda, but in 1961 Airfix felt strong enough to manufacture their rival product and continued to do so throughout the 1960s. Their bullishness is evident from the statement: 'A particular advantage of the new Betta Bilda series is that the manufacturers also market 1s.6d. boxes of supplementary and spare parts for owners who wish to extend or replace their components.' LEGO, of course, did precisely the same, but the fight concerning any plagiarism was some way off.

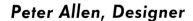

Peter Allen, Designer

Model-maker turned designer Peter Allen joined Airfix in 1962. (I've known Peter since the early 1980s when I was writing *The Model World of Airfix*.) 'There were only six of us in the Drawing Office – nowadays

Above: Roy Cross's fine painting of the 1/72nd scale Bristol Fighter – the classic WWI 'Brisfit'

it would be called "Design",' he told me. 'The atmosphere was friendly, with a lot of mickey-taking and other fun happening. There was a degree of competition to make your component that bit more advanced and interesting than previous designs.'

Peter was relieved to be at Airfix because he had only recently been made redundant from Tri-ang, for whom he had been working at their premises in Merton, Surrey. Ironically he was one of the team working on Arkitex, Tri-ang's building set. Trained as an apprentice tool maker, whilst at Tri-ang Peter had been seconded to the experimental department where, working as a model maker, he fashioned by hand the initial prototype components for the unveiling of Arkitex at the Brighton Toy Fair. In fact Peter was asked to demonstrate the new construction toy at the fair, it being deemed too fragile in prototype form for the potential rough handling of interested buyers. It's worth pointing out that there was never a fear of younger hands wrecking Tri-ang's handiwork, one of the curious things about the Brighton Toy Fair being the total absence of children!

Peter provided me with some additional details about his and Airfix's involvement with construction toys.

'Whilst at Tri-ang I worked on a building set based on the LEGO size and principle but about half as thick as the LEGO brick. This went into production but I cannot recall the name. To progress the design we had details of the patent of a German system, a larger brick than LEGO but the same principal. Bayko to me does not relate closely to the other systems as it slots

> between metal rods. Tri-ang had two Arkitex ranges,
> HO-OO and I think 1/42nd, to line up with Spot-On.
> Its design is not close to LEGO or Bayko. It was designed to compete with the
> Chad Valley set. LEGO tried a court action on us and we had to withdraw one
> brick from production, I think this was a long brick that had six studs.'

Whilst with Tri-ang Peter was involved with the ongoing development of another famous British toy range – Spot-On cars. Developed at the Belfast factory of Tri-ang's parent company Lines Brothers, these were die-cast models of mainly British cars, such as the Ford Zodiac. Many Spot-On cars were redesigned to include headlights that were battery powered. Others featured detailed interiors, with well-dressed drivers and passengers. Peter had the task of adjusting individual car designs so that they could accommodate the additional components required to make miniature headlights operate reliably. Consequently Peter was delighted that once at Airfix he was encouraged to get even more intimately involved with product design. 'Airfix was the greatest company to work for. You were encouraged to develop and extend your knowledge of the products and processes relating to production.'

The First Airfix Catalogue

In 1962 there was another publishing first for Airfix and the beginning of a perennial favourite which survives to this day: the very first Airfix catalogue. Then it was priced at only nine old pennies; today, mint copies of this landmark booklet are worth around £200.

Below: The Battle of Waterloo Assault set shown in this selection of Playsets has recently been re-released. But there's nothing like the original...

'As you flip through the pages of this catalogue, you will see details of over 135 constant scale plastic construction kits,' the introductory copy explained. 'In developing the Airfix range we recognise the special requirements of the advanced modeller as well as the beginner. Although Airfix kits are simple to construct, the enthusiast specialist will find that adaptations and variations of standard kits are easy for him to make.' Good for him. Bearing in mind Airfix's earlier comment about large kits being potentially unpopular with a modeller's wife or mother, it's clear that the company was making no concessions to political correctness in the early 1960s. Airfix was making models for chaps, pure and simple.

Airfix's inaugural catalogue also referred to the issue of the previous year's two scales of aircraft models. The Skyking range was 'an addition to the Airfix range and will in no way replace the 1/72nd scale series', the catalogue reassured its readers.

The first edition of the Airfix catalogue is a social historian's dream, a real time capsule full of retro delights. Hard-top and convertible Sunbeam Rapiers, Saunders-Roe SR53 research planes, the prototype Hovercraft SRN1 ('for demonstration purposes it has carried 20 fully equipped soldiers'), jostled for attention with Spitfire MkIXs, Hurricane MkIVs, Messerschmitt 109s and SS Canberra.

The first edition of the Airfix catalogue is a social historian's dream, a real time capsule full of retro delights.

In the three years from 1960 to 1962 Airfix had added more than 50 new models to their range. It's easy to see why the company felt it was time to print a full-colour, multipage catalogue. Looking through the very brief selection which follows, model fans will see many Airfix classics, lots of which sustained the range for years to come. However, they weren't all brand new models. Proof of Airfix's commitment to the serious modeller was their 1960 release of a modified version, a second tool, of John Edwards's famous Spitfire MkIX. John's skills and knowledge about the practical possibilities of plastic moulding had come on immeasurably in the five years since his first version of Battle of Britain ace Johnny Johnson's Spitfire fighter plane was released in 1955. He felt he could improve the model still further, and Airfix management acquiesced to his costly request to revisit and re-cut the mould tool. Modellers appreciated his efforts and Airfix's determination to provide the best possible scale replicas.

In 1960, together with a much improved late mark Spitfire, Airfix provided modellers with a wide variety of new kits, such as a really good replica of the first operational jet fighter of the Second World War, the Me-262, a less than perfect model of the RAF's ill-fated Boulton Paul Defiant, a neat model of the SRN1 Hovercraft, the tiny predecessor of the giant hovercrafts that would regularly criss-cross the English Channel later in the decade, a neat 1/72nd scale model of the new Bristol Bloodhound surface-to-air missile system, which came with a tiny Land Rover and an RAF regiment guard complete with Alsatian dog on lead. Henry VIII and Joan of Arc joined Edward – Woodstock – the Black Prince in the 1/12th scale figure range, while the British battleship HMS *Hood* was added to the growing 1/600th scale ship range. The Airfix HO-OO railways range grew considerably with the addition of kits of an Esso Tank Wagon, Water Tower, Engine Shed and Railbus. Models of the stalwart Douglas Dakota and equally reliable Fokker Friendship completed the 1/72nd scale aircraft range.

In 1961 new Airfix kits included models of British warships HMS *Daring* and HMS *Campbeltown*, the hero of the famous Zeebrugge commando raid where the vessel was used as a battering ram to smash through the lock gates of the Nazi-controlled dry dock at the port.

The HO-OO armoured fighting vehicle range was considerably reinforced by the addition of models of the Panther, Sherman and Churchill tanks. Vehicle fans were treated with 1/32nd scale miniatures of a Sunbeam Rapier, Austin Healey Sprite MkI, Renault Dauphine and Morris Minor – all of which are now very collectable. Richard I, Oliver Cromwell and Charles I were added to the popular figure range. Amongst lots of other kits, highlights included a 1/72nd scale replica of the RAF's Handley Page Halifax heavy bomber, which joined the existing Airfix Lancaster and Wellington bombers. Finally there was a model of the brand new liner, SS *Canberra*, built for P&O at the Harland and Wolff shipyard in Belfast and launched in March 1960.

In 1962 more Airfix classics joined the range, most of which were destined to be made by generations of modellers for many years to come. The German 75mm Assault Gun and its Second World War adversary the Soviet Stalin 3 tank joined the range (although as all true enthusiasts pointed out in the letters pages of *Airfix Magazine*, the Mark III version of this Russian tank entered service too late to see action in the war). And at last tank fans had a suitable transporter when the mighty British Scammell also joined the range. Aircraft enthusiasts were delighted by the addition of a Heinkel He III to the range, although somewhat disappointed that again it was a late war Mark H variant and not the Mark E of Battle of Britain fame. Even to the novice the differences between the two were quite distinctive. Another equally famous Second World War bomber, the USAAF's B17 G Flying Fortress, completed the series of major wartime heavy bombers.

The Great War Bus

Airfix's lovely 1/32nd scale Edwardian Omnibus B Type joined the vehicle range in 1962. It was updated four years later, appearing as The Old Bill Bus, complete with British Tommies in Great War uniforms. Designed as a miniature facsimile of the type of London omnibus pressed into military service on the Western Front, this new kit was very well received.

However, once again, it was the details, or lack of them, that disappointed serious modellers. Most enthusiasts would have preferred to paint moulded plastic replicas of the wooden shuttering used to clad the outside of each vehicle, acting both as a base for hastily applied

Assembled version of the 1910 London Omnibus and the Old Bill conversion of the vehicle used as a troop transport during the Great War

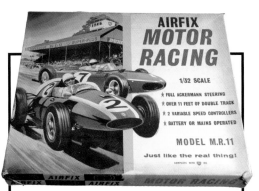

khaki camouflage and also as rudimentary armour. Instead, modellers had to make do with detaching the pre-printed cardboard component and glueing them on to the vehicle's bodywork. This cheap addition and the sprue featuring the admittedly excellent soldier figures and their rifles were the only really new bits in the box. There was, however, one other saving grace. When the army version of the London bus appeared in 1966, the new box top featured some really striking artwork by the legendary Roy Cross, the artist and illustrator having begun a ten-year contract with Airfix in 1965.

Giving Scalextric a run for its money (ironically they are all now part of the same family) in the 1960s Airfix slot racing outfits like this MR11 boxed set helped satisfy the enormous demand for that generation's equivalent of the PlayStation.

Slot-Car Racing

Obviously a lot was happening to Airfix in 1962. Along with Crayonne, who manufactured plastic household utility items, and Semco, a pre-war manufacturer of toy dolls, Airfix acquired the slot-car racing firm Model Road Racing Cars to supplement their small existing range, and for a while their products were released under the Airfix MRRC banner. Later in the 1960s, however, a variety of sets of these slot racing cars were sold under a new brand name, Airfix MotorAce. Six exciting sets were on offer, each featuring a variety of circuit layouts and items of track such as double straights, banked sections and inner curves. The Monte Carlo Rally set included super 1/32nd scale motorised Mini-Coopers, and equally striking Ferrari 250s and Porsche Carreras could be found dotted throughout the other sets alongside the more traditional Lotuses and Brabhams.

 SLOT RACING

In the 1950s and 1960s the slot-car racing craze swept the US and UK. In an attempt to grab some of this action, in 1962 Airfix purchased Model Road Racing Cars Limited (MRRC), a manufacturer of slot cars located in Boscombe in England. Airfix produced slot racing cars with the popular front-wheel Ackermann steering, which featured a swinging front axle and could be purchased as a separate unit. This was used extensively by scratch builders. Later, Airfix made conversion kits so that their non-motorised 1/32nd scale kit cars (such as the E-Type Jaguar, Mini Minor, Sunbeam Rapier, Ford Zodiac, MG1100, Lotus Cortina and Vauxhall) could be made to run on slot racing circuits. The first Airfix MRRC set featured Ferrari and Cooper cars and an 11-foot figure-of-eight track.

On the Move

Because of Airfix's rapid expansion, in 1963 chairman Ralph Ehrmann decided that it was unfair to manage such a large group from the Haldane Place premises in Wandsworth, principally the home of the kits division, Airfix Products. He didn't want to be breathing down the neck of John Gray, with whom he had worked closely for so long. So, to cut some slack for those responsible for construction kits, premises more suitable for such a large toy group were acquired in Kensington, and the rest of Airfix Group was relocated there.

Above: Sir William Cockerall's SR-N1
Hovercraft joined the Airfix range in
1960. This is Charles Oates' packaging

Right: The assembled SR-NI

The Second Catalogue

It seemed that everything at Airfix
was being smartened up, for in
1963 the second edition of the
Airfix catalogue was published with
a much more striking design than the first edition. It also contained a few more pages but
remained at the bargain price of nine pence.

The range of kits continued to grow. 'This new Airfix Catalogue contains details of over 150
plastic construction kits. From the photographs and brief description you will get an idea of
what the finished models will look like. But not until you begin to build them will you feel the
excitement and satisfaction of creating miniature, exact scale models of the real thing.'

Subsequent Airfix catalogues, surviving examples of which are all very collectable, became
more and more elaborate. The third edition included a replica of a Ford Zodiak [sic] Mk.III.
The typographic error wasn't repeated in the kit's description: 'All the luxury and detail of the
exciting 100 m.p.h. Ford Zodiac Mk.III is reproduced in full by this superbly scaled 55-part
Airfix kit. Complete with a choice of registration numbers.'

If the thrill of being able to construct two replicas, each in a different colour finish and with
its individual number plate, wasn't enough, aspiring boy racers might opt for a Series One
kit of the streamlined Ariel Arrow motorcycle. 'This brilliant high-performance machine was
voted the Motor Cycle of the Year in 1960. This kit comes complete with transfer markings and
display stand.' Original examples of this venerable kit are rare enough, but the most prized

Above: Roy Cross's mid-1960s revision of Oates' artwork

version, Ton-Up-Tony, one of Airfix's short-lived Weird-Ohs range, which depicted an Ace Café renegade racing the wrong way down the new M1 motorway, is as rare as hen's teeth and didn't appear until the fifth edition of the catalogue.

The Weird-Ohs range was produced in collaboration with the owners of some old moulds developed by the US kit manufacturer Hawk, the company that had pioneered cartoon-style models. This new fun range made use of mould tools, such as the Ariel Arrow, acquired when Airfix bought the ailing British Kitmaster brand of model trains and transport items in 1962.

Pooling Ideas

Throughout these years of rapid change and expansion *Airfix Magazine* reported each development and encouraged debate from its readership about any aspect of plastic modelling which took their fancy. In the days before the internet the publication provided one of the only national forums for fans to voice their likes and dislikes. *Airfix Magazine* built a community as real and active as any to be found today on Facebook or MySpace.

One of the most useful services *Airfix Magazine* provided to the modeller was the consistently high standard of articles from a variety of experts who showed modellers how to hack a bit off here and cement some plastic card there, transforming existing Airfix kits into something new

Top: Kitmaster railway kits. Above: Airfix's reboxed Kitmaster Evening Star. Right: 25 Standard Couplings. Bottom: Kitmaster Deltic Diesel – one of the tools Airfix acquired but never released

RAILWAYS

Shortly after it began making plastic construction kits in the early 1950s Airfix included a range of HO-OO scaled accessories, such as buildings and railway station accessories, with which enthusiasts could enliven their model railway and die-cast toy layouts. In 1956 the railway Trackside Series was launched with No.1 The Country Inn. However, it was not until it acquired the established Kitmaster model train range from rival manufacturer Rosebud in 1962 that Airfix's model railway range really expanded. In the 1970s the railway range was further extended with the addition of the GMR (Great Model Railways) series of working electric models, which were designed to directly compete with the more familiar products of manufacturers like Hornby.

and different. A common feature in more or less every article was the requirement for the enthusiast to add a component, an aerial or bracing wire perhaps, made from stretched sprue. Youngsters growing up today would never be encouraged to hold a piece of plastic over a naked candle flame and then, the moment it begins to go limp and pliable but before it burns, gently pull it in opposite directions so as to manufacture a thin filament of polystyrene. I often used this neat technique without immolating myself!

In June 1964 Chris Ellis, specialist writer, expert modeller and later one of the editors of *Airfix Magazine*, penned an article in the publication's 'Military Modelling' series explaining how to make an original Churchill Bridgelayer from the parts of Airfix's Churchill Tank. Throughout his piece Chris, or C.O. Ellis as his byline read in those early days, explained how his conversion was quite simple and used bits and pieces of existing kits, such as the piston motion rods from the wheels of the Airfix Pug Loco kit together with a couple of unwanted Biro tubes.

Airfix Magazine conversions always required the reader to possess a plentiful spares box and some unwanted kits to cannibalise for additional parts. For example, in his Churchill Bridgelayer piece Ellis also advised: 'A large piece of spare plastic is required for the lifting arm – I used an Airfix Booking Office canopy – from which a rectangle, 86mm x 9mm, is cut to form the arm. Drill holes at 10mm centres to represent the openwork pattern of the real thing and cement the arm to the sleeve already on the axle. Two lugs need to be cemented 28mm from the foot of the arm to take the linking section from the dummy hydraulic piston. The cocktail stick you use for this will need to be at least 60mm long (preferably a little more) and the Biro tube for the cylinder must be 10mm shorter than this.'

Upon such genius the British Empire was built. It's little wonder that the letters page abounded with letters from detail fanatics. In the same issue North American reader Frank Allan, from Glenside, Pennsylvania, wrote: 'A close observation of the photograph of the Airfix Scharnhorst, on page 243 of the April issue of *Airfix Magazine*, reveals that the floatplane featured on the model is a biplane, probably the Heinkel He-114. After some research I found that the Scharnhorst received the well-known Arado Ar-196 which, in fact, is included with the Bismarck kit. Scharnhorst operated this type of aircraft from August 1938 until she was sunk. All criticism aside, I would like to congratulate Airfix on their fine models.' This letter is a typical expression of the kind of inclusiveness, the bond of loyalty, Airfix had engendered between its brand and customers.

In 1965 Airfix decided to rationalise the price and packaging of their popular 1/12th scale figure range. Up until then the 11 figures in the series were available in either Series One or the more expensive Series Two ranges. This was somewhat confusing for customers, as they seemed to get more or less the same number of parts regardless of the price. Airfix's solution was simple – the entire range was put in 'attractive new full-colour boxes', classified Series Two and sold for three shillings each.

In the February 1965 edition of *Airfix Magazine*, Chris Ellis wrote another of what would amount to numerous articles, not just by him, about improvements required to get the recently released German Armoured Car up to scratch. Immediately upon its release in 1964 modellers everywhere, Chris Ellis amongst them, had pointed out glaring inaccuracies in the design of the vehicle – its mudguards in particular. Ellis had a tip for getting them right: 'Last of all come those long mudguards, best cut from paper and supported by strips of styrene sheet or scrap plastic previously cemented just below the angled edges on each side.' Correcting the occasional design mistake became a rewarding challenge. It was never a chore or the subject of the kind of consumer criticism with which we are familiar today when manufacturers get things wrong.

The following extract from a 1965 letter to *Airfix Magazine* is a typical demonstration of the enormous bond of loyalty Airfix had encouraged in little more than 10 years of large-scale kit production. 'I have always found the letters to the editor section of *Airfix Magazine* very interesting,' wrote C.M. Sharp of Southwick, Sussex. 'But, like a few other people, I get sick and tired of readers suggesting why don't Airfix come out with this model and

Fred, the Homepride Flour mascot – manufactured by Airfix!

Above: 1/32nd scale Ford Escort (1969). Below: Stunning original artwork for 1/12th scale Black Prince figure

that model. To me, any kit that Airfix produce is satisfactory.'

Another letter to *Airfix Magazine*, headed 'Cheap Windows', recorded a novel way of scratch-building window frames. Hailing from London E9, D.J. Hutchings wrote:

'A type of plastic hair roller can be bought, about three inches long, over an inch in diameter and with quarter-inch spikes protruding all round. The end is open, so it is a simple matter to select only those with an oblong web. Cut off the spikes and open out … window and door frames of practically any size required for HO-OO scale can be obtained in this way, and some suitable for 1/32nd scale.'

All You Need Is Love?

The year 1966 is often characterised as the pinnacle of the Swinging Sixties. Doubtless some modellers were radicals, pacifists or advocates of sexual liberation and free love, but I think it unlikely that many readers of *Airfix Magazine* joined the growing number involved in the demonstrations against the war in Vietnam or much cared for the hedonistic excesses of the wilder elements of the rock and pop community.

Under the heading 'Lazy Modeller' in a letter to the August 1966 edition of *Airfix Magazine* is a reassuringly sober example of how modellers carried on regardless of the Summer of Love. 'As a dedicated but lazy modeller from the brass sheet days,' wrote D. Payne, from Auckland, New Zealand, 'I think plastic kits were invented for me! However, even confining myself to cars, I am hard put to keep up with new Airfix kits without becoming involved with much in the way of heavy conversion work – as in *Airfix Magazine* for April 1966, where a Mini was converted to an Elf. But it's nice to read about such industrious modellers.' In the same issue G. Newton from Carshalton, Surrey, wrote: 'I have an idea for readers who like to display their aircraft in a flying position. When completed, the model's propeller appears to spin. First take a sheet of clear, thin, stiff celluloid and cut out a disc the size of the propeller. Then find the centre. After that, depending on the number of propeller blades, draw fuzzy lines from the centre getting wider towards the edge (it is best to use a marker pen for this), allow to dry. Then stick on to the front of engine, last stick the spinner in place.'

I take back what I previously said about the 1960s mood of sexual liberation perhaps not extending as far as the readers of *Airfix Magazine*. In the April 1967 edition Miss Audrey Sanderson of Middlesbrough, Yorkshire, stepped on to the platform of the Letters to the Editor page to have her say. Beneath the heading 'Horses Wanted' she wrote: 'On looking through the catalogue of Airfix assembly kits I find that the majority of the kits are of aircraft, ships and railway models, etc. As one of thousands of an eight to thirteen age group who are interested in horses and horse riding I believe that a

Below: Roy Cross illustration for Airfix's release of their newly acquired 1/16th scale Ariel Arrow motorcycle

Right: The Ariel Arrow box from circa 1965

Left: One of the least successful kits Airfix ever released, yet ironically one of the most collectable – the Boy Scout from 1965. Right: Dating from the late 1960s, what collectors term brown box, 1st issue examples of Airfix's long-running 1/32nd scale polythene figure ranges are the most highly valued

series of models of types of horses in the 1/12th scale would be a profitable project.' Let us hope that Ms Sanderson was still making kits in 1975, when Airfix released their famous 1/12th scale Showjumper, allegedly modelled on HRH Princess Anne.

A letter in the same edition headed 'Matt to Gloss' was perhaps another expression of the prevailing mores. From Leighton Buzzard, in Bedfordshire, reader Dane Loosley wrote: 'Reversing the normal advice, readers may be interested in a way of altering a matt finish to a gloss one. When the matt paint is completely dry, coat it with clear nail varnish and allow to set. Though modellers would rarely need to do this, it helps when a specific paint shade is not available in gloss or when only a small part of a model needs a gloss finish.' Chaps speaking of using nail varnish … in a serious way, bring it on. But in the days before you could purchase every conceivable shade of paint and every type of varnish imaginable, such expedient solutions were a godsend.

Right: Although modeller's preferred Humbrol enamels and even Airfix's house publication, *Airfix Magazine*, recommended the paints of a competitor, throughout the 1950s, 60s and 70s Airfix persevered with its own brand

In 1962 Kitmaster was acquired because ownership of its existing model railway moulds would provide an enormous supplement to Airfix's relatively modest HO-OO trackside range. Along with a vast range of locomotives and rolling stock, most of which Airfix re-released, curiously they also acquired a single motorcycle tool for the Ariel Arrow

An Epic Line-up

By the time the sixth edition of the Airfix catalogue appeared in 1968, inflation and success had conspired to increase the cover price to one shilling and ninepence. This is still less than 10p in today's prices and was a bargain price even then. At the time of writing, perfect examples from this period are worth between £75 and £100.

'Airfix have the world's largest selection of Construction Kits plus new models every month. So no matter whether your interest lies in Aircraft – Tanks – Cars – Ships – Historical Figures – Rolling Stock or Museum Models, Airfix have it covered.' Not bad for a company that had only entered the construction kit market in earnest some 15 years previously.

The 1968 catalogue was one of the first times Airfix used a technique they would repeat in other catalogues, particularly throughout the 1970s – a large-scale photograph of almost the entire range laid out on the studio floor to reveal Airfix's products in tantalising detail.

Keen-eyed observers will notice the arrival of the famous Blue Box packaging for Airfix's HO-OO scale soldiers – the new Commandos being displayed front and centre. Oh, how I remember assembling the tiny kayaks and leaning miniature scaling ladders against bundles of sweaters, which in my imagination were perfect substitutes for the rocky cliff faces of Norwegian fjords, up which my tiny warriors were clambering as part of their mission to pinch a radar set or two from the dastardly Nazis.

Also in the photograph and part of the aforementioned Museum Models series was an example of Airfix's Beam Engine. Kits such as this, and the Maudsley Oscillating Cylinder Paddle Engine of 1827, the 1804 Steam Locomotive (Trevithick's) and the later Four-Stroke Engine were all intended to be motorised. To be honest, however, I've never met anyone who actually managed to animate their models. The friction generated by polystyrene rubbing against polystyrene and the pernicious action of stray blobs of polystyrene cement combined to prevent the free movement of moving parts. Fortunately for those more persistent and perhaps more careful modellers out there, *Airfix Magazine* was on hand to explain how the judicious use of suitable lubricants such as graphite dust (the filings of lead pencils) and Vaseline could be employed to enable moving parts to run freely.

Classic HO-OO
scale blue box
R.A.F Personnel

The August 1968 edition of *Airfix Magazine* built on the impression of almost limitless models suggested by that year's catalogue. But even more new kits had been added to the range since the sixth edition appeared at the beginning of the year in time for January's annual toy fair which, in those days was still held in Brighton, not in London, the current home for this industry jamboree.

The cover of this magazine featured a painting by the famous aviation artist Frank Wooten. The picture was of a Saladin Mk2 armoured car, and was described in the caption as 'the subject of a recent Airfix model'. This wasn't true, there was no new Airfix kit of the British Army's popular and successful FV601 – the six-wheeled armoured car built by Alvis as a replacement for the AEC armoured car used during the Second World War.

Interestingly, in the 1970s Peter Allen designed a 1/32nd scale Saladin, battery operated and moulded in ABS. It was part of the toy range. Managing director John Gray said it was the last time Airfix would design such a toy, as it was very nearly a kit. 'Well, the customer did have to clip a few bits together, I suppose,' recalled Peter. There is a Saladin in Airfix's current range, however, but this is only because of the recent acquisition of the 1/72nd moulds created by British company JB and subsequently rebadged Airfix.

The cover of the August 1968 edition of *Airfix Magazine* is also notable for showing Airfix's commitment to fine paintings. Interestingly, the late Frank Wooten, who painted it, was a hero of another master painter, Roy Cross, an artist who would single-handedly transform Airfix packaging and who had joined the company in 1965, at the beginning of an exclusive tenure which would last a decade, finishing in 1975.

A full-page advertisement in the August edition of *Airfix Magazine* gives a pretty good idea of the variety of available Airfix kits. Large-scale Classic Ships such as HMS *Victory*, the *Royal Sovereign* and *Cutty Sark* competed for attention with old favourites like the 1/12th scale figure of Edward, the Black Prince (it was important to let the face of Edward III's eldest son dry before you tried to fit or remove his great helmet, otherwise a scuffed nose would result) and the Hurricane MkIV. New kits included a delightful 1/32nd scale replica of a Ferrari 250 LM and a 1/72nd scale replica of the new US swing-wing F111A listed in a Stop Press panel and announced as 'Over 1ft. long and priced at 7/11d'.

Figure Sculptors

Between 1963 and 1970 Airfix released about 170 new kits, not to mention countless HO-OO scale figures and lots of similarly scaled ready-assembled polythene tanks and vehicles to support them. Also released towards the end of the decade, was a series of larger, 1/32nd scale polythene figures, sold in boxes that included a bumper selection of around 30 of these figures. More

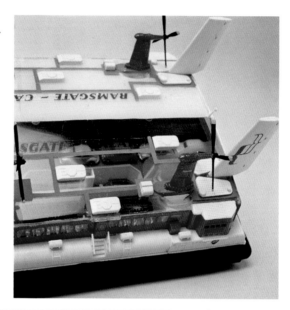

Above: For me one of the highlights of 1969 was the release of Airfix's stunning SRN4 – Hovercraft. My paternal grandmother bought one for me and appropriately she lived in Ramsgate, from where the cross-channel hovercraft embarked for the continent. This kit featured a transparent roof moulding so that the machine's internal detail and cargo of motor cars could be more easily viewed. Below: Original Roy Cross artwork for the SRN4's box

Original box-top sketch for James Bond Autogyro – probably by Roy Cross

than toys, although these model soldiers were very inexpensive, they were often the work of expert sculptors. Indeed luminaries such as John Niblett and Ron Cameron often fashioned master figures for Airfix, although they are perhaps better known for their work for other manufacturers.

Ron Cameron, for example, designed figures for Airfix but also sculpted much of Britains' famous Deetail range – the plastic successor to their Swoppet figures. John Niblett started working freelance for Airfix in 1956. He was the original designer of the HO-OO range of figures, creating their first set – Guardsmen – in 1958. Niblett worked for Airfix until 1974 and is responsible for many of the company's 1/32nd scale polythene figures and many of the 54mm Napoleonic figures released early in that decade. Whilst working as a designer for Mettoy (the original owners of Corgi die-casts) he met and became close friends with Les Higgins, and went on to sculpt many figures for Les Higgins Miniatures.

The efforts of the various skilled artisans who patiently carved the clay masters and cast maquettes to be used as patterns for Airfix's toy soldiers ranges (though to model fans they were always much more than toys) are now prized more highly than ever. All Airfix figures, but especially the military ones, are enthusiastically collected. Original cartons of the first edition 1/32nd scale figures, packaged in what collectors call the Brown Box, realise the highest prices.

Hits of the Sixties

There are far too many new kits to study in detail here, but I want to single out a few notable examples from the 170 manufactured in the seven years between 1963 and 1970.

Since it first appeared in 1963, Airfix's classic 1/32nd scale E-Type Jaguar has popped up time and again, but there's nothing quite as iconic as the original bagged version of this stylish car.

Following their acquisition of Rosebud's Kitmaster range in 1962, primarily purchased so that they could increase their HO-OO model railway range at one fell swoop, in 1963 Airfix wasted no time releasing a rebranded version of the Kitmaster Ariel Arrow Motorcycle.

Airfix's perennial HO-OO scale Bren Gun Carrier with its tiny 6-pounder anti-tank gun accompaniment first appeared in 1964 and has been beloved of military modellers ever since.

The following year Airfix issued a real turkey in their 1/12th scale figure range with the release of their Boy Scout. In sales terms it bombed and was only available for a short time. Consequently, this woggle-wearing chap in shorts and sporting a shirt bedecked with numerous proficiency badges is now very scarce and much sought after by collectors. A neat 1/12th scale diorama of James Bond and Odd Job from the smash hit movie *Goldfinger* was Airfix's first collaboration with Eon Productions, the 007 rights owners. Several more kits based on vehicles depicted in later films from the franchise would be released during the years that followed.

In 1967 one of Airfix's largest kits up until that point, a 1/72nd scale replica of the Luftwaffe's only heavy bomber, the inefficient Heinkel He 177, joined the range. Roy Cross's stunning box-top artwork was perhaps the best thing about this kit.

Quite a disparate selection of new kits joined the growing ranks of Airfix models in 1969. There were tanks like the HO-OO Anglo/US Lee/Grant of western desert fame; state-of-the-art jets like the brand new Hawker Harrier; and two kits associated with that July's moon landings – the Lunar Module itself and the Sikorsky Sea King helicopter which subsequently plucked it from the Pacific Ocean after it had splashed down. And then of course, there was a massive 1/144th scale Apollo Saturn V – the rocket that actually propelled the US astronauts to the lunar surface. Another rocket released that year, but an entirely fictitious one, was the Orion Space Craft from Stanley Kubrick's epic *2001: A Space Odyssey*. The fact that Airfix's financial success had enabled the company to purchase the largest injection moulding machines available is illustrated by the fact that 1969 also saw the release of large kits such as the 1/72nd scale Lockheed Hercules, an aircraft which came complete with Airfix's existing Bristol Bloodhound missile system stored in its cargo hold. Though of

I'd wager that every boy who grew up in the 1960s made at least one of these classic Airfix military vehicle models. They sold in their millions and are still available today. Clockwise from top left: Stalin, Sherman, Tiger, T-34, German Armoured Car, Panther and Lee

a smaller scale (1/144th) Airfix's latest addition to its Skyking range, a Boeing 747 Jumbo Jet, also made its maiden appearance in 1969. One of the largest and most complex kits released that year has to be the SRN4 Hovercraft, which had just started carrying vehicles and passengers from Ramsgate to Calais.

The highlight of 1970 has to be the release of the inaugural kit in Airfix's block-busting 1/24th scale Superkit series, their highly detailed Supermarine Spitfire MkI. This fine replica set new standards for kit production when it was released, and although many of its inherent mould design features have been superseded, even after nearly 40 years this impressive model cuts the mustard with kit fans.

The December 1970 edition of *Airfix Magazine* marked the end of the decade. The cover featured an interesting Second World War colour photograph of a vintage USAF P-51D Mustang in Royal New Zealand Air Force service in 1958 a short time before this aircraft was deemed obsolete by the antipodeans. Curiously for what would have been the Christmas 1970 issue there was no editorial from Chris Ellis, who still resided in the hot seat at *Airfix Magazine*. Chris was clearly occupied with Letters to the Editor.

Asking for the Moon

'Moondust' was the heading for a rather topical letter. 'I have found a very effective means of forming a layer of moondust on the patch of moon provided with the Airfix Lunar Module,' wrote M. Crellin of Taunton, Somerset. 'The entire surface should be painted light grey, and before this is dry, sprinkle a fine layer of fine cigarette ash on to the paint, and smooth out. The area directly under the nozzle should be sprinkled over. Then blow gently on this area. The ash should spread outwards.'

It's little wonder that wives and mothers were often left distraught by the activities of modellers in their families. Scratches on the dining table caused by a slip of the craft knife, or gloss enamel paint splashes on saucers press-ganged into service as makeshift palettes was bad enough, but being caught emptying a filthy ashtray on to a dripping wet kit and then blowing the detritus all over the lounge must have been the final straw. 'Mr Crellin sent us a most convincing sample of this miniature moondust,' noted the editor at the end of his correspondent's missive.

Let's close the decade with the words from one of Airfix's ads from the period. 'Get every detail right with Airfix' was the headline of a long-running campaign that had served the company well for a number of years. Beneath a photo of Airfix's new 1/600th scale HMS *Fearless* amphibious assault ship, a paragraph of copy stated the firm's claim to excellence. 'It's the little things – like the helicopters, operating stern ramp and landing craft – that really make the model! And that's why Airfix Construction Kits are so fantastically popular. Every model is accurate to the smallest detail – a perfect replica of the real thing! There are 19 different series, each made to a constant scale. Over 300 kits, at prices from 2/11 to 23/6. At all good hobby shops and F.W. Woolworth. Ask for the catalogue.'

Actually this advertisement wasn't entirely accurate, for only a few pages further inside the magazine another ad from Airfix about the new 1/24th scale Spitfire MkIa quoted a suggested retail price of 35 shillings. However, when you consider that this was less than £2 and that at the time of writing the current average retail price for the kit, still very much part of the Airfix range, is at least £40, it makes you think. I must be getting old …

With all the armour surrounding the enemy Gun Emplacement it's little wonder the troops within hadn't already surrendered! The Pontoon Bridge was a classic and popular toy and the ideal accessory for Airfix's cheap and robust plastic military vehicles and virtually indestructible HO-OO figures

AIRFIX - 144 SCALE
R.N4 HOVERCRAFT

Above: Spanning the decades. Late 1960s packaging for large 1/144th scale SRN4 Hovercraft and early '70s packaging for 1960s veteran SRN1 Hovercraft. Below: From 1976 an ad promoting plastic ice cube trays. Airfix was a big player in housewares

AIRFIX KIT CATALOGUE 17th EDITION

50p

NEW 'Pop-Up' Ice Cube Trays from Winfield.

Just a twist and up they pop.

2 FOR 49p

Wonderful Value. Great Quality. THAT'S THE WONDER of WOOLWORTH

CHAPTER 4

AIRFIX TAKES ON THE WORLD

As the 1970s dawned, Airfix's progress appeared unstoppable. The company was releasing newer and better kits at a prodigious rate every month. Airfix Group chairman Ralph Ehrmann told me that at this time 100,000 units was considered the right figure for the initial run of each new kit. (He also said that when Airfix went bust in 1981, for the larger kits this figure had fallen to only 5,000 units.)

By now kits were Airfix's core business and the product for which the brand was famous. But it had never abandoned toys or craft products, and around this time it actually expanded this sector of its business when it acquired some of the biggest names in the British toy industry through its purchase of Meccano-Tri-ang.

This new trading name had been adopted by Lines Bros. Ltd in 1970. A cosmetic improvement, it did little to alter the fortunes of the ailing British toy giant. In 1971 Meccano-Tri-ang went into voluntary liquidation and Airfix snapped it up for £2,740,000, getting the famous Meccano/ Dinky factory located in Binns Road, Liverpool, as part of the package. At the same time, North American combine General Mills purchased the majority of shares of Meccano France S.A., renaming the French company Miro-Meccano.

Above: In the early 1970s it was still perfectly possible to find examples of all types of Airfix packaging. This selection of nautical items is typical of what could be found

From *Airfix News* (1976), a photo of MD John Gray and chairman Ralph Ehrmann, admiring the firm's new model railway system

Tri-ang had always belonged to Lines Bros., a company founded by brothers William, Walter and Arthur (three Lines making a triangle – hence Tri-ang) shortly after their return from the Great War.

Now in one fell swoop Airfix had become Britain's largest toy company.

A Blistering Year

In fact, besides the cherry-picking of Lines Bros., 1971 saw an awful lot of other interesting things happening to Airfix.

This was the year that Airfix's iconic Series One plastic bags were consigned to the dustbin of history, being replaced by much sturdier, vacuum-formed blister packs, introduced to prevent the contents from being damaged whilst still allowing customers an opportunity to see the contents of the kit. Two years later this ingenious packaging won a prestigious award. Ironically, even though it was introduced for its robustness, fewer examples of intact kits in mint blister packs survive today than do complete models in the flimsier poly bag with paper header combinations. The reason is simple: bagged kits can be opened, examined and then returned from whence they came – and, with the addition of a couple of staples, the entire package made to look as good as new. To examine individual pieces inside blister packs the packaging must be ripped open, thereby permanently destroying its value to collectors.

1971 also saw Airfix win the Queen's Award to Industry for its export achievements. Surprisingly, although as winners of this award they were entitled to display a royal crest, Airfix apparently never applied such a flourish to its corporate communications.

Further developments in 1971 saw Airfix Plastics absorb Kingston Plastics and Declon Foam Plastics. Airfix Footwear was also incorporated that year. There was a divestment of equity, however, in 1972, when Airfix sold its shares in Airflow Housewares.

Despite this Airfix was still very much involved with the domestic market. The company manufactured many household items that could often be found in large retailers like F.W. Woolworth on sales-floor display only a few aisles distance from its better-known plastic kits.

An Award for Input

Airfix's 1962 acquisition of Crayonne, then a manufacturer of bath accessories, had developed into quite a big deal a little more than ten years later. The 1974 Design Council Awards for

Airfix manufactured the Cascade Cassette Storage Case for manufacturer Warwick

Contract and Consumer Goods were featured in the April 1974 issue of the product design industry's prestigious *Design Magazine*.

Their main criteria being innovation, fitness for purpose, ease of use and good appearance, six judges, each a highly regarded member of the product design community, chose a range of award winners including industrial light fittings, an all-season ski slope, a compass attachment and a hi-fi amplifier. They also chose the Input Range of heavy-duty abs resin containers made by Crayonne Ltd of Sunbury-on-Thames, Middlesex. Designed by Conran Associates, these bright items each retailed at between 85p and £4.00. This is how *Design Magazine* described them:

'Two years ago, Airfix Plastics, one of Britain's biggest injection moulding companies, initiated a design programme aimed to give plastics the kind of improved image already well established on the continent. The company approached Conran Associates, design subsidiary of Habitat, with a view to jointly producing a range of products for the home or office. A happy association between the two companies was soon formed and in May 1973 the Input range was launched, designed by Conran Associates for Crayonne, a newly formed division of Airfix.

'Research had shown that everybody needed "something to put things in" and these things could be anything from fruit and flowers to pencils and paper clips.

The Input range consists of 21 such "containers", all made from heavy duty ABS [Acrylonitrile Butadiene Styrene, a common thermoplastic used to make a huge variety of light yet rigid moulded products] plastics. This material was chosen for its strong, solid finish and its scratch- and shatter-resistance. A particularly low rate injection moulding cycle enabled the units to be made nearly twice as thick as other abs products, adding to the impression of solidity. The range is built up logically, all units being based on the same diameter and height ratios, which gives them an integrated quality. The Input range is only the first of a series of products planned by Crayonne. Soon to be launched is a range of bathroom fittings this time in pastel colours. Input has already won the Living Award for Good Design (sponsored by *Living Magazine* in conjunction with the Design Council).'

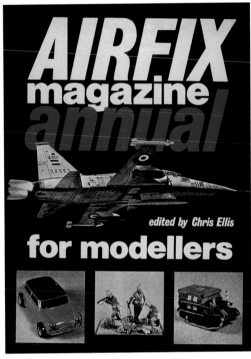

Airfix Magazine Annual – 1st edition 1971

Superkits

Under chairman Ralph Ehrman's steady stewardship Airfix knew no bounds.

Kits were always the core of Airfix's business, of course. They had begun the decade with the launch of the superb 1/24th scale Spitfire Mk1A, the first of their famous Superkits. In 1971 its famous Battle of Britain adversary, the Me 109E fighter, joined the range. Like its predecessor, the box for the 109 featured another simply stunning painting by Roy Cross, the doyen of Airfix artists.

Another terrific large-scale kit was also about to join the Airfix range. However, this one was a replica of something that flew down the track not along a grass airfield. After 18 months' hard work, Peter Allen's 1/12th scale, 4.5-litre supercharged Bentley finally made it to the shops in time for the 1971 Christmas rush.

The first model car Peter had designed for Airfix was the 1964 Vauxhall Viva, Airfix having decided to make miniature modern cars in 1961 (previously, as with the Classic Ships range, Nicholas Kove had insisted that Airfix cars should only be models of antique subjects). Peter's second car was another classic – the 1902 De Dietrich released in 1967 – but his third was both modern, bigger and arguably more exciting: the 1/24th scale James Bond Toyota 2000 GT Roadster, as featured in the film *You Only Live Twice* and in the shops in 1968.

Airfix planned further additions to this larger 1/24th scale vehicle range and, knowing his love for classic cars, chief designer John Edwards proposed that Peter have a go at a new 1/24th scale Bentley (John had created the existing 1/32nd scale Bentley in 1956). Consequently,

Peter and chief draughtsman Jack Armitage were dispatched to a meeting of the Bentley Owners Club, who were then celebrating W.O. Bentley's 80th birthday, and Peter was invited to peruse the rows of vintage Bentleys on display and decide which should be the subject of his new model. Peter chose to model his new kit on the vehicle owned by Neil Corner, financed by Lady Dorothy Padgett and known as 'the Pau car', after the location of the 1930 French Grand Prix where it had come second. The car was based in County Durham, and Peter and John Edwards later flew up there to take photographs and measurements.

Back at Airfix, competition from larger 1/8th scale Japanese model car kits prompted management in London to suggest making their new Bentley even bigger. Peter considered 1/8th just too big – to maintain the necessary rigidity in the plastic body shell mouldings, for example, precise scale accuracy would have been compromised. Peter felt that a 1/8th scale Bentley would look 'more like a toy' and suggested 1/12th scale as the best compromise. This was agreed, and then began the lengthy and difficult process of creating accurate engineering drawings for each component in the mould tool, a process made far more difficult because the plans for the Bentley were stored at a Rolls-Royce warehouse (RR having bought Bentley in the 1930s) which the Luftwaffe had destroyed during the Blitz!

The R&D and tooling costs alone came to £80,000, then an enormous sum. Nevertheless, despite the trials and tribulations the Bentley was warmly received. Sadly, John Edwards died before this superb kit made it to market.

In a panel edged with a thick black line the May 1971 edition of *Airfix Magazine* paid the late designer a glowing tribute. The obituary read: 'Chief Designer of Airfix Products Ltd, Mr Edwards had held this position since 1956 and was responsible for the design of virtually all Airfix construction kits produced since then. His energy, guidance, and imaginative leadership in the design field will be sadly missed and we extend our sympathies to his wife Anne, and his colleagues at Airfix, at this sad loss. For all of us, however, Mr Edwards leaves a fine memorial

Since their first appearance in the mid-1960s Dog Fight Doubles were a very popular way for Airfix to combine two related kits in one box. Aided by Roy Cross's stirring artwork designed to trigger the imaginations of young purchasers, this series was an enormous success. This WWI Bristol Fighter and Fokker Tri-plane is in a mid-1960s red stripe box.

in the big range of kits he has designed and which continue to give pleasure to millions of modellers throughout the world.'

After John Edwards died Airfix employed Barry Wheeler as their technical researcher. 'The first time Airfix had employed what we affectionately called a nutter – someone with the most amazing aviation knowledge,' chuckled kit designer Peter Allen when he thought back to his days at Airfix during this time. 'Barry was always keen to make a 1/24th scale Mosquito and now, years later, Trevor Snowden has realised this ambition.'

In fact Peter can remember being in a meeting with Barry Wheeler and Jack Armitage, Airfix's new chief designer, when the subject of a Superkit version of the Mossie was first raised. 'Where the hell can you display a monster of that size?' asked Armitage.

Peter Allen was more concerned about the practicalities of moulding such large pieces in polystyrene whilst attempting to achieve scale accuracy: 'Certainly with our knowledge of injection moulding we would have been very concerned about distortion of the wing components. We would have also expected them to be produced in two conventional halves, so that they

Opposite page: Beaufighter & Me 109 duo from 1973 and Stormovik & Fw 190 (1973)

This page: WWI Roland & R.E.8. (1973) and WWI Camel & Albatros (1973)

would lie either side of the fuselage to keep the overall box size to a minimum.

'Our standard moulding thickness was .045" [45 thousands of an inch or just over 1mm]. To mould any thicker than this would have resulted in shrinkage and possible distortion, because on thick mouldings the plastic cools fastest on the outside whilst remaining molten at the core. When the centre cools it has a tendency to pull the outsides inwards, distorting the outside wall of the moulded component.'

Pat Transfield

At this time Pat Transfield, formally a design lecturer at a technical college, joined Airfix as a freelance pattern maker. He had a very good knowledge of aviation, but was really more of

Spitfire & Me 110D (1975)

a model maker. In his spare time he used to build scale flying models. 'He had no knowledge of the intricacies of injection moulding at all,' said Peter, 'and at times Airfix designers would have to guide him through this process. His skill was in producing the pattern, but he couldn't fabricate the mounts required to hold the pattern in position in preparation for casting.'

Peter Allen and his team would take Pat's patterns and use them to produce engineering drawings which showed where the tooling 'shut-offs' should be located as part of the mould manufacture.

Because Pat Transfield was really a model maker rather than an engineering pattern maker, it was the responsibility of Peter's design team to provide the tool makers with accurate dimensions and locations. 'I believe Pat Transfield's first involvement with Airfix was on the 1/24th scale Me 109E Superkit,' said Peter. But although Pat fashioned the wooden patterns for the Messerschmitt it still required an in-house draughtsman to produce the engineering GA (general arrangement) drawings. These were always prepared in house. 'I don't think we would have ever trusted someone from outside to prepare drawings to our satisfaction,' Peter told me.

Pat also did lots of pattern work on the 1/24th scale Harrier GR1, but these were based specifically on Peter Allen's technical drawings. Similarly, Pat produced the patterns for the 1/24th scale Ju 87 Stuka, but these were entirely based on the drawings of the designer, Norman Sorrell.

Growing Pains

The early 1970s saw Airfix introduce a lot of new types of kits and make ever more complex ones in their familiar aircraft, cars and military vehicles ranges. There was even a plan to follow up the success of the 1/12th scale Bentley with an even more elaborate replica of a Rolls-Royce 1912 Silver Ghost in the same large size. This project was taken so seriously that all the general arrangement and detailed component drawings were completed. However, despite all the time and effort involved this kit was never manufactured.

Above: Complete 1/32nd scale Combat Pack (1978)

Right: The Combat Pack Pillboxes actually fired missiles – these looked rather more like *Star Trek* Photon Torpedoes than WWII vintage .303 calibre bullets!

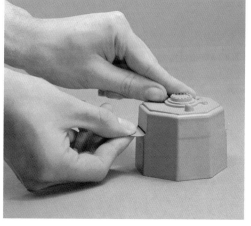

'Airfix didn't proceed with the 1/12th scale Rolls-Royce purely because of the escalating costs involved,' said Peter Allen, the kit's designer. 'The patterns were made and cast in resin. The steel for the bolsters, the main body of the mould, was already on site in Wandsworth, the moulds were to be tooled in Airfix's own tool room. The final bill was estimated at £243,000 and we simply couldn't afford it.' Commenting on Hornby's recent decision to release their signature Airfix kit, a 1/24th scale De Havilland Mosquito, Peter said: 'If we had wanted a flag waver we would have gone for the 1/12th scale Rolls-Royce rather than a large aircraft kit. As Jack Armitage said, "It's too big – where do you put it?"'

The enormous popularity of *Waterloo*, the 1970 Soviet-Italian film directed by Sergei Bondarchuk, encouraged a surge of interest in all things Napoleonic. Lead-alloy metal miniatures had always been in abundant supply for figure modellers with a leaning towards Chasseurs, Scots Greys and Inniskilling Dragoons. Recently the French plastic construction kit firm Historex had demonstrated the eagerness with which those more familiar with polystyrene embraced 54mm soldiers of the period.

AIRFIX

HO-OO SCALE NORTH AFRICAN OUTPOST

MODEL KIT · MODELE REDUIT

NEW

CONSTRUCT THIS WARTIME NORTH AFRICAN OUTPOST COMPLETE WITH PRE-FORMED BASE AND MILITARY VEHICLES

NEW

AIRFIX

GERMAN RECONNAISSANCE SET OO

SCALE

MILITARY SERIES

BRITISH EIGHTH ARMY

AIRFIX

29

32nd SCALE FIGURES

ACTUAL SIZE

Opposite page

Bottom: In the early 1970s Airfix changed the packaging of their 1/32nd scale soldiers from the so-called brown boxes to a much more contemporary style collectors know as target boxes

Top: Just as they could with the larger 1/32nd scale figures and vehicle sets, fans of 1/72nd scale military construction kits could extend the possibilities of their purchases with dioramas and multiple vehicle sets

Right: Assembled German WWII Reconnaissance Set

Reacting to market demand, Airfix initiated a new series of Napoleonic figures. They began in 1971 with the release of a 54mm 1815 period British Guardsman and mounted Hussar and quickly followed these up with a 2nd Dragoon (Scots Grey), a kilted 42nd Highlander, a Polish Lancer, a French Imperial Guardsman, a 95th Rifleman, a French Cuirassier and, a bit later, a French Napoleonic Line Infantryman.

The range proved enormously popular and in 1976, the year of the US bicentennial celebrations, Airfix added a British Grenadier, a North American Minuteman and a mounted figure of George Washington to the series.

Having spent many years focusing on military vehicles and figures in HO-OO scale, Airfix now saw that the much larger 54mm, or 1/32nd scale was the way to go. Consequently, starting in 1972 with a superb model of General Montgomery's Humber staff car, complete with a lovely figure of Monty wearing his distinctive beret featuring tiny miniatures of the two cap badges that only he could get away with wearing, Airfix embarked on a series of military vehicles in this larger size. They followed Monty's Humber with a 1/32nd scale replica of Rommel's Hannomag Halftrack, so that the two adversaries of the Western Desert could slog it out amidst the barren wastes of Mum's dining table. Soon after the release of these two kits Airfix added a superb 1/32nd scale miniature of the 8th Army's Crusader Tank and also released a highly detailed copy of a 17-pounder Gun, Britain's answer to the scourge that was the dreaded German 88.

This new range was designed to accompany another figure range released by Airfix in the 1970s – the superb Multipose figure range of soldiers from each of the major belligerents of the Second World War – except, for some reason, any Soviet troops. Not surprisingly, Multipose figures of soldiers from Monty's 8th Army and Rommel's Afrika Korps were the first to arrive, soon to be followed by other British and German soldiers and miniatures of US and Japanese troops. Sales of these were poor, however, and the range was withdrawn.

Japanese Advance

Here came the rub, however. Choosing to model such figures and vehicles in 1/32nd scale was inspired by the success of the original Napoleonic figures manufactured in the scale internationally accepted by painters of connoisseur figures. However, the scale internationally

A delighted customer with his new 1/24th scale P-51D Mustang, a Superkit first available in 1972

Below: HO-OO WWI German Infantry in 1978 box

adopted by military modellers who made plastic kits was that bit smaller – 1/35th. What's more, this was the scale adopted by Japanese modellers, and manufacturers from Nippon had almost cornered the market in Second World War tanks, figures and accessories. Indeed by the mid-1970s Japanese manufacturer Tamiya's hegemony in this field was almost absolute. Airfix not only had to contend with the disparity in scales between their kits and the enormously popular imports flooding into the UK via importer RIKO (Richard Kohnstam), they also had to keep a weather eye on the quality of such kits. Tamiya were fast setting new standards in the field of kit design and mould manufacture.

In the event, Airfix lost out, as previously had US manufacturer Monogram when they tried to sell tanks and plastic soldiers to 1/32nd scale. The winner was 1/35th scale. This unhelpful situation was exacerbated by the mismatch resulting when Tamiya soldiers from their much more plentiful range were introduced into dioramas featuring Airfix vehicles. When placed around the Airfix German Half-track, 1/35th scale Tamiya Afrika Korps figures appeared to be young boys wearing shorts!

Left: Anonymous box-top rough for
HO-OO scale Scorpion light tank

As we have seen, Airfix were at least committed to 1/32nd scale in one way – their growing range of cheaper polythene soldiers was manufactured in this scale. This didn't really matter because, excellent though they were, these figures were rarely integrated with polystyrene kits. The reason was simple: you couldn't paint them without enormous effort.

Since the early 1960s the pages of *Airfix Magazine* had been littered with features explaining how to get the most out of the war game potential of Airfix's cheap and plentiful HO-OO scale figures. We were told that all you had to do was coat each tiny figure in a layer of white PVA glue and wait for it to set, when it would dry and go clear, shrinking around each tiny 20mm figure like a tight corset. We were also told that Airfix or, more likely, Humbrol enamel would adhere to the new surface perfectly. It did work after a fashion but *Airfix Magazine* never properly dealt with the hazard of fluff sticking to these, temporarily at least, adhesive figures – they always fell over because it was almost impossible to remove the remaining pip of plastic on the bottom of each soldier's base after you had removed it from the sprue. Neither did the experts really get round the problem that, being composed of a softer and more pliable material than polystyrene, HO-OO figures and their larger 1/32nd scale counterparts never possessed really sharp details. The layer of glue, however carefully applied, reduced what little relief there was.

The result was that few modellers bothered to mix the softer figures with polystyrene kits. This didn't matter as the larger 1/32nd scale figures were excellent and cheap playthings in their own right. It wasn't long before Airfix supported this burgeoning range with a series of ready-assembled polystyrene military vehicles to maximise their play value. As with most things associated with Airfix, however, these were produced to such a high standard that they were embraced by serious modellers who soon discovered ingenious ways to super detail them and, being manufactured from polystyrene, they were easy to paint. The series soon included superb replicas of items such as the British Army's then modern Alvis Stalwart Amphibious Lorry, a Second World War Matilda Tank, a German Half-track, a Bedford Lorry, a Wombat Field Gun, an Afrika Korps PzKpfw IV and a Daimler Armoured Car.

In no time Airfix could field inexpensive armies in two scales – the larger 1/32nd scale and the tiny and more iconic HO-OO scale. I should mention that the smaller scale figures had been supported with vehicles and Playsets since the late 1960s. By the mid-1970s youngsters could choose to encourage their little soldiers to attack coastal gun emplacements or cross pontoon bridges in a fleet of 6x6 lorries or, if they were in the mood for playing with bigger warriors, could get their 1/32nd figures from the toy box, line then up alongside some military vehicles (or perhaps in their 1/32nd scale Strongpoint) and even assail them with a hail of tiny discs, which could be fired from a spring-loaded pillbox!

Magazine Issues

Airfix kits and catalogue in 1972

In January 1976 *Airfix Magazine* increased in size in every way, at last becoming A4, in keeping with nearly every other periodical on the newsstand, and also getting thicker, with 56–60 pages in each issue. The editor at the time was Bruce Quarrie. However, by the mid-1970s the popularity of plastic modelling created a market for numerous rival magazines. Previously *Airfix Magazine* had only to contend with *Military Modelling* and *Scale Models*, and many modellers bought copies of each.

Airfix was of course expected to underwrite its supposed affinity publication. By this time, however, the fact that *Airfix Magazine*, exhibiting its much admired impartiality, frequently criticised Airfix kits whilst heaping praise on the models of competitor manufacturers, was seriously beginning to rankle with Airfix management.

On 17 April 1974, Airfix managing director John Gray sent a memo to Barry Wheeler, who had taken over John Edwards's research and development duties following the latter's untimely death.

'Attached is a galley of a future article on modifying the Airfix Heron to a different mark,' wrote Gray regarding the proof of a forthcoming *Airfix Magazine* article he had just been given. 'I felt you should see it as it criticises the kit quite openly, justifiably in my opinion, but I am not sure on the rules of *Airfix Magazine* pulling apart its own products so to speak. I have checked out the comments made and have found them correct – the kit needs some work on it and the fit of some parts is very poor. I understand the kit is one of the temporarily withdrawn items. May I have your ruling on this article?'

John Gray attached the aforementioned galley proof and had circled the most damning criticism. Here's a flavour of reviewer Alan Laird's piece: 'The kit is basically accurate but contains one or two annoying errors. The type of canopy supplied in the kit is of the bulged type like the Dove's and unfortunately very few Herons of either type were fitted with this. However, this is of minor importance since the canopy does not fit anyway.'

For the managing director of a massive kit company, perhaps the most famous one in the world, to get involved in minutiae like the above was extraordinary. John Gray doubtless had far more important things to do. However, this snippet is an example of the kind of focus both he and chairman Ralph Ehrmann could bring to bear. Mr Gray's memos with their hastily scribbled additions of either 'Yes!' – denoting his approval – or 'No!' – his dissatisfaction – were legendary.

Any friction behind the scenes wasn't apparent to the readers of *Airfix Magazine*, of course, and everything carried on as normal.

For some time now *Airfix Magazine* had included a boldly designed feature entitled 'News from Airfix' (previously entire issues would be published without any mention of anything new from Airfix, unless there was an ad from the company or a reader's comment on the letters page). The January 1975 issue at least gave Airfix the prominence it deserved with a double-page spread advertisement in the centre of the publication promoting a quite eclectic selection of new kits. Beneath a 1/8th scale replica of the Suzuki TM-400J Cyclone, with 'a wealth of superb detail including chrome forks and suspension springs, brake and throttle cable and thick tyres' a 1/12th scale figure of Anne Boleyn in the newly titled Famous Women of History range was juxtaposed with the new HO-OO scale German Reconnaissance Set, which included an Sd.Kfz 222 armoured car and VW type 82: 'Popularly known as the Kubelwagen, very much the workhorse of the German Army'. Original examples of each of these kits are now really valuable, especially the Suzuki motor cycle because, as with motor cars, the popularity of bikes is directly associated with contemporary fashions. When they go out of vogue neither the real things nor the miniature copies of them are produced. As a consequence they have a limited shelf life and soon become quite scarce.

'News from Airfix' included a review of the all-new 1/72nd scale P-51D Mustang, an excellent kit made all the more perfect by the brand new drawings and patterns produced for it – it wasn't simply a reduction of the 1/24th scale Superkit as is commonly thought.

Elsewhere in this issue there was an advertisement for the Airfix 1975 Calendar, which stated: 'Airfix have long been renowned for the superb artwork used to depict in graphic detail the world's largest range of construction kits. From the collection of Roy Cross originals we have made up a 13-page calendar that ranges from aircraft from both World Wars to an airliner and the Harrier of today, as well as ships and a profile of the 3½-litre supercharged Bentley. The calendar measures 14¾ in. x 19¾ in. and is printed on heavy weight smooth white cartridge to give truly faithful reproductions of the originals. A limited number will be printed and we advise ordering now to avoid disappointment.' The calendars cost only £1.85, which included postage and packaging. They have since become enormously collectable.

> Original examples of each of these kits are now really valuable, especially the Suzuki motor cycle because, as with motor cars, the popularity of bikes is directly associated with contemporary fashions.

Airfix Artists

The mention of Roy Cross's artwork in the 1975 Airfix Calendar invites consideration of the work done by Roy and all the other talented artists and illustrators who have made Airfix packaging so distinctive down the years.

Charles (Charlie) Oates was Airfix's resident illustrator at the time the company branched out into construction kits in the 1950s. Best known as an artist on television, Oates is nevertheless to be credited with some eye-catching graphic design. He created the distinctive half-colour and half-white division behind all of the product illustrations on early Airfix boxes and poly bag headers. He also illustrated many of the original full-colour box-top artworks for kits including the F4U-1D Corsair, Walrus, Stormovik, Avro Anson, Black Arrows' Hawker Hunter, Bristol Beaufighter and Douglas Boston.

Howard Jarvis, RSMA, was the other artist producing work for Airfix, though not to the extent of Charlie Oates. Jarvis illustrated many of the original 1/600th scale Royal Navy warship range, including classics such as HMS *Daring*, *Campbeltown*, *Hotspur* and *Suffolk* as well as the aircraft-carrier HMS *Victorious*. He also illustrated some of the early Airfix motor vehicles and model railway kits. He died in 1964.

Roy Cross

With Jarvis gone and Charlie Oates becoming increasingly unwell, Airfix were in the market to employ a new packaging artist. How fortuitous then that in the year Jarvis died Roy Cross, having seen Airfix kits in abundance in his local Woolworths – the majority of which featured colour paintings of aircraft, a subject at which Roy was particularly proficient – decided to write to the manufacturer suggesting he could do a better job. Airfix invited Roy for an interview and he passed the inquisition with flying colours. In fact he produced virtually every new Airfix illustration for the next ten years, leaving in 1974 to return to his one great passion, marine art.

Roy Cross was born in London in 1924. Like many in his peer group he was an air-minded kid and in 1938 joined the Air Defence Cadet Corps, later the Air Training Corps (ATC).

During the Second World War Roy provided drawings to the *ATC Gazette*. His first published work, *US Army Aircraft*, appeared in 1942 when its author was only 18. Roy was employed as a technical draughtsman at the Fairey Aviation works in Hayes, Middlesex, where he produced easy-to-understand perspective line drawings in pen and ink for pilots' manuals and handbooks.

After the war he went freelance and illustrated *Know Your Airliners* for Shell as well as writing and illustrating other books including *Supersonic Aircraft* and *Jet Aircraft of the*

Artist Roy Cross at home in his Kent studio

World. In 1952, as the result of this work and other classic illustrations, including his famous cut-away drawing of the Gloster Meteor jet for *The Aeroplane*, he applied for and was accepted for membership to the Society of Aviation Artists, in the company of artists including Terence Cuneo, David Shepherd, Gerald Coulson and the great Frank Wooten. At about this time he started doing a lot of illustration work for London's advertising agencies and also began drawing for the *Eagle* comic.

Roy is, of course, most famous for painting some of Airfix's best artwork. He started working for the kit company right at the beginning of 1964. Dated 7 January, his first invoice, for the not inconsiderable sum then of £78.15s., was for his box-top painting of the 1/72nd scale Luftwaffe Do 217 bomber of Battle of Britain vintage. First released in 1959, this was one of the many kit illustrations Roy was asked to revisit, changing Charles Oates's rather graphic line representation into a stirring full-colour action scene in Roy's hallmark style.

Working 'half-up', that is at a size 50 per cent larger than the printed illustration, Roy generally used designer's gouache for his paintings. This is essentially rather thick, opaque, watercolour paint and is ideal for use by graphic artists as it allows them to cover or revise areas needing amendment – and if John Gray wanted even the tiniest detail changed, amendments there would be! Although Cross hated what he called 'the stupid letterbox shape' – the generally narrow rectangular box area within which he was expected to fit all manner of shapes – he

There's no doubt that his efforts were a contributing factor to Airfix's successes in the 1960s and 70s.

soon became adept at fitting the maximum excitement into this restricting canvas. There's no doubt that his efforts were a contributing factor to Airfix's successes in the 1960s and 70s. They certainly inspired me. I would rush home from the toyshop eager to try to recreate the events suggested by Roy's box-top painting. I rarely did, however, but still had enormous fun consigning my often still dripping wet creation to a toxic funeral pyre.

The list of Roy's work for Airfix is truly stupendous. He painted virtually flat out for them, exclusively, for ten years. Reliable, consistent and prodigious, Roy was capable of painting as many as four of the smaller ones in a month. Pointing to the surroundings of his lovely detached home where he lives in a village near Tunbridge Wells in Kent, he proudly told me that Airfix had effectively paid for it, so much work did they give him!

All of Roy's work is of the highest standard, but amongst the long list of classics he painted, my favourites include his stirring depiction of a battle-damaged RAF Wellington MkIII skimming the waves of the North Sea as it returns from a bombing sortie, his painting of the massive Short Stirling heavy bomber being loaded with its deadly cargo, the mighty US B-29 Superfortress emptying its bomb load over a battered and blasted Japan and, of course, the marvellous paintings he did for Airfix's 1/24th scale Superkits, especially the Spitfire Mk1a and Me 109E.

Roy's last paintings were produced in 1974. They were of the new Airbus kit in the 1/144th scale Skykings range and the 1/600th scale Second World War German cruiser Prinz Eugen. Airfix paid him £590 for the pair.

With Roy planning to leave Airfix and concentrate on high art – particularly his marine paintings for which his gallery owners had said there was a ready demand – Airfix looked to other illustrators to replace him.

Above: HO-OO blue box of Washington's Army, box illustration by Brian Knight. Below left: His original pencil sketch for Airfix HO-OO Washington's Army box. Below right: The magnificent original painting for Airfix HO-OO Washington's Army figures

Brian Knight

Knight was quite well known in the kit industry because he had painted many box tops for rival manufacturer Revell. He had started doing the occasional job for Airfix prior to Roy's departure. When Roy Cross left, Brian's workload increased dramatically.

Like many a youngster of his generation, Brian aspired to be an airman and hoped to one day join the RAF. He made model aircraft and furiously drew pictures of them. During the Second World War Brian joined Miles Aircraft as an apprentice draughtsman, quickly graduating to their design section. After several other jobs, including one for the Atomic Research Establishment at Harwell in the early 1960s, Brian went freelance. It was about this time that he began working for US model giant Revell's UK subsidiary based in Potters Bar.

At this time Brian began to attend a great many toy and hobby industry trade fairs. Not surprisingly he made contact with Revell's competitors and soon came to the attention of one of the fastest growing amongst them – Airfix.

Brian was told that Airfix had a requirement for more artists – especially for their new larger scale Classic Ships range. Brian's first commission for them was HMS *Endeavour*. Soon, vessels from the age of sail became Brian's speciality. He progressed to produce the stunning artwork for the entire series, including such masterpieces as *Victory*, *Wasa*, *Prince* and *Royal Sovereign*. His last large-scale Classic Ship was the *St Louis*.

Above: The late Brian Knight seen leaning against one of the floats of a Supermarine SE 6B in the Southampton Hall of Aviation in 2003. Below: Original box-top artwork for 1975's 1/32nd scale Rommel's Half-Track (either by Ken McDonough or Brian Knight)

Original Brian Knight pencil sketch of his 1/32nd British Commando figure artwork

As Knight was getting his teeth into sailing vessels for Airfix, he was approached by Charlie Smith, the firm's buying manager, who said, 'Brian, we are thinking about a new series. What are you like at figures?' Although many of Roy Cross's works included figures, the master artist never liked painting or drawing them. He was more comfortable with aircraft, vehicles, sailing ships and, of course, stunning landscape backgrounds.

Thus began another strand in Brian's career with Airfix and he began to prepare each and every piece of artwork for the entire HO-OO polythene figure range.

Actually, one of the factors that encouraged Airfix to ask Brian to switch to figures was that the firm had run out of subjects for sailing ships! Meanwhile, such was the success of these little and very inexpensive figures that Airfix could barely keep up with the demand.

I think the most memorable work that Brian ever did for Airfix was for the 1/32nd scale figure range. Each of these boxes has an illustration of almost cinema poster impact in which the viewer's eye is led back from two or three figures interacting in the foreground to a dramatic scene that extends beyond the middle distance to a panoramic background. Brian was paid £125 per box top, and they often took a fortnight to complete.

Cruelly for such a gifted artist, in his later years Brian was struck down by Parkinson's disease, and he died in December 2007.

Ken McDonaugh

A contemporary of Brian's, and another fine artist who is sadly no longer with us, was Ken McDonaugh. Born in 1920, he died in 2002 after suffering a stroke, which put paid to his artistic talents. Like many illustrators of his generation. Ken was adept working in full colour with paint and brush and equally at home producing more technical line artwork with pen and ink. He wrote and illustrated the book *Atlantic Wings* and provided illustrated articles for *Aeromodeller* magazine. Ken McDonaugh created a great deal of fine artwork for Airfix, much of it illustrated here. Of particular merit are Ken's paintings for the 1979 re-release of the 1/72nd scale Bristol Bulldog biplane and a new version of the Boulton Paul Defiant turret fighter, depicted over London during the Blitz. However, for me his best painting is the one he produced for Airfix's new 1/48th Spitfire VB in the late 1970s.

Sanitising the Box Top

Going back to Airfix's progress through the 1970s, it is worth pointing out two significant things that happened in 1977. This was the year Airfix acquired Scalecraft, a company that since the 1960s had produced snap-together polyethylene models capable of being motorised.

Airfix's famous unfurling banner logotype had been steadily developed since its introduction in the 1950s. In the early 1970s this motif changed radically into a circular but equally striking form. In 1977 it was amended into an oval design. These details are important because they enable collectors to gauge the age of individual kits.

More significant perhaps was that 1977 saw the start of a complete repackaging programme, removing all depictions of violence from box artwork. The origins of the decision to sanitise Airfix artwork began with a move of German origin. 'We had to remove swastikas from the artworks – Matchbox had run ads featuring this emblem – although it was illegal to use it a blind eye had been turned for many years,' said Peter Allen. 'Europe then became very anti-violence so we removed any such depictions.'

Sometimes the box tops were altered by cutting out the aircraft from the original artwork and replacing it on an airbrushed background.

Another reason for the decision, allegedly, was that the Australian government had also decided to ban depictions of violence from children's playthings and it was understood that the European Economic Community (the predecessor of the EC) would soon follow suit. Certainly legislation in the US, which was introduced in the 1970s, decreed that a toy-box illustration should depict exactly what was inside the package, and supposedly it was in response to their American master's wishes that in the 1980s Palitoy replaced illustrations with photographs of poorly made Airfix models on kit boxes. Peter Allen disputes this long accepted theory, however, saying: 'At Palitoy the US legislation did not apply to us, the US did their own models, as often the decals changed. The new packs were a marketing decision.'

Just as imperfections and colour variations

AIRFIX ARTISTS

Other talented artists who have provided illustrations for Airfix include the following:

● **KEN RUSH**, prior to producing illustrations for Airfix, worked for Rosebud, illustrating some of the Kitmaster model train range (much of which was purchased by Airfix).

● **GEOFF HUNT**, like Roy Cross, is now a respected marine artist. A fine example of his facility for nautical subjects is his striking illustration of Airfix's 1/72nd scale Vosper RAF Rescue Launch.

● **RON JOBSON** illustrated several Airfix kits including the 1/72nd scale Ilyushin IL-28 which can be seen on page 174 complete with original box-top roughs. Ron Jobson worked for Tudor Art, one of the studios Airfix used to prepare, amongst other things, camera-ready artwork for instruction leaflets. He has illustrated scores of books, particularly about aviation, and occasionally teams up with an expert writer such as Bill Gunston.

● **DOUG GRAY** re-worked Roy Cross's famous Wellington artwork, as required by the insurers following the devastating fire at Humbrol in 1988.

● **GAVIN MACLEOD** was responsible for introducing the airbrush to Airfix artwork. He painted most of the company's new kits released in the 1990s, including stunning artworks for the 1/48th scale English Electric Lightning supersonic jet fighters, released to such acclaim in 1998.

● **KEITH WOODCOCK** has recently painted lots of the box art required by Airfix for the ex-JB models, including the 1/72nd scale LWB Landrover (soft top) and Trailer.

● **MIKE TRIM** illustrated the 1/400th scale destroyers HMS Montgomery and HMoNS St Albans (the designation relates to the Royal Norwegian Navy-in-exile in 1941).

● **JOHN D. JONES** was invited to work with Airfix in 2003. Since then he has already completed numerous stirring illustrations for the company, ranging from aircraft and warships to military vehicles. He provided the striking cover for the 2005 Airfix catalogue (the one featuring the then brand new TSR2), and painted the 1/48th scale Canberra and its US conversion the famous B-57, the popular Severn Class Lifeboat and the Lockheed U2 spy plane. Most recently John's artwork has graced the box of Airfix's acclaimed 1/72nd scale Nimrod MR2.

Produced in association with the US MPC's Fundimensions division, Colossal Mantis was twinned with another US monster – the Rampaging Scorpion

add value and entertainment to other collecting hobbies – notably with philately and die-cast cars – the acquisition of two Airfix boxes, apparently identical but with the bomb blasts, muzzle flashes and columns of smoke removed by the censor's airbrush on one of them, makes kit collecting all the more enjoyable.

New Releases

In the mid-1970s Airfix released new kits at a prodigious rate. The year 1975, for example, saw no fewer than 17 new kits. Amongst them were superb 1/72nd scale replicas of the RAF's Scottish Aviation Bulldog trainer and the USAF's North American Sabre, the aircraft involved in the world's first jet-versus-jet duel when it fought the MiG 15 over North Korea in 1950. A very popular HO-OO scale kit of a Second World War Forward Command Post provided military modellers with a useful diorama accessory. The existing RAF Rescue Launch was joined by its wartime adversary, a 1/72nd scale German E-boat.

In 1976 a total of 18 new kits of all sorts were released. Quite a few new 54mm figures were added to the existing 1815 range, including a mounted British Lifeguard, as well as a superb Bengal Lancer from the days of Queen Victoria's Indian Raj. A new range of English Civil War figures was begun with a Pikeman from 1642. A French Legionnaire joined the existing 54mm figure range, and there was also a large 1/12th scale French Imperial Guard figure. However, because this was produced to the same size as the 1/12th scale master sculpture and not reduced down from a larger original, as the 54mm figures were, it is somewhat soft in surface detail.

Airfix also began its curious love affair with dinosaurs and wildlife of the hedgerows, releasing both a model Tyrannosaurus Rex and a diorama featuring Bullfinches that year. For me, however, the highlight of 1976 has to be the superb 1/24th scale Ju 87 Stuka, a kit with which Airfix once again raised the bar.

The following year a small but beautifully detailed 1/72nd scale Luftwaffe Me 163 Komet rocket plane joined the range, and the 1642 Pikeman was joined by a 54mm figure of a Musketeer. The English Civil War range was further supplemented by the addition of a

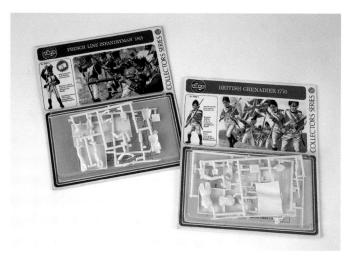

Above left: In 1973 Airfix finally did away with their iconic plastic bags. New blister packs were their replacement. This award-winning packaging enabled customers to scrutinise kit components but the stout vacuum-formed design protected vulnerable pieces and made storage, packaging and despatch much easier. Above right: Promotional photo of new 1/24th scale Hawker Harrier jump jet. Below: 1/24th scale Harrier GR1 Superkit (1974)

mounted Cavalier/Roundhead figure, one kit providing sufficient pieces to create a cavalry man of either the King's or Parliament's forces.

Amongst the many other aircraft released, the 1/72nd scale Fw-190 A8/F8 made an exquisite addition to Airfix's range of aircraft kits.

The Parting of the Ways

The situation with *Airfix Magazine*, which would eventually lead to the kit manufacturer parting company with its eponymous magazine, rumbled on.

On 7 December 1977, a meeting was held with Patrick Stephens Ltd (PSL), which Stephens himself attended. Airfix was represented by John Gray, who had moved over to Airfix Group's HQ in Kensington, and John Abbott, the managing director of the kits division. Bruce Quarrie, the editor of *Airfix Magazine*, and Darryl Reach, who had edited it during the 1960s, were also present. It was noted that *Airfix Magazine* was being subsidised to the tune of £14,000 per annum and that circulation was 37,000 while its competitor *Military Modelling* was selling 50,000 copies. PSL argued that there were fewer serious kits being produced and that, in any case, their competitors received information about new Airfix kits before they did. They also said they needed even greater editorial freedom and wanted to increase their page rate from £110 to £130.

The typed minutes John Gray showed me concluded: 'After much discussion it was agreed that Airfix did not wish to be involved in future books [PSL had produced numerous small *Airfix Modellers Guides* and earlier still a series of individual studies of Classic Kits from the 1/24th scale Superkit range and the large-scale Historic Ships series, as well as a number of *Airfix Annuals*] but are prepared to consider proposals to continue to allow PSL to have the use of the Airfix name on such publications if they continue to produce them.' The crack in the machine was turning into a chasm.

In September 1978 an announcement in *Airfix Magazine* said that PSL would no longer be publishing it. By this time the magazine's sales had fallen from a peak of 100,000 copies per month to just 30,000. The next month, Gresham Books of Woking, Surrey, accepted responsibility

The following series of artworks, including those opposite, show how, during the late 1970s, Airfix rather crudely sanitised valuable original artwork in their efforts to remove all traces of violence. 40mm Bofors Gun and Tractor in original gung-ho form

Top: Original 1979 vintage Geoff Hunt artwork for the RAF Rescue Launch. Above: Just a nice day on the water. RAF Rescue launch without any evidence of WWII

for publishing *Airfix Magazine*. The sudden collapse of Airfix in January 1981 disrupted things, and following this seismic event there were a number of subsequent publishers of the magazine including Kristal, Darter, and Ray Rimmel's Albatross. Following Humbrol's acquisition of Airfix in 1986, publication of *Airfix Magazine* was temporarily suspended. When it reappeared, in November, it was published by Andrew James.

Airfix Magazine changed hands again in 1988 and seemed to be born again under Alan W. Hall (Publications) – the September 1988 edition was called Volume 1 Number 1. The editor was Jim Wood.

Right: Bill Stallion was the artist responsible for Monty's Desert Rats. The figure in the foreground is a self portrait!

Below: Multipose Afrika Korps and 8th Army frozen in time

Below right: Bill Stallion's Africa Korps artwork. The artist enrolled his neighbour, BEA pilot Steve Brown, as an alternative model

The last ever *Airfix Magazine* was a bi-monthly edition, cover date October/November 1993. By now the circulation had dropped to only 5,000 or so per month. Michael J. Gething has the dubious honour of being the last editor.

Strong Finish to the 1970s

There were several significant new Airfix kits released in 1978. Amongst them were some great 1/32nd scale Multipose sets of British and US Infantry of the Second World War. To the irritation of many modellers, however, the military vehicle released to accompany them that year, a US Army Cargo Truck, was not to the same scale and it was not even an Airfix original. Designed by Peerless Max, this bought-in vehicle was, like a number of other releases, manufactured to the significantly smaller 1/35th scale. Airfix released an excellent 1/600th scale replica of the US Navy's mighty aircraft-carrier *Forrestal*. Science fact and fiction also played a part in that year's releases with the addition of a superb kit of the then brand new Space Shuttle and the release of the Star Cruiser, allegedly designed by none other than Gerry Anderson, the mastermind behind countless Supermarionation TV shows, but I have since been told by Peter Allen that, in fact, Gerry Anderson never designed a kit for Airfix!

In 1979 Airfix decided to release a new, state-of-the-art addition to their 1/72nd scale Spitfire series with the introduction of a faultless Mk1A. New 1/72nd scale kits of the Luftwaffe's veteran Fw 190D fighter and modern MBB 105 Helicopter and a superb range of 1/48th aircraft: a Spitfire MkVB, Me Bf-109f and Hawker Hurricane, were added to the kit range.

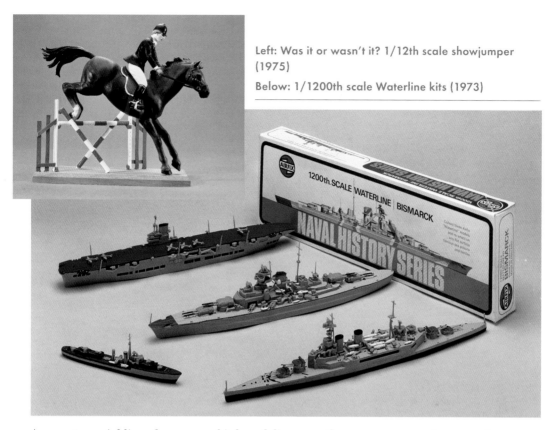

Left: Was it or wasn't it? 1/12th scale showjumper (1975)

Below: 1/1200th scale Waterline kits (1973)

Amongst a sprinkling of even more birds and dinosaurs there were some real gems such as a 1/72nd scale RAF Rescue Launch, a large 1/12th scale Bengal Lancer and highly detailed, and now highly collectable, 1/8th scale model of a Norton Motorcycle.

Despite growing industrial uncertainty and the extreme polarisation of political opinion in Britain following Mrs Thatcher's election victory in May 1979, a subject to which we shall return in the following chapter, for Airfix the 1970s ended with the company continuing to reign supreme. Together with all the real kits that actually made it on to the shelves of hobby shops, staff at the company were even afforded the luxury of regularly contemplating a wish list of potential subjects. Like any provisional plans the majority of opportunities discussed never got beyond concept stage. However, I thought I'd end this chapter with one or two 'might have beens' from a foolscap sheet, dating from the late 1970s, that Peter Allen retrieved from his archive.

As one might expect from Airfix, the suggestions are enormously diverse, ranging from a suggestion to convert the existing 1/12th scale Showjumper into a Cowboy to large-scale dioramas revealing sections through a Tin Mine and a Coal Mine. There was an idea to produce kits of individual Gun Turrets from Second World War bombers, a Large Scale Windmill, a model of an Oil Rig and even a kit of the Skeleton of a Pre-historic Monster. So, plenty of boys' toys but, to the potential disappointment of those of us who preferred macho items, there was also a note to 'Increase Wildlife Series' with the addition of Swifts, Swallows, Thrushes, Kestrels and even a Fish 'mounted on a wall plaque'!

CATALOGUE OF

AIRFIX

CONSTANT SCALE CONSTRUCTION KITS

FIRST EDITION 1962 · PRICE 9d.

CATALOGUE OF

AIRFIX

CONSTANT SCALE CONSTRUCTION KITS

THIRD EDITION   PRICE 9d

CHAPTER 5

TROUBLE LOOMING?

For Airfix, the 1980s couldn't have been more of a contrast with the preceding decade. Whilst the 1970s were characterised by awards, expansion and increased commercial success, the new decade displayed the flip-side of the coin, exposing the problems particular to a closely knit group of companies and especially those which befall businesses to whom export trade is crucial.

Elsewhere, I have chronicled the specific problems that beset Airfix Industries Group and in particular those of Airfix Products, the kit division, in 1981. I do not intend to repeat them in this book. Suffice it to say, however, that although the Airfix construction kit business was profitable, its progress was being impeded by the mounting problems within Dinky and Meccano, both of which it owned and both of which were embroiled in industrial action. In 1979 pickets surrounded the manufacturing plants at Meccano and Dinky's famous Binns Road factory in Liverpool after Airfix said it intended to close the plant.

Opposite top: Airfix Catalogue Number One from 1962. Now a real collectors' item. Below: Third Edition Catalogue 1965

Above: Not surprisingly, the Falklands War provided inspiration for Airfix's legion of military model fans as the cover of this October 1982 edition of *Airfix Magazine* suggests

Bullfinches, 1976

During this period those in the know recognised that the inordinate amount of time Airfix management committed to negotiating with Liverpool shop stewards caused them to take their eye off the ball in other areas, perhaps preventing them from investigating every business solution and unfortunately letting other, perhaps solvable problems, fester. As Airfix's own stockbrokers, Grieveson Grant, put it, 'Had the Meccano closure proceeded smoothly the group would be in a stronger position.'

Events beyond Airfix's control conspired to heap further problems upon them.

Rising oil prices and trade union militancy had led to a recession under the Labour governments of Harold Wilson and James Callaghan, which became the worst slump to hit Britain for 40 years. Inflation peaked at more than 20 per cent as prices of basic goods rocketed. In 1979, following the so-called Winter of Discontent, Labour lost power and for a few years, until it turned things round, Margaret Thatcher's Conservative government presided over a biting depression complete with rising unemployment, civil unrest, even riots.

Going Down

Stanley Lerner joined Airfix in 1976 as its chief internal auditor, having previously been a partner in the external auditors. He recalled those years for me:

'My brief was to ensure that all the accounts of subsidiary companies were in order and that there were no major surprises or differences when the final audited accounts were produced. And I am pleased to say that this was the case from 1976 to 1979.

'My brief also included the toy subsidiaries in both Germany and the USA (my schoolboy German came in very handy). In May 1979 I was seconded to Meccano, where in essence I was the deputy MD. I returned to Airfix HQ in Kensington in January 1980 following the departure of the then financial director and company secretary through ill health.

'I was appointed company secretary in early 1980 and tried to hold the financial fort until the repackaging deal was worked out; when I was appointed as the financial director. Unfortunately Mrs Thatcher was not a lover of manufacturing, which, together with the stronger pound, seriously affected Airfix Products' export market. In addition, the financial advisers of the repackaging forgot to take into account a signed commitment when arriving at the proposed overdraft facilities needed for the projected ongoing business.'

Stanley told me that the Airfix Group was suffering from a variety of difficulties at the time, but that these perhaps could have been dealt with, if it had not been for the problems which the situation at Meccano certainly exacerbated. 'Given a prevailing wind I think the smaller toy group could have survived, but that is only my personal thoughts,' he reflected. 'Meccano should have been closed when one of the unions demanded an increase, even though we were already paying more than union rates. Unfortunately, egos became involved, with the result that demands that Meccano could not afford were acceded to – thus increasing the losses.'

Nevertheless Stanley remembers his time at Airfix with fondness. 'Airfix, certainly the toy side, was a family, and as the remaining trustee of the Airfix Retirement Plan I have still kept in touch with many of the old pensioners over the last 25 years, together with some of the management of Airfix Plasty in Germany (the firm's distributor there). The trouble is I am beginning to feel my age!'

Not surprisingly, amidst all this social and economic turmoil, toy sales were in steep decline.

Not surprisingly, amidst all this social and economic turmoil, toy sales were in steep decline. Airfix wasn't the only big name suffering. British toy industry giant Dunbee-Combex-Marx, owners of the Pedigree brand in the UK, the manufacturers of Sindy, was placed in receivership in 1979. Lesney, the company behind the Matchbox range of die-cast toy cars, shed some 1,300 jobs. It declared a trading loss in 1980, finally going into receivership in 1982.

Airfix was haemorrhaging money. To stem the flow it desperately needed to close at least some of its five factories, but the unions threatened to close them all if Airfix shut even one. Nevertheless, just before Christmas 1979, with the loss of 900 jobs, Airfix closed the iconic Meccano factory in Liverpool.

In an effort to raise cash and counter the problems of the financial shortfall stemming from the loss of production and consequent loss of sales, and because its vital export business was suffering owing to the high pound, in November 1980 Airfix sold its profitable Crayonne and

Left: Cotton Craft – young girls rushed to fashion butterflies from multi-colour threads

Right: Racing Champions New Artist set 1970s

 **ARTS & CRAFTS**

It was natural that Airfix would supplement its enormous product range, which by the late 1960s included not just plastic kits but toys, games, slot-car racers and even plastic housewares, with products aimed at those consumers with an artistic bent. Painting by numbers was all the rage in the 1960s, and Airfix quickly released their own sets using this method. Graham Westoll spent five years at Airfix as joint manager (with Sue Godfrey) of the Arts & Crafts and Games development section. He was responsible for introducing subjects of greater appeal to boys to Airfix's Painting By Numbers range and soon football champions, fighter pilots and rock and rollers joined canvases like Pony Show, Furry Kitten and Ballet Nocturne. Airfix's arts and crafts range extended far beyond painting sets, however, and in keeping with the zeitgeist of the 1970s Airfix also manufactured pictures designed to be completed not by the application of pencil or paintbrush but by winding multi-coloured threads around a series of pins pushed into tracings revealed in velour backing boards or by sprinkling glitter on to patterns traced in glue!

Declon plastics businesses for nearly £5 million.

This cash injection only provided a short-lived tonic. There was an enormous loss of revenues from export – Airfix kits were good but not so good that overseas customers would pay twice as much for the same kit they had purchased only a year before. Ralph Ehrmann, who was still Airfix Industries' chairman in 1980, told me that at the time his company depended on exports for nearly 80 per cent of its income.

When Airfix's results for the financial year 1979–80 were finally filed they showed a pre-tax loss of more than £2 million. Interim figures posted in December 1980 forecast a similar amount of loss for the first half of financial year 1980–81, but this sum was for only six months' trading, and based on a declining turnover. Things were getting worse.

Despite their best efforts, both Airfix Industries' group chairman Ralph Ehrmann and managing director David Sinigaglia's proposals for Airfix's financial restructuring, placed before their UK bankers, were rejected (Ken Askwith had the misfortune of being managing director of Airfix Products, the kit division, at this time). 'We were very surprised the banks were not prepared to accept our proposals as presented,' Ralph Ehrmann told me. 'They seemed very reasonable to us and our advisers.'

Ehrmann is equally bitter that Airfix Industries, a manufacturing group employing countless workers up and down the country and which had won countless awards, many for export sales, received no government support. He pointed out that when similar situations arose overseas they attracted immediate government support. Indeed, Airfix's foreign competitors had often enjoyed official subsidy whilst it had had to fight its battles on its own, without support. In the end Airfix's wounds proved mortal.

Ken Askwith, managing director of Airfix Products during the fateful period in 1981 when everything imploded was, of course, intimately involved with every development. In fact he was closer to many of the goings-on than others because he had temporarily been seconded to Meccano in Liverpool as assistant MD to Ray McNiece.

In his view Airfix didn't stand up to the very militant unions active in the North-

CONSTRUCTION TOYS

Since the 1930s the introduction of plastics had encouraged a boom in new construction toys, previously the province of Meccano, famous for their system of slotted metal plates, strips, wheels and gears. Bayko and Minibrix were two of the most famous competitors to Frank Hornby's Edwardian concept, but by the late 1950s Airfix became involved with the release of their No. 1 Building Set. This quickly expanded into the very popular Betta Bilda range in the early 1960s. However, similarities to the Danish LEGO system meant that Betta Bilda was short-lived. Consequently, surviving mint and boxed sets are now coveted by collectors.

Above left: Too close for comfort. In the early days Airfix got away with any similarities to a well-known Danish construction toy. But by the late 1960s the threat of legal action for infringing the Lego's IP quickly brought an end to Betta Bilda

Above: Early Betta Builder sales leaflet

Left: Scheduled for release in 1969 to catch the wave of enthusiasm surrounding the Apollo Moon Landings, this Betta Builder Rocket Set featured a very, very, simplified replica of a Saturn V rocket

West at that time. However, he concedes that perhaps this wouldn't have achieved anything, because when Airfix tried to reach an agreement on a percentage of redundancies at Meccano to save the majority of workers there, the union firmly resisted even a single job loss, threatening to go on strike if any were attempted.

'Meccano was a big millstone around Airfix's neck,' Ken told me. 'With the benefit of hindsight, perhaps we should have moved manufacturing overseas, to Hong Kong, for example, where we already had connections with factories.' He knew what he was talking about, for manufacturing was in Ken's blood. Prior to his ten years with Airfix, he had been production director at Hotpoint.

A report prepared for Ken Askwith in January 1981 was intended to reveal specific areas of growth, or lack of it, in the kit division. Whilst it showed some areas of concern, especially in larger kit – Series 10 models revealing a massive drop in sales from £555,000 in 1979 to only £108,000 in 1980, a reduction of more than 50 per cent – it also highlighted some increases. The venerable HO-OO figure range, for example, was up by nearly 5 per cent and generating more than £800,000 income. The larger 1/32nd scale figure range was doing even better, up by 8 per cent with income of nearly £500,000.

Right up to the last moment, Ken reminded me, the kits division was profitable. In fact, his staff at Airfix Products in London were totally shocked that the business in which they worked, and which was self-evidently busy and successful, was about to close, and that they would lose their jobs. But the Meccano issue, the cross-guarantee nature of Airfix's financing and their bankers' reluctance to extend credit, together with a property development deal in Manchester which effectively tied up what funds were available, meant that in those recessive times Airfix was doomed.

The *Star Wars* Millennium Falcon from 1982 even included a working lighting loom with which to illuminate Han Solo's rebel spaceship

Like many in Wandsworth, I guess, Ken Askwith thinks it was a shame that while it was the success of plastic kits that enabled and encouraged the development of the wider Airfix Group, it was ultimately the various pressures created by the nature of a large and extended business network that, in the end, ultimately destroyed the kits division. The cruel irony was that right up to the last day the manufacture of plastic kits was still a real money-spinner.

No Fun at the Fair

Airfix ceased trading in January 1981 and was immediately put into the hands of the receiver. Salt was rubbed into the wounds of the famous company when the announcement was made on the eve of the British toy industry's forum of sales and enterprise, the national Toy Fair, which in the 1970s had relocated from Brighton to London's Earl's Court exhibition centre.

It was inconceivable that a group which until recently was at the top of its game and which owned not just Airfix, but numerous other great icons of the British toy industry, could be allowed to disappear for ever.

Those employed by Airfix learnt the sad news the previous day. Designer Peter Allen, who was at a sales conference in Cobham, first realised something was up when, of all people, Airfix's sales director, Peter Mason, didn't turn up for the first part of the day's session. He had been called back to Haldane Place for an extraordinary board meeting.

For Airfix management, particularly those in sales and marketing for whom the Toy Fair represented the highlight of the year, this was a particularly cruel humiliation. Months in the planning, Airfix's stand was receiving the finishing touches and being stocked with boxes of new kits and displays of assembled models as well as copies of Airfix's 1981 Model Kit Catalogue. How ironic its introduction must now have seemed! 'Airfix believe that 1981 will mark the beginning of another new period in the company's history and provide more products that are both innovative and exciting,' it began.

Few thought that a brand name as famous as Airfix would be left on the shelf for long. Even back in 1981, anything to do with what had already become a national treasure achieved column inches. The broadsheets were awash with stories about the famous toy company. It was inconceivable that a group which until recently was at the top of its game and which owned not just Airfix, but numerous other great icons of the British toy industry, could be allowed to disappear for ever.

Because of their relatively long lead times, the first couple of issues of the monthly *Airfix Magazine* published in 1981 made no mention of the recent disaster that had befallen their namesake. The then proprietors, Kristall Publications Ltd, carried on delivering the popular magazine under the terms of their contract. In any case, advertisements had been booked and paid for well in advance, so there was no imperative to alter anything.

In 'Editor's Notebook' in the January 1981 edition, Chris Ellis wrote: 'Airfix go into the new year with their contribution to the new snap-together marketing development, Snap'nGlue, which we welcome, in particular because it will encourage youngsters and that is all to the good.'

There was, however, an ironically titled colour advertisement from Airfix on the inside front cover of the January 1981 edition. A rather striking full-page advertisement for Airfix's then new 1/72nd scale BIII kit was headlined 'Seeing is Believing'. Like me, few modellers who

purchased this edition, probably before Christmas 1980, could have believed their eyes when a few weeks later they read that Airfix, designers of this all-new version of the RAF's Second World War heavy bomber, had been shot out of the sky.

'If you were coming in on a wing and a prayer … you'd be glad that it was an Airfix model Lancaster,' read the caption under the photo. On a wing and a prayer Airfix were still aloft that Christmas, but they'd already damn near bought it.

New Owners

As we know, the dark cloud of sudden collapse had a silver lining. Not surprisingly, there was a queue of interested purchasers ready to pluck Airfix from the administrator's grip at a bargain price. A strong suitor was the Yorkshire-based Humbrol, ostensibly British through and through like Airfix, but in fact part of American-owned Borden. Humbrol put in a solid offer, but it was outbid by General Mills, another American company – one with much deeper pockets.

General Mills was a huge combine, made up of numerous businesses. Most of them were in its core foodstuffs sector, but since its rapid expansion in the 1960s it also included a large number of familiar international toy brands in its leisure and entertainment realm. One of them was Palitoy, based in Leicestershire, in England, and this subsidiary was chosen as Airfix's new home.

The firm had been founded by Alfred Pallett as Cascelloid Ltd in 1919 to exploit the new market for household items manufactured from celluloid, one of the earliest plastics. By the mid-1930s the company had a new name, Palitoy (a nod to its founder Mr Pallett) and a new product range of toy dolls and cars. In 1968 its then owners, British Xylonite Ltd (BXL), sold Palitoy to General Mills. Palitoy had already been manufacturing Action Man under licence for Hasbro, and from 1968 onwards the US giant wasted no time ramping up production of this phenomenally successful doll for boys in the UK, ultimately giving Palitoy the freedom to extend the Action Man range even more than its originators had done with GI Joe in North America. Indeed, amongst other innovations, Palitoy can be credited for introducing Action Man's revolutionary Gripping Hands.

This, together with the fact that by the early 1980s General Mills was the world's largest toy conglomerate, suggested that Airfix was in very good hands indeed.

General Mills had its origins in two mid-19th-century flour mills situated on either side of the Mississippi River in Minneapolis, Minnesota. Until it went on an acquisition spending spree in the 1960s the company was perhaps best known for its association with the famous Pillsbury dough brand and its range of cereals, many of which were linked to television shows, such as the popular *Adventures of Bullwinkle and Rocky* series, via a range of successful sponsorship deals.

In the 1960s General Mills' formidable toy division included such names as Play-Doh, toy maker Kenner Products and Parker Bros, the manufacturers of Monopoly and Risk. General Mills really struck gold in 1977 when Bernard Loomis, then president of Kenner, purchased the merchandising rights to the *Star Wars* franchise. Kenner's three-inch tall character replicas of *Star Wars* characters were a success from the start, as they are today more than 30 years after they first appeared. In fact this deal transformed the world of toy licensing, but that's another story.

The addition of Craft Master Corporation (famous for its various 'painting by numbers' sets)

Kamov Ka-25A/C
helicopter in rather
lacklustre Palitoy
packaging

and its subsidiary, Model Products Corporation (MPC) added craft kits and Lionel trains (America's Hornby) to its expanding product range. Craft Master and MPC were then placed under the Michigan-based Fundimensions brand.

Immediately after General Mills' acquisition of Airfix it tasked Palitoy to reorganise things. For weeks the famous factory at Haldane Place in London had lain idle, managed by a skeleton crew of only four employees, including Peter Allen, who were by then either employed by General Mills or on short-term contract to them.

Peter put paid to what he calls the 'urban myth' that original kit artworks, patterns and artefacts were dumped in a skip. He told me that firstly the patterns were stored at Charlton, not on site, and that these were all moved to Palitoy's HQ at Coalville, in Leicestershire. 'All the artworks and current production box mechanicals were stored in the art store in the Drawing Office, and Artefacts were stored in the Library – also in the Drawing Office,' he pointed out. 'The keys to both of these stores I held, and the contents of both were sent to Palitoy. Yes, there was one skip, and into this Barry O'Dwyer, the ex-head buyer, and I emptied the contents of the Buying Office Store. This included some toy artworks mainly from the Poly Tank range, plus box mechanicals, most of which dated back many years. What was thrown away relating to the Kit range was in my control.' So there. You've been told.

The famous Garrett Lane factories that Airfix inhabited for so long live on today. They are now part of developer Workspace Group's London Heritage Properties and have the new name Riverside Business Centre. Fittingly, the area is still a hive of industry, as it has been since the 1870s when the area around the River Wandle first became popular with manufacturers – then mainly of paper, not plastic kits.

Airfix's most valuable asset was its mould tools, and these were treated with more respect, as befitting something that accounted for a large proportion of the purchase price. One of the last tasks before Airfix's move to Leicestershire was the transfer of these heavy items – to France. Airfix works manager Derek Sharpling had overall responsibility for the safe handling of these crucial items.

Palitoy owned the Miro Meccano factory in Calais, built in 1959 for the manufacture of French Dinky Toys and now owned by General Mills who, following Airfix Industries' collapse, owned both Meccano UK and Meccano S.A. in France (which they had purchased in 1971) so it made sense to shift all manufacturing operations there. Soon afterwards Airfix models started appearing with 'Made in France' on the boxes. (Today, incidentally, collectors tend to pay more for apparently identical vintage Airfix kits from this period if they bear the legend 'Made in England'. Ah, patriotism.)

A glance through the yellowing pages of List of A.F.T.O. Moulds, a surviving document from this period, makes fascinating reading. A.F.T.O. stands for AirFix Take Over, and the list tells exactly how much General Mills paid for each chunk of Airfix machine steel.

Not surprisingly, the brand new models commanded the highest prices. The mould tool of the Mig 23 Flogger cost a whopping £11,800, compared with only £400 for the veteran line-side Thatched Cottage. Airfix's HO-OO Platform Fittings cost even less – they were snapped up for only £250. Not surprisingly, the 1/24th scale moulds of the Superkit range cost top dollar – literally, I suppose – the FW 190 A5 costing a whopping £44,100. Interestingly, the mould tool for the SS *France* is listed (valued at £3,800). It has since disappeared and the model is considered a rarity by collectors.

Peter Allen told me that when the manager of the French shippers, who had brought a 'non-stop fleet of flatbed lorries' in order to transport the hundreds of moulds to France, saw the readiness with which the tools were loaded prior to their dispatch, he exclaimed with incredulity that such a thing would never be tolerated in his country. Heritage stays where it belongs. This is particularly interesting when you consider that years later, as will be explained in a following chapter, these self-same moulds did in fact leave France without interruption when they were dispatched back to Hornby in Kent from an even more distant location: Heller's

Classic Roy Cross artwork for the 1971 Douglas Invader...

... and what Palitoy had done to it in little more than a year. Which version is likely to stimulate the purchaser's imagination?

plant at Trun, near Falaise. One might have thought that after so long the French might have considered these tools part of their heritage.

Peter told me that after the closure of Airfix's famous Haldane Place premises in London, only four people who had worked there were immediately employed by General Mills. 'We all had a sound grounding in specific areas,' he said.

Naturally, Palitoy were committed to stick, as much as possible, to delivering the range of kits promised in Airfix's now very rare 1981 catalogue, distributed to the trade by reps at the London Toy Fair and mailed internationally to hobby and model shops during the run-up to this jamboree. Also, as previously mentioned, the pages of *Airfix Magazine*, which had gone to press weeks before calamity struck, were dotted with features and ads promising new products. Chief amongst them at the beginning of 1981 was the new 1/24th scale FW 190 A5 kit.

The new Airfix catalogue dedicated a whole page to the new Series 16 kit of the FW 190. It really was a superb model and raised the bar once again as far as precision design, pattern making and mould making were concerned. The description in the catalogue was gushing but it certainly wasn't hyperbole. 'One of no less than three versions can be built and a number of optional items are provided including canopies, guns, a bomb or drop tank plus the different sets of decals. Full engine detail and a complete cockpit interior make this a true masterpiece in miniature.'

Airfix Magazine said that the latest edition to Airfix's 1/24th scale Superkit range was 'well worth waiting for'. Saying that the kit was fantastically detailed, the review continued: 'As a 1/24th scale model it is likely to be acclaimed as one of the most realistic yet, having full engine and cockpit detail, hinged control surfaces, provision for a concealed motor within the engine block, and an undercarriage which can be put down or retracted.'

Given the financial constraints on Airfix which ultimately led to its collapse early in 1981, it is something of a miracle that this impressive kit ever made it beyond concept stage. That year, not surprisingly, Airfix managed to release very few new kits. In fact, for the aviation modeller there was only one other new tooling – that for the 1/72nd scale Sikorsky H.H.53C Jolly Green Giant helicopter – another superb kit well up to Airfix's new high standards.

Those modellers who enjoyed making kits of birds, a rather thin constituency it has to be admitted, did as well as the aircraft buffs. In 1981 Airfix released their Little Owl and Robins kits. They further patronised those modellers who would rather not make kits of war machines – girls – by releasing four dinosaur kits. However, good as they were, Airfix's Tyrannosaurus Rex, Triceratops, Pteranodon and Corythosaurus kits received only a lukewarm reception.

Across the Atlantic, the coolly branded US Airfix (USA, geddit?), the British firm's North American subsidiary, based in Hewitt, Texas, also released a new catalogue for 1981. Reflecting the US modeller's preference for automobile kits, it was packed with model cars. 'New for 1981 super detail is built into the latest Snapfix Datsun King Cab 4x4 Pick Ups,' said the catalogue blurb. Along with dozens of flashy motors the catalogue also featured the rest of the British Airfix range originated in London, though these were far less prominent than the hot rods and custom cars.

> It wasn't until 1982 that Palitoy could make its mark on Airfix's product range and signal its serious intent to British modellers.

It wasn't until 1982 that Palitoy could make its mark on Airfix's product range and signal its serious intent to British modellers. That year's new releases dwarfed those that reached the shops the year before. It wasn't that my friends in the design office, Peter Allen, Keith Melville and David Wicks, were working far harder (I'm sure Peter would claim that he always worked as hard as he could!), rather that with Airfix now part of General Mills its range could be supplemented by kits originated on the other side of the Atlantic at Craft Master or MPC within GM's Fundimensions brand. Consequently, along with kits originated either in London before Airfix's January 1981 collapse or from the drawing office at Palitoy's Coalville HQ, numerous US originals were added to the range.

The 1982 catalogue did include some notable new Airfix originals such as the superb 1/72nd scale replicas of two of the US's latest front-line combat aircraft, the F-18 Hornet and F-16A Fighting Falcon, a delightful 1/48th scale Ju 87 Stuka (scaled down from the drawings of Airfix's giant 1/24th scale Luftwaffe dive-bomber released in the 1970s), and a couple of new 1/600th scale Second World War Royal Navy warships (*Repulse* and *KGV*). The majority of new items, however, were of American provenance.

These included some superb kits and introduced an eye-catching range of automobile models and, five years after the movie was released, some great *Star Wars* kits at last. Some, like the large kit of Han Solo's Millennium Falcon, were from the original movie, but others, including dioramas such as Battle on Hoth, an impressive armoured AT-AT and Encounter with Yoda, were from the second, or fifth instalment in the series if you are a true believer, *Star Wars Episode V: The Empire Strikes Back*, released in May 1980.

The various car kits included a smattering of items licensed to the then popular TV series *The Dukes of Hazzard*, first aired in 1979: Duke's Digger, Cooter's Cruiser, Boss Hogg's Hauler and, naturally, a replica of the boys' General Lee Charger, their iconic 1969 Dodge.

Meanwhile Airfix persevered with their birds and dinosaur kits, also releasing a Woodpecker and Brontosaurus in 1982.

There were two distinct oddballs released that year: a Star Destroyer and a Flying Saucer, the former allegedly being designed by Gerry Anderson, the man who gave us *Thunderbirds*, *Captain Scarlet* and *Space 1999*. Because these kits were purely fictitious and didn't appear in their own series, unlike the ever-popular Airfix Angel Interceptor from *Captain Scarlet*, this pair of sci-fi models didn't sell well. Ironically, because they were destined for a short production run and did not outstay their welcome, like another Airfix failure from an earlier age, the ill-conceived Boy Scout, the futuristic duo are now eminently collectable.

A Different Way of Doing Things

Perhaps because it was run along American lines, the structure of Palitoy was quite different from what those recruited from the old Airfix staff were used to.

Integrating the three disciplines of marketing, product design and development and actual manufacture, Palitoy expected every member of its staff to operate along clearly defined paths and answer to set reporting procedures. All this was obviously designed to get the utmost from each employee and let individual departments do what they did best as they focused on core skills and disciplines.

Peter Allen told me about an incident immediately after General Mills' acquisition of Airfix. 'One of their high-powered executives asked me, "Why were you allowed to cross over into so many different areas of manufacturing, including marketing?" I told him that this was the way it had always been. We liked it that way and got involved in every aspect of a project, which was very rewarding.'

I have seen a flow diagram of the structure Palitoy imposed on Airfix. The marketing department got involved in initial briefing meetings and throughout the entire product development stage, but particularly when it came to agreeing pack mechanics and artwork, and of course they were heavily engaged in every aspect of advertising and promotion of the finished kit including via PR, at events and directly to the trade.

Within the product design, research and development sphere were numerous critical disciplines involving product tooling and safety assessments, estimates of the number of parts, and production of drawings, even a prototype. All these stages led up to a meeting that would decide whether the project would actually go ahead. If it did, the design department had to liaise with tool and jog makers and of course the manufacturing company, the third sector in this new triumvirate.

All of the time cost estimates for each required stage were being assessed, time and motion studies undertaken, and a detailed schedule of production management implemented.

Palitoy's flow chart features more arrows than probably fell at the Battle of Little Big Horn – each one pointing to the precise stage in this complex relay when one department handed the baton to their peers next door. Responsibilities were clearly labelled and everyone knew what they were expected to do.

Though comforted by once more being employed in a stable organisation with a clearly defined game plan, Peter felt somewhat pigeonholed. At old Airfix he worked intimately with other designers, briefed pattern and tool makers, liaised with Airfix's own injection moulding staff and even briefed illustrators such as Roy Cross regarding box-top artwork. 'You were allowed to expand your knowledge and involvement – which provided enormous job satisfaction,' he told me.

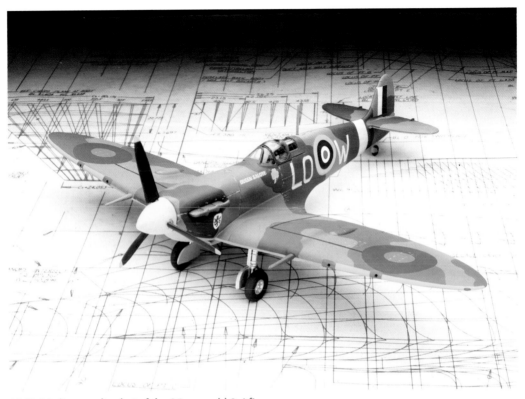

1980s' Palitoy studio shot of the 25 year old Spitfire

Although when he joined General Mills his opinions were respected and he was considered an expert on all matters Airfix, Peter soon discovered that he no longer had the freedom he had been used to. In his day the Drawing Office was a law unto itself, even issuing purchase orders to freelance contractors. He had been involved in every aspect of a model's development.

> 'Since Airfix, though I joined companies who paid me a lot more money, I never again had that degree of job satisfaction.'

'Since Airfix, though I joined companies who paid me a lot more money, I never again had that degree of job satisfaction,' he mused. 'Suddenly the Production Department were doing their own thing, Marketing was doing things independently. Often my Design Department refused to approve and sign things off because they weren't up to the standard to which we had become accustomed. To a degree this made me unpopular, I suppose, and I sometimes felt that I had perhaps made a mistake joining the operation at Palitoy. Things had become fragmented. Perhaps previously we had had too much responsibility.'

Above I mentioned the time and cost involved in deciding which kit should proceed to final production. Although a reasonably large proportion was spent on concept work, research, preliminary drawings and sometimes even pattern making, this was a fraction of the investment required to actually tool, manufacture, package, market and distribute the finished kit. An investment which would be wasted if the new kit turned out to be a turkey.

General Mills insisted on a three-year payback period for any new kit. If the return on the tooling and production investment was estimated to require a longer period, they simply wouldn't proceed – pure and simple. Peter Allen told me that, before their collapse, Airfix amortised the costs for their new 1/600th scale battleship *King George V* over a forecast 25-year period. General Mills would have considered this to be financial suicide, and in the light of future events perhaps it was.

When he joined Airfix, Peter said they were just completing their 1/168th scale kit of HMS *Royal Sovereign*, or *The Sovereign of the Seas*, one of the most important ships in the history of the Royal Navy, built at Woolwich in 1635, which along with their 1/120th scale HMS *Endeavour* (used by Captain James Cook during his scientific expedition of 1768) began Airfix's large-scale sailing ship series. These models were released in 1963. Peter told me that John Edwards, the modeller who had boldly criticised Airfix for the inaccuracies of their first Spitfire kit (BTK) and who after joining the company had quickly risen to the post of senior designer, claimed the significant cost of tooling for the *Royal Sovereign* (the first release of the two vessels) would be paid for by F.W. Woolworth's initial order alone.

Deep Waters

General Mills' much stricter rules concerning their return on investment meant that there was much more pressure on Airfix management to be certain that any new kit would succeed. I can confirm here that Peter Allen played a significant part in the demise of the fabled *Nautilus*, Captain Nemo's submarine in Jules Verne's novel, *20,000 Leagues Under the Sea*.

Conspiracies theories abound concerning the actual existence of this fabled kit. Did it or did it not exist? Why was an illustration commissioned and the new product advertised in the 1981 Airfix catalogue, the last such publication produced before the company was acquired by General Mills?

Well, Peter had the answer. 'When we went into liquidation the *Nautilus* mould existed, as did that for a butterfly we were going to release in our wildlife range. The instructions, even the box art proofing were all complete for the *Nautilus*.'

Even though Peter had been involved in a lot of the design work on it, when General Mills took over and asked him if he thought the *Nautilus* should go ahead, he said 'No' and killed it stone dead. He reckoned that Walt Disney's *20,000 Leagues Under the Sea*, the 1954 film starring Kirk Douglas as Ned Land and James Mason as Captain Nemo, on which the design of Airfix's *Nautilus* was based, was far too long in the tooth to appeal to youngsters and help drive sales. Perhaps one of the reasons Airfix had thought the kit might succeed was because of the numerous TV repeats of this old movie. Maybe it was because the original sets had been part of a famous walk-through attraction at Disneyland between 1955 and 1966. In 1981 the *Nautilus* submarine ride at Walt Disney World Resort's Magic Kingdom, which opened in 1971, was still a popular attraction, surviving until 1994. Perhaps this was a driver. Who knows?

News from Palitoy

Palitoy News was the expanding toy company's in-house newsletter. Like all such publications it suffered from a lack of regular features and contributions. In only its second edition, the editor Sue Berkeley, based in London at Airfix's PR company Munro Deighton, was writing in her editorial: '… we could use a few more suggestions from you – after all you're who the paper's for. And I'd like to see some of those photos I'd been promised turning up.' Ms Berkeley was keen to remind her readers that to 'make for a brighter more cheerful news-sheet' she didn't want any photos of weddings, christenings or 'what you personally did on the Marathon'.

Certainly the photographs used to illustrate a prominent, full-page article, 'Airfix – the Inside Story', were anything but parochial. The five images of a boyish and very dapper Peter Allen, Airfix's design manager, exhibiting the general arrangement drawings, wooden patterns, steel mould tool and resulting test shots of the new 1/72nd scale Harrier GR3 he had designed, were about as businesslike as you could get. Peter of course was an expert on the jump jet, having spent a considerable amount of time with a Harrier squadron at RAF Wittering, when he was working on his fantastic 1/24th scale replica of the GR1 variant.

Some of the text in this feature somewhat contradicted what Peter felt had changed since he was at Palitoy. 'At Airfix they always try to keep the design of a product under the control of one designer, rather than spreading it to several. This has the obvious advantage of allowing the designer to sustain his interest in the product from the beginning of the creative process right through to the end result. Also, it means that he is familiar with all aspects of the product from beginning to end.' As we have heard, Peter felt that overall his involvement with every aspect of a model's journey from concept to distribution was now rather reduced because of the increased involvement of the sales and marketing departments. However, the article concluded:

> 'In the past eight months an excellent working relationship has been built up between the Airfix and the MPC personnel, their American counterparts. MPC does already have a connection with Airfix reaching back some eight years. Airfix used to have their own American company tied up with MPC, and the two companies worked together prior to General Mills coming along … Airfix has obviously come a long way since the days when a certain Mr Nicholas Kove started a company to manufacture rubber, air-filled toys.'

On 22 February 1983 a presentation was given to Airfix and Action Man marketing manager Andrew Low in which it was claimed that the forthcoming year's introduction programme was 'the strongest new release programme ever'. Thirty-three new releases were scheduled at a rate of three per month, the major items being six *Star Wars* and *Return of the Jedi* kits, three vehicles from the popular TV series *The Fall Guy* starring Lee Majors, and two long-awaited Airfix originals, a superb 1/72nd scale RAF Vulcan V-bomber and a 1/48th scale RN Sea Harrier. However, the report did note that the only issues which could pose a threat to this ambitious programme were 'engineering and production delays'.

The key objective of the presentation and its findings was to ensure that Airfix quickly generated a profit to cover General Mills' acquisition costs. To achieve sufficient revenues, manufacturing volume and sales had to be increased and tooling costs reduced. Naturally the only way to achieve this was to buy in kits originated elsewhere – hence the numerous US-made kits that were added to the Airfix range.

The presentation document is very interesting for a variety of reasons, not least the statistics on a page entitled 'Historical Background'. The document claimed that Airfix's high point came in 1975, when the company had a UK market share of an impressive 75 per cent, selling nearly 20 million kits each year. Airfix's projected share of the 1983 market was only 40 per cent, with kit sales of only 2.3 million units. These were forecast to generate sales revenues of £2.7 million, of which nearly half was to be generated by aircraft kits alone. In 1983 F.W. Woolworth's hegemony as Airfix's principal retailer was challenged by Boots, the erstwhile chemist's sales now approaching a third of Woolies' figures. Interestingly, the report stated that one of the reasons for Airfix's collapse in late 1980 was the entry of Matchbox on to the market in the mid-1970s with their 'new kits, two-colour moulding and wholesale distribution'.

Nevertheless, even after its recent troubles, Airfix was still a major player in Europe, accounting for an impressive 10 per cent of all kit sales in both Spain and the Benelux countries and 75 per cent in Germany. In France, by contrast, Airfix had only 2 per cent of the kit market, Heller grabbing the lion's share there with 40 per cent. Nevertheless, in 1983 sales of Airfix kits across Europe were forecast to increase by a few percentage points, even in France, against those achieved in 1982.

Another interesting revelation from this document is on the page headed 'Box Tops'. New 'strongly branded artwork, colour coded and in eight languages' was required. This could be achieved by 'model photography, new artwork, repro and films' and would cost £300,000. So, this is the source of Airfix's infamous decision to replace all its stunning *Boy's Own* artwork with photographs of poorly assembled and painted kits …

The overview of competitors in the report praised the models of Japan's Tamiya Corporation as 'excellent kits' and said that the US's Revell enjoyed a massive range and could offer substantial discounts. Revell had not yet joined forces with its American rival Monogram, whose range was considered biased towards the US market but, the author conceded, was gaining popularity in Europe.

> 'Airfix provides the ultimate in satisfaction derivable from a leisure construction activity by providing both an absorbing, creative challenge in assembly and subject matter that is appealing, realistic and detailed.'

In its summary the report proposed a positioning statement: 'Airfix provides the ultimate in satisfaction derivable from a leisure construction activity by providing both an absorbing, creative challenge in assembly and subject matter that is appealing, realistic and detailed.' To achieve a new target of net sales of £3 million and above as well as its profit margin to boot, Airfix was going to appeal to the key demographic in its target market – 'Children, primarily boys aged 7–15' – by convincing them that 'putting together a true to life Airfix kit provides an absorbing creative challenge that cannot be beaten for play value. Airfix should be seen as exciting yet authoritative – a brand that is charismatic in the kit market.'

In April 1983, Airfix's US partner MPC also produced a detailed survey of the plastic kit market. Their *Model Kit Industry Review* showed that even in the US, after a steady increase in volume throughout the 1970s which reached a peak in 1981 of more than $130 million, by 1982 the domestic kit market was contracting. As might be expected in the nation that gave us the automobile production line, automotive kits represented the biggest market segment. In 1982, it noted, 33 per cent of US modellers assembled car kits as opposed to 21 per cent who built model aircraft.

MPC's report included a page entitled 'Manufacturer Market Shares (%)' – an interesting section, which showed Monogram as having the largest share of the US market in 1982, with

When dinosaurs ruled the Earth. Dimetrodon originally released at Haldane Place in 1979 but shown in Palitoy period packaging

a whopping 30.3 per cent of the hobbyists' spend. Revell wasn't far behind, however, having a 25.6 per cent share. MPC was hanging in there as a serious contender with 20.1 per cent. By comparison US Airfix was a lightweight, possessing only 1.6 per cent.

MPC had some of the bestselling US kits in its range, however. In fact they had the best seller of all, the Millennium Falcon from *Star Wars*, which was soon to join Airfix's range. MPC had seven kits in the top 20 and they were all in the top ten, so it was doing really well. There were only two aircraft kits in the entire top 20, however: MPC's snap-together quarter scale SR-71 Blackbird, the long-range, supersonic reconnaissance aircraft capable of flying at Mach 3.2, and Revell's 1/32nd F-18 Hornet jet fighter.

Throughout 1982 and 1983 Palitoy kept up the effort to get new products on to the market, albeit that the majority were US-originated kits based on the blockbusting *Star Wars* movie series or on hit US television series. Fortunately there were some classic Airfix originals including their superb F-16s and 18s, a modification of the Jolly Green Giant helicopter resulting in the CH 53G variant, new battleships *KGV* and *Repulse*, an A10 Tankbuster and an F 105 Thunderchief – the famous Vietnam War era Thud.

For me and many other British modellers, however, the highlight of this period has to be the release of Airfix's lovely 1/72nd scale Avro Vulcan. British modellers had long clamoured for a kit of this distinctive delta wing bomber – it had been in service since the 1950s after all – and now at last Airfix had done it. In doing so they had stolen a march on any other manufacturer who could just be deciding, following the plane's recent celebrity during the Falklands War when it was used to crater Stanley airfield, that the publicity it received might help drive sales.

'Building on Success', screamed the cover of Palitoy's 1984 catalogue. Certainly the inventory of famous brand names on the front cover suggested unstoppable progress within the British toy industry. Airfix was there, of course, but it was only one brand amongst many others, all serious players in the early 1980s. They included Parker Family Games, Parker Video Games, Strawberry Shortcake, Action Man and Action Force, Play-Doh, Meccano, Mainline Railways and Care Bears, the delightful little creatures featuring prominently within the cover design.

The first thing to confront the reader on opening the catalogue was some detailed sales spiel about each of the aforementioned brands. 'Airfix is the outright leader in the kits market with a 40 per cent share,' read the blurb beneath the kit company's distinctive logo. 'Over 1984 Airfix will expand its share of the market through the introduction of new prestige kits for committed purchasers and easy to build kits for beginners.'

The 1984 Airfix catalogue certainly included announcements of some all-new kits which delighted serious modellers. The best amongst these included the Soviet Kamov Hormone helicopter; the Rockwell B-1B – the first true stealth bomber and an impressively large kit even in 1/72nd scale; a replica of the notorious Lockheed U2 spy-plane of Gary Powers/Cuban missile crisis fame, and a 1/48th scale Hughes Apache AH-64 helicopter gunship. As British modellers had come to expect, however, the majority of kits in the catalogue actually originated in America at MPC.

MPC's own 1984 catalogue featured many Airfix originals alongside a plethora of muscle cars, the staple diet of US modellers, it seems. Airfix's new Mil Hind 24 helicopter, their Avro Vulcan and Rockwell B-1B were lauded, as was the large 1/12th scale Bentley Blower designed at Wandsworth in the 1970s by Peter Allen. The Bentley had been elevated to MPC's Masterpiece Collection and now came with a distinctive plastic base. Other MPC peculiarities included the US firm's repackaging of Airfix's veteran HO-OO tanks into a duo of pretty impressive dioramas, Attack: Rhineland (featuring the DUKW, Panther, Sherman, Pontoon Bridge and various opposing soldiers, together with a 12"x18" vacuum formed base) and Attack: Normandy (Tiger, Sherman, soldiers, Burned Out Building – the old HO-OO Command Post – and soldiers, but with a smaller 10"x14" base). Naturally all the *Star Wars* kits, for whose licences General Mills had paid such a hefty price, were also there in profusion.

As far as people actually working at Palitoy were concerned, such as Peter Allen, the list of new kits featured in both Airfix's and MPC's 1984 catalogues was old news by the time of publication. They were already working on the schedule of kits due for release in 1985!

Early in March 1984 Peter attended a meeting with marketing manager Andrew Low and Steve Buck, Palitoy's product manager. The 1985 Airfix range was the main subject of conversation. During discussions about the possible modification to the 1/24th scale Harrier, designed to upgrade it to a GR3 model, and investigations into the practical possibilities of producing both a Soviet YAK Forger and Backfire Bomber, Peter was asked to consider adding

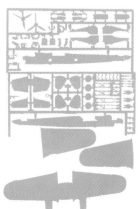

a US M1 Abrams tank to Airfix's existing HO-OO military vehicle range. The possibility of including some Israeli military vehicles and aircraft was discussed, but it was agreed that nothing should be done about these until the effect of such kits on existing sales in the Middle East in general was considered. It was also agreed that Airfix would carry a maximum of 200 kits for 1985, a reduction from the level in 1984, when 225 were scheduled for availability to retailers.

Another detailed internal analysis of Airfix's current status was prepared in April 1984. Projected UK sales income was estimated at £4.1 million. Of the three million sales of individual kits forecast to generate this total, nearly 35 per cent would be models of aircraft. Interestingly, however, 26 per cent of all Airfix kit sales were forecast to be models from the *Star Wars* range.

Although the name of the author of this book does not appear in the report, it gets a mention by proxy, because 1984 saw the release of *The Model World of Airfix*, and it is included under '1984 New Intros'. Fortunately for my ego it was listed along with Airfix's new Vulcan and B1 Bomber kits in 'Major Items'. This, my first ever volume, was in effect a book and kit compendium. The literary component, such as it was, consisted of a slim, perfect-bound paperback, which came with two specially packaged kits (Imperial Airways' HP 42 Heracles and the new Kamov Hormone helicopter). Everything fitted neatly into a robust cardboard slip-case.

I first thought of writing a book about Airfix shortly after I learnt of the company's collapse in 1981. In 1983 it had become reality. *The Model World of Airfix*, published by Bellew & Higton, was effectively sponsored by Palitoy, who purchased virtually the entire print-run to use as a promotional tool.

One thing the 1984 report identified as a real problem at Airfix was the profusion of different box sizes.

One thing the 1984 report identified as a real problem at Airfix was the profusion of different box sizes. There were 41 in total, and this was considered to be far too many and distinctly uneconomical. The report recognised, however, that doing much about the disparity in shapes and sizes would be costly and would take a long time. Re-releases, for example, if packaged in new boxes would require two years' sales to recoup the cost of their redesign and manufacture.

The report included some fascinating qualitative research findings that I guess confirmed what most people at Airfix already knew – times were changing, and buying habits in the toy sector were changing too. Although the report said that Airfix should be optimistic, because model making was still understood and respected and there was no basic difference in the individual motivations and attitudes of youngsters, it recognised that the tempo of life had accelerated, resulting in individual consumers possessing less manual dexterity than previous generations. In 'Negatives', plastic kits were considered fiddly, prone to breaking – even too daunting. Boxes were often found to bear little relationship to the size of finished kits – another black mark.

A meeting was held in May 1984 to discuss ways of reducing production costs, and Peter attended it, accompanied by his boss, design director John Hawkes. Ex-Airfix himself, John had moved to Palitoy in the role of designer some time before the 1981 collapse. He thought highly enough of Peter to recommend Palitoy to take him on, and in his new role as design director he was able to make such recommendations formally. John Hawkes was 'one of the influences behind Palitoy's decision to employ me', Peter told me. Before joining Airfix, John had worked for die-cast toy car manufacturer Matchbox. Also present at the meeting were Roger Morrison, the tooling manager, and designer Steve Buck. Peter and Roger were on the same level – which meant, said Peter, that they had better company cars than Steve!

The meeting concerned itself with ways of reducing costs by restricting the number of components, perhaps leaving out optional pieces. 'Further reductions could be achieved in deleting armament,' Peter said. 'However, it seems pointless to remove these components as this reduces the excitement of the product. For example, the Stuka is famed as a dive-bomber. Propellers, where fitted, have been left as moving parts. A saving of one moulding per kit would be achieved if these become solid. However, the research did highlight a desire for moving parts amongst consumers.'

Nevertheless, Peter did prepare a list of savings that could be achieved if certain, nonessential components were omitted. These included: deleting the outer wing drop tanks from the modified Hawker Hunter FGA 9 kit; moulding an integral tail-wheel to the 1/72nd scale Me 109's fuselage; moulding the crew's seats integrally to the floor of the SA 341 Gazelle helicopter; deleting the port and starboard retracted undercarriage components from the 1/48th scale Spitfire VB kit and doing the same on the smaller 1/72nd scale Spitfire Mk1a, and deleting four pieces of unspecified armament from the components provided with the veteran Lockheed F104G Starfighter kit. These amendments would reduce costs in the long term, but to achieve the economies a certain amount of work blanking off and modifying elements of the mould tool would have to be budgeted for up front.

In June 1984 *Airfix Magazine* ran a piece about the forthcoming publication of my new book, *The Model World of Airfix*. Entitled 'Airfix – A Personal History', the article by editor David Taylor featured a photograph of a much younger author – I was 24 years old then – together with my friend Peter Allen, the kits design manager, brandishing a test shot of the new 1/72nd scale B1-B bomber, flanked by kit designer Keith Melville and tooling section leader David Wick.

Later in June the Palitoy company held another intense meeting where it looked critically at the ongoing programme of re-releases. I've seen some notes from this meeting and they provide a good picture of what the management considered Airfix's best and worst seller during the period. The old Supermarine S6B, the Schneider Trophy-winning seaplane, was thought unlikely to sell in sufficient volumes. 'The product is rather crude,' read a comment in the margin. Not surprising really when you consider that the tool design dated from 1957. The Bristol Belvedere helicopter was considered 'a bit old hat … do not recommend it', and the 1/72nd scale Douglas Boston and Fairey Battle bombers were considered more worthy alternatives.

The Model World of Airfix book/kit compendium 1984

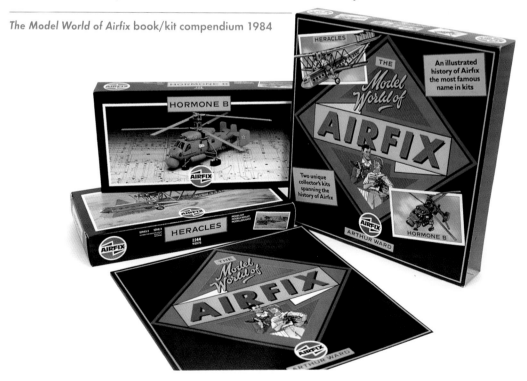

THE BOYS' BOOK OF AIRFIX

In late July an Airfix brainstorming session was held at Palitoy, attended by representatives from each internal department involved with the design, production, marketing and sales of Airfix kits. Carol Deighton and Francis Rosati from Palitoy's London PR firm, Munro Deighton, were also present.

Several short-term development projects were identified. Four key things were proposed, one of which was the inclusion of self-adhesive decals – which as we know didn't receive the go-ahead. Neither in fact did a proposed in-pack questionnaire for market research purposes. A couple of innovations do have their genesis at this meeting, however: on-pack skill levels and the redesign and simplification of instruction leaflets.

Under the subheading 'Long Term Development Projects', Duncan Billing, the author of the minutes, who was then Airfix's marketing manager, wrote: 'The idea that you have singled out as being the big idea – glue and paint pens – was also the favourite of the meeting as a whole.' However, despite his determination to test similar products already on the market from Airfix's competitor Tamiya, and then commission research prior to briefing Grey, Palitoy's advertising agency, the glue pens came to nothing. 'Clearly it is important to get this project rolling as quickly as possible,' he wrote. 'To that end Grey will have formulated a research proposal to test the idea amongst boys of seven to eleven … Once we have the results from the research and if they look promising I will then draw up in conjunction with product development and the agency a more detailed critical path.'

Unknown to Billing, decisions being taken at General Mills HQ in the US would result in the huge corporation withdrawing from the toy industry altogether and would ultimately put paid to the notion of Airfix paint and glue pens. In the meantime, as far as the outside world was concerned, things at Airfix continued as normal.

Trouble from Mills

In fact, as a result of some drastic decisions at General Mills HQ – the first step in their planned withdrawal from the toy business – the career paths of many at Airfix came to an abrupt end.

In a move which, Peter Allen suggested, required a Stateside accountant to do little more than erase a column of figures from his ledger, Palitoy's entire design and development department was shut down.

'As a company Palitoy had, like most big toy companies in the early 1980s, seen a drop in its profits, indeed was showing losses,' Peter told me. 'I knew we were close to our cut-off point too. A couple of weeks before the 1984 closure we had an offsite meeting for a day to relocate design into a refurbished offsite from the main factory.' But within two weeks all of Palitoy's design capability, including all R&D and creative functions relating not just to Airfix but also to Action Man, Play-Doh, and Mainline Trains – the whole design function – was closed for good.

'Big US companies do not give reasons for closure,' recalled Peter. 'When I first joined Palitoy I was told that General Mills had bought them and a few years later Chad Valley (one of the oldest UK toy companies) because they both held Royal Warrants – despite the fact that Chad Valley had a dated product range and was losing money. The factory was soon closed and the name was lost for many years.' The Chad Valley brand finally re-emerged, to be used by F.W. Woolworth.

'Traditionally toy companies could be very prosperous, which is why corporations like General

Mills invested in them and encouraged their growth during the good times,' Peter said. 'However, few of the new management teams, put in place to run businesses outside of their parent's core disciplines and understanding, knew what to do when times got tough.'

The downturn in the global toy market was clearly having a negative effect on Palitoy's bottom line. Peter recalls with bemusement some of the jargon arriving in memos from those at their US parent determined to put a positive spin on an apparently negative situation. 'We were bombarded with lovely phrases like "we've made controlled losses", which amused us all enormously despite the underlying danger they concealed.'

Those in the know within the UK toy industry were aware of forthcoming changes at Palitoy. Indeed at the 1984 Toy Fair Peter had been approached by a headhunter to see if he might consider jumping ship then. In the event he didn't follow it up, out of loyalty to his employer, a decision he regretted some months later when Palitoy told him that his department was to be closed and its staff made redundant. 'I telephoned the recruitment company,' said Peter. 'I knew the MD, Derek Dodds, because fortunately he had once been the head of Personnel at Airfix. He told me that the position had not been filled, and it was with Milton Bradley (MB Games). By then they had a freeze on recruitment as the company was being taken over by Hasbro, but because of my toy background I was taken on immediately.' Peter spent many years at MB designing for Playskool, and in later years worked on designs for Sindy and Action Man.

Palitoy basically carried on as a marketing company, guided by its US masters, but its profitability continued to suffer.

The 1984 closure of all Airfix's R&D and design functions naturally clarifies why the range of new kits was thinner in 1985 and, of course, why there weren't any new kits in 1986

TAILGUNNER WARD

Below: Heartbroken by public reaction to 'The Model World of Airfix' Gunner Ward prepares to do the decent thing.

I WOULD like to initiate my tenure here at *Airfix Magazine* with a warm greeting to all its many readers.

I have enjoyed and collected plastic kits since my childhood but my earliest memories are certainly Airfix — the Series 1 bagged type! As friends invested in George Best football boots and 'Jetex' powered aircraft I eagerly consumed the contents of the latest Airfix catalogue and handed over my pocket money in return for an Auster Antarctic or Bristol Superfreighter.

It was this fund of happy memories of collecting and constructing plastic kits combined with my career interest in books

photography was especially commissioned and in finally selecting the illustrations the most dif… …cide what to leave ou…

The te… proofed… young la… al error… onto pa… ings w… artwor… returne… colour… made a… comp…

TAIL GUNNER

In December 1984, I further strengthened my relationship with Airfix and with its magazine in particular when I began to contribute 'Tail Gunner Ward', my monthly page which, as the name suggests, was placed right at the back of the magazine.

The accompanying photograph of the author was taken by my dear friend, the late Wing Commander Bill Wood, OBE. Showing me standing alongside the tail gun-turret of the RAF Museum's Lancaster bomber, it seemed especially relevant. I should have noticed that the muzzles of the turret's .303 Browning machine-guns were directly aligned with my head. Never one to pass up the opportunity for some good-natured humour at a contributor's expense, editor David Taylor, who by then had become a firm friend, captioned the photo thus: 'Heartbroken by the public reaction to The Model World of Airfix Gunner Ward prepares to do the decent thing.'

For a year after my inaugural 'Tail Gunner' article, I was fortunate enough to write, literally, the last word in Airfix Magazine (if you exclude the premium ads inside and on the back cover, of course). I must say I enjoyed it immensely and felt very proud to be even a small part of a publication I enjoyed as a youngster.

and 1987. Despite the fact that, as we shall see, Humbrol took Airfix over in 1986, they had to start from a clean sheet as far as the design, pattern making, tooling and manufacture of entirely new models was concerned. It is all the more remarkable that in 1988 there actually were some new Airfix kits, and that Humbrol had been able to get new product off the drawing board and into production in around 18 months.

Scaling Down

New kits for 1985 were very thin on the ground. There was only one aircraft and that was merely a modification of the existing 1/72nd scale Tornado mould, converting it to an F2 ADV variant. The only other kits were definitely US focused. There were two vehicles, the Pick Up and Coyote from the TV series *Hardcastle and McCormick*, which starred Brian Keith as Judge Milton C. Hardcastle and Daniel Hugh Kelly as ex-con and racing car driver Mark 'Skid' McCormick. Also in the malnourished 1985 range, and again from a US television series, were the Streethawk Car and Streethawk Bike. These came from the hit show about a police officer and former amateur dirt-bike racer secretly picked to test a top secret project named Street Hawk – a high-tech motorbike capable of speeds in excess of 300 mph. There were some more *Star Wars* kits in the new range, but these, featuring integral wind-up motors, were distinctly childish and very, very un-Airfix. Demand was low and few were made. However, as is always the case with Airfix items produced in small numbers, the wind-up C3PO, AT-AT, Scout Walker and R2-D2 are now particularly sought after by collectors, of whom there are thousands amongst fans of Luke Skywalker and his pals.

Airfix's 1985 catalogue, a distinctly lacklustre affair, reflected the lack of new activity at Palitoy. Perhaps fittingly, it even featured a rather sombre plain black cover.

Airfix's 1985 catalogue, a distinctly lacklustre affair, reflected the lack of new activity at Palitoy. Perhaps fittingly, it even featured a rather sombre plain black cover. To make matters worse, and especially upset aircraft fans, in the photo section located in the centre of the catalogue a photograph of an Avro Lancaster is described as being a De Havilland Mosquito. Kit modellers had the right to expect those at Airfix, of all people, to know the difference.

The tough market of the mid-1980s forced Airfix to exhibit a breadth and variety across its range that suggested they were as big as ever and that kits of all types were popular. In reality, Palitoy management were encouraged to offer only the fastest moving items. They were told to 'reflect, to a certain extent, the breadth of the entire range' and were assisted in achieving this goal by the production of 'attractive, efficient' in-store 'Plannagrams', an innovation in retail marketing used by General Mills among others to describe the layout and positioning of kits on a retailer's shelves. Traditionally, the larger kits were positioned on the deeper shelves at the bottom of the unit. Regardless of precise position, if carefully arranged, a selection of kits could do wonders to the appeal of a brand like Airfix and, consequently, satisfy the retailer as well.

In an effort to generate revenues in perhaps the easiest possible manner, during 1985 Airfix sold its entire railway and trackside ranges to Wales-based Dapol. All except the venerable Airfield Control Tower, that is, which surprisingly began life as an accessory for model railway layouts. The majority of these tools weren't in fact of Airfix origin. They began life as Kitmaster tools before Airfix purchased the brand in the early 1960s. The legendary Deltic Diesel loco tool passed to Dapol among the job lot of items, although as fans know this kit was never issued when owned by Airfix, which makes the original Kitmaster model of even more value to collectors.

There was no new tooling scheduled for 1986. This was hardly surprising, because in February General Mills sold Airfix to Humbrol. It was hardly surprising either that the 1986 catalogue was a bit late arriving in the shops. When it did arrive, the introduction boldly stated that the new acquisition marked 'the dawn of a new era in the model kit industry'. Humbrol had at last got their hands on the prize, and for enthusiasts Airfix could be seen to have come back home. 'Possibly the world's most famous name in model kits is now owned, managed and serviced by a company dedicated to the model kit industry, with all the expertise, resources and professionalism required to maintain Airfix in a position of brand leadership.'

Above: Before proper catalogues there were price lists like this one from April 1961

Below: Fifth Edition Catalogue 1967

A BRUSH WITH HUMBROL

Following in his father's footsteps, Douglas Barton embarked upon a career in the oil business, becoming a broker in marine engine oils and, in the 1890s, operating in Yorkshire from premises in Kingston upon Hull and Bridlington. In 1919 he consolidated his affairs and set up the Humber Oil Company in a small workshop in Burton Street, Hull.

The firm produced cycle oil and calcium carbide for bike lamps. By the early 1930s the company had a 30-strong workforce and a new factory. It specialised in cellulose lacquers and paints and, when the Second World War broke out, supplied these to munitions factories and defence establishments under government contract. The original factory was destroyed by bombing in 1941 and, after a period in temporary premises, in 1947 Humbrol moved to its long-time base in Marfleet, a suburb of Kingston upon Hull. Douglas's son, Gerald Barton,

Opposite: Humbrol packaging. Studio shot 1990s

Above: Humbrol Authentics raised model paint manufacture to new heights

was the driving force behind the firm's move into the field of hobbyist paints in the 1950s and 60s. During this period Humbrol paints developed an enviable reputation as the best model enamels money could buy.

The company's belief in and support for the serious modeller was demonstrated by its active involvement in the development of specialist matt and gloss enamels. Humbrol's little 14ml tins, their lids coloured to illustrate the paint colour inside, and each featuring an embossed reference number, are iconic objects. Well, they are for us modellers! Better still was Humbrol's famous Authentics range. These were formulated from the finest pigments and came in an enormous range of shades, each designed to precisely match specific military finishes and combat colour schemes. In fact Airfix manufactured its own matt enamels, which for a long time were supplied in distinctive glass bottles as opposed to Humbrol's famous and more practical tinlets.

Together with its hugely successful paint range, Humbrol also produced a popular range of adhesives, under the name Britfix, and masking fluids called Maskol. The adhesives, even the polystyrene cement used by plastic modellers, were a pretty logical development from the epoxy-based compositions in the various puncture repair outfits Humbrol had marketed since the late 1930s along with its bicycle touch-up paint range. By the early 1970s, within the global community of plastic modellers at least, Humbrol was an internationally famous brand.

In 1976, the year of the US bi-centennial celebrations, the Barton family ceased to play an active part in the company when it became part of the international Borden Group of Companies, based in America. In 1961 Borden and Uniroyal had joined forces to become one of the largest and most integrated chemical companies in the world, and throughout the 1960s the huge company went on an acquisition spree, finally purchasing Humbrol, which in 1976 became part of its growing Hobby Products Group.

Frustrated in its ambition to purchase Airfix when its much larger US rival, General Mills, moved in and bought it off the administrator, in 1981 Borden acquired a French company, plastic kit manufacturer Heller, and added this firm to its Hobby Products Group instead.

However, in 1986 Humbrol finally acquired Airfix when General Mills sold it as part of a planned withdrawal from the toy market to refocus its efforts on its core food manufacturing business.

In fact, when General Mills began divesting itself of its toy business in 1985 it was the largest toymaker in the world, with playthings, fashion and non-apparel retail items accounting for 25 per cent of all its business. Incidentally, General Mills' former president E. Robert Kinney became head of the spun-off Kenner Parker Toys Inc.

The spring 1986 acquisition of Airfix positioned them alongside Heller within Borden's Hobby Products Group. The Airfix moulds remained in France, but were moved from Palitoy's Calais plant to Heller's under-utilised factory at Trun, near Falaise. Unlike the French company, however, which had its kit designers and moulding engineers on site, Airfix's production management would be operated from Humbrol's HQ in far-off Yorkshire.

However, as we learned in the previous chapter, Humbrol had really only purchased title to the Airfix brand, its tool bank and existing stock. Effectively Humbrol had purchased the brand, complete with its extensive back catalogue, only a small proportion of which was actually in production. To invigorate the increasingly tired range, Humbrol would have to pick up the baton Peter Allen and his colleagues had been forced to drop nearly two years before when

In the early 1970s Humbrol teamed up with British manufacturer FROG to produce a series of construction kit and paint combinations

Palitoy had made them redundant, ceasing any new design and development. Fortunately, Humbrol possessed in Trevor Snowden a research and development engineer who came from a similar background to Peter Allen and who relished the opportunity to take responsibility for the trusteeship of such a famous name.

Whilst all this reorganisation took place, naturally there was uncertainty about Airfix's future. In 1986 the editor of *Airfix Magazine* was the well-known author and First World War aviation expert Ray Rimmell. In March, the publication majored on the celebrations commemorating the 50th anniversary of the Spitfire's first flight. The cover featured a stirring illustration of the prototype Spitfire K5054 painted by the late Brian Knight. Brian was then a leading light in the prestigious Guild of Aviation Artists. Like Roy Cross, he had long since stopped painting for Airfix, but unlike his contemporary he had stuck with aviation art and was at that time regularly illustrating covers for Windsock, Ray Rimmell's own publishing company.

Humbrol had really only purchased title to the Airfix brand, its tool bank and existing stock.

Writing in 'Editorially Speaking ...' in the March edition of *Airfix Magazine*, Ray Rimmell touched on the subject of the confusion regarding Airfix's future. 'Amongst many rumours concerning the diminishing availability of Airfix kits,' wrote Mr Rimmell, 'many readers are naturally anxious to know the true story and what the future holds for the brand. I've no intention of adding further ill-informed speculation to what has already been circulated, but as soon as the true facts do emerge, Airfix readers will be among the first to know ...'

Ray Rimmell addressed the above under the heading 'Airfix kit availability'. Earlier in his editorial, beneath the heading 'Airfix Magazine availability', he had also dealt with the issue of the irregular distribution and erratic publication of the magazine, which was then published by another of his imprints, Albatross Publications, on behalf of Kenner Parker UK Ltd just before they relinquished title ownership to Humbrol.

Although the 1986 Airfix catalogue appeared somewhat later than usual, fans hoped that its arrival would signal an upturn in the kit company's fortunes. However, when it did appear, although it was marginally more colourful than its predecessor, it was still rather lean in extent and, aside from a brief introduction from Humbrol and the addition of their logotype on the back cover, it looked for all the world like just another Palitoy production.

This was of course entirely due to the fact that to get it printed at all, Humbrol had no choice but to work with the artwork and transparencies they had acquired when they took over Airfix lock, stock and barrel. Nevertheless, the publication of the 1986 catalogue did at least put paid to all the rumours about Airfix's future. It was now time for Humbrol to make its mark.

Whilst Airfix's mould tools moved south, albeit in France, from Calais to Trun, back in England the company's human component headed north. They were relocated to Humbrol's HQ in Marfleet, East Yorkshire.

Trevor Snowden

Trevor Snowden, Humbrol's senior R&D engineer, was given responsibility for restarting production and releasing new kits after Borden's acquisition of Airfix. There were two factors that made Trevor's job somewhat easier. Firstly, Trevor loved kits, especially model aircraft, and was a skilful model maker himself. Indeed, Trevor is a life member of IPMS, the International Plastic Modelling Society, the respected association of serious modellers that acts as a useful lobby group by virtue of its close association with kit manufacturers, many of whom like Airfix are keen supporters of the hobbyist. It also hosts a number of international exhibitions where expert modellers can compete for prestigious trophies.

Apart from his understanding of the modeller's needs and desires, the other advantage Trevor possessed was that he worked for Humbrol, who as part of Borden's Hobby Products

PACKAGING STYLES

Like every company with such a lengthy heritage, Airfix has regularly changed or amended its product packaging to keep up to date with changes in fashion and graphic design styles. Enthusiasts use these changes to help them determine a release date and to grade the rarity of individual kits. There is lengthy debate about individual types and formats and often the tiniest differences between boxes. Much of this is beyond me, as alterations were often simply the result of artworking expedience and not part of some grand plan. However, it is rather easy to tell the difference between
Charles Oates' two-colour linear designs of the 1950s, Roy Cross's marvellous illustrated box tops and headers in their red-strip boxes of the 1960s with their unfurling banner logos, and the more precise packaging of the 1970s, which featured firstly a new circular logo and then an oval one. The 1980s were the era of Palitoy's photographic box tops, and in the 1990s Humbrol's white boxes held sway.

Below: Beam Engine (Roy Cross artwork)

1: HO-OO scale Indians and Wagon Train in 1st issue boxes from the early 1960s

2: Still going strong after nearly 50 years! Current releases of Indians and Wagon Train

3: Humbrol 1/24th scale Spitfire Mk1A

4. Beam Engine (Roy Cross artwork)

5: Late 1960s blue box HO-OO Wagon Train

6: In an homage to the earliest Airfix HO-OO figure boxes, soldier manufacturer HäT, who manufacture some Airfix figures under licence, recently produced this set of their own Assyrian Army figures

7: 1990s Humbrol packaging for veteran 1953 vintage *Golden Hind*

Group were partnered with the famous French kit manufacturer, Heller. Indeed in the early 1980s this relationship had been put to good use with Humbrol's own Bobcat kit range and some other own-branded construction kits. Because Borden had a sizeable foothold in the kit industry, Humbrol's bid for Airfix obviously made much more commercial sense this time than in 1981, when they were pipped at the post by General Mills and Palitoy.

Trevor is still very much with Airfix and now does the job he has grown to love with new owners Hornby. There's a detailed interview with him later in this text, but it is worth pointing out that he has been a key factor in Airfix's success for more than 20 years.

Like many of his generation, Trevor had been familiar with the Airfix brand since his youth and saw the opportunity of being a kind of custodian for a cherished brand as a distinct honour. Of course, having a real liking for plastic kits also helped.

Trevor told me that Airfix's mould tools didn't immediately transfer from the Miro Meccano factory in Calais to Heller's plant in Trun. Apparently at the time when General Mills was divesting itself of Palitoy, Airfix and its other toy industry assets, management at this French factory successfully organised a management buy-out, enabling production to resume there in the short term.

Once Trevor had successfully managed the transfer of Airfix tools from the Calais region to Trun, he was able to continue where Palitoy had left off, but it wasn't until 1988 that he was able to make his mark on new Airfix kits.

I've mentioned the almost stop-gap catalogue that Airfix distributed to the market in 1986. Given its lateness and all the turmoil, the fact that it featured Humbrol branding was at least a reassurance for the kit fans. Airfix was back in safe hands.

Tom Cruise is On Board

The 1987 catalogue was much more like what fans had come to expect from the annual publication. It was bright and clean, thicker than before at 24 pages, and displayed a large selection of the kit range fans had grown to love. However, there wasn't anything really new. In fact, about the only surprise was a trio of aircraft kits based on the principal aircraft featured in *Top Gun*, the film starring Tom Cruise and Kelly McGillis. Although of interest perhaps to film buffs, these 1/72nd scale kits were a disappointment to aircraft modellers because they were replicas of 'pretend' planes. In the film the MiG, for example, was actually an F5-E Tiger II. This gave Airfix an opportunity to drag out their veteran F-5 tool but was of no real consequence to serious modellers. Maverick's F-14A Tomcat was a better proposition because it was based on a much newer Airfix kit, but the third airframe in the trio, Jester's Skyhawk, was just a tarted-up version of Airfix's old A-4 kit, which first appeared in 1958! By 1987 many other manufacturers produced much better versions of an F-5 or an A4 than those packaged in the 'Paramount Pictures' Top Gun' branded boxes.

For a really significant Airfix catalogue true fans had to wait until 1988. Airfix's 1988 catalogue is important for lots of reasons. I've already mentioned that it included the announcement of a kit that never made it to the model shop shelves – the BAe/McDonnell-Douglas Goshawk – but it also features the first kit released from an existing tool actually modified by Humbrol. Previously, the company had been content to release tools manufactured by Airfix at their

Wandsworth factory or those created under the aegis of Palitoy in Leicestershire. Mind you, despite featuring a number of kits marked 'New', in reality other than the Goshawk only one other kit was truly original and only a small part of it at that.

The converted kit? Pattern number 02080, the Series 2, 1/72nd scale BAC Lightning F3 modified from Airfix's existing F1.A. The revised tool featured a new tail fin and two infrared Firestreak missiles. It was not much, but at least it was something.

Several kits marked 'New', including the 1/72nd scale De Havilland Chipmunk, had actually first appeared years before – the Chipmunk in 1970; both the Ilyushin IL-2M3 Stormovik and the Dassault Mirage III C as long ago as 1964; the Dornier Do 217E/J in 1959, and the German pocket battleship Graf Spee in 1971. Another notable feature of the brochure was the absence of any introduction or copy explaining Humbrol's recent involvement and future plans. Many thought this a great marketing opportunity missed.

Perhaps the most notable feature of the year, at least as far as Humbrol was concerned, was the devastating conflagration that engulfed their Marfleet premises. Said to be one of the largest factory fires in post-war Hull, the blaze destroyed warehouses containing amongst other things the remaining unsold copies of my book *The Model World of Airfix*, which had been published five years previously.

> By the early 1990s Airfix involved itself in mould sharing, as it was far cheaper to repackage an existing kit than to design, tool and mould one from scratch.

Mould Sharing

The years 1990 to 1993 were arguably Humbrol's busiest. An enormous quantity of new kits were released during this period, though it has to be admitted that the moulds of some of them, such as the 1/72nd MiG 29 Fulcrum, the Su 27A Flanker, the Boeing AWACS E-3D Sentry, the YF-22 Lightning II, the F-117A Stealth and the 1/48th scale Etendard, were shared with Heller. So were a particularly large number of vehicles, ranging from Ferraris, Triumphs and Mercedes cars to Scania Eurotrucks, Semi Trailers and refrigerated lorries.

In keeping with most other manufacturers, by the early 1990s Airfix involved itself in mould sharing, as it was far cheaper to repackage an existing kit than to design, tool and mould one from scratch. However, it must be pointed out that unlike today, when finished kits can be brought by the bucketload from a wide variety of manufacturers who provide them with pieces attached to a numbered sprue (or runner) in polythene bags, Airfix's earliest mould swaps were transacted only with its sister company.

Despite this new development there were still a good number of Airfix originals such as superb 1/72nd scale Shorts Tucanos, Super Etendards, Mirage 2000s and both a Harrier GR5 and a GR7. In 1992 Airfix released a 1/72nd scale version of the all-new Eurofighter EFA and excellent larger, 1/48th scale replicas of the RAF's Tornado GR-1A and Argentinian Etendard IVP. In 1993 Airfix upgraded their late 1970s Avro Lancaster, producing a BIII Special Dambuster version, perhaps the most famous variant of this classic RAF heavy bomber but one which had never appeared in the Airfix range.

The highlight of 1994 has to be the release of Airfix's 1/48th scale H.S. Buccaneer S2B, but their conversion of Heller's existing Gloster Javelin T3 to a FAW 9/9R variant was also very well received.

Above: Mint Same Day Flyer Spitfire (1975) and Changeable Charlie toy, early 1960s

GAMES & TOYS

In its earliest days Airfix supplemented a range of utilitarian items such as rubber airbeds and injection-moulded plastic combs with a variety of cheap toys and novelties. Until the 1981 collapse, toys and games remained an important part of the company's product offer. In the 1970s Airfix released a new series of toys, including the famous Weebles series, aimed at youngsters. Weebles were marketed under licence from Hasbro's Playskool, a range which in turn was linked to Romper Room, a US pre-school TV and toy franchise that originated in Baltimore in 1954. By the 1970s Airfix produced a huge range of toys including many ready-assemble military playthings, which mimicked the type of products available in their construction kit range.

Bottom left: At the 1978 London Toy Fair Airfix Products managing director John Abbott unveiled the Micronauts range. He told visitors to Airfix's stand that whilst the company's commitment continued to be towards plastic kits, the threat of activity toys, such as skateboards, of which some 25 million had been sold in 1977, required his company to introduce some energetic toys to the range. Consequently the introduction of Airfix Eagles, a series of 3" figures of the kind growing in popularity since the introduction of the groundbreaking *Star Wars* figures and the Micronauts robots were announced

Below: Weeble Cabin Cruiser 1973

Right: Flight Deck – Could you land the carrier-borne Phantom jet?

Anti-clockwise from the left: Weeble Zoo Cage 1973 / This mid-1970s Datamatic Car could be programmed to negotiate a pattern of traffic cones / In 1979 Airfix allegedly sold £2 million worth of Micronauts, which put against around £20 million average annual sales across the board represented an excellent achievement for such an innovative toy / Sky Diver – chuck him in the air and hopefully he would come back to earth without getting tangled in the branches of a nearby tree / Junior Driver. In the 1960s young boys purchased hundreds of thousands of these popular toys and Airfix manufactured most of them

Left: SuperGyro – Just how many of mum's ornaments were trashed when this miniature helicopter got out of hand inside the living room is anyone's guess. Below left: A hugely popular toy in the 1960s – Airfix's FN Rifle. Doubtless the company sold lots of these because parents were forced to replace those whose fragile barrel's snapped off. Below right: You could even buy spare bullets for your FN Rifle. Above: Airfix Eagles Adventure Sets

The end of an era. The last ever edition of *Airfix Magazine* October/November 1993

However, the other big news at Airfix that year was Borden's sale of Hobby Products Group to Irish investment company Allen, Maguire & Partners Ltd, who restructured their new purchase under the Humbrol banner.

The following year Airfix extended their 1/48th scale Buccaneer range with S2, S2C, S2D and SMK50 variants. Conversions to their 1/48th scale Tornado GR1B and 1/72nd scale D.H. Mosquito NF. XIX/J.30 further supplemented the massive existing aircraft range.

Trevor Snowden really put his stamp on Airfix's aircraft range and delighted kit fans to boot with the 1996 releases of stunning 1/48th scale replicas of both Supermarine's late war Spitfire F22/24 and the carrier-borne Seafire FR46/47.

Under Allen, McGuire's management, in 1997 Humbrol diversified into the craft and science sector with the acquisition of the plaster moulding company Supercast and the following year bought a number of former Bluebird Plc brands. Bluebird

A range of so-called Airfix Junior kits was about all that was new in 1997.

made the Young Scientist Anatomy Set, and it was a model in this series that hit the headlines in 2000. In 1996 the artist Damien Hirst had produced a 20-foot bronze sculpture, Hymn, which bore a striking resemblance to Humbrol's Anatomy Man, designed originally by Norman Emms. At the time Humbrol was selling more than 10,000 of these sets each year. Interestingly, Charles Saatchi had paid £1 million for the Hirst sculpture. Humbrol took Hirst to court for breach of copyright but settled for an undisclosed sum to be donated to charity.

A range of so-called Airfix Junior kits was about all that was new in 1997, but in 1998 Trevor Snowden delighted kit fans once again with the release of two smashing 1/48th scale Electric Lightning variants: an F-2A/F6 and an F-1/F-1A/F-2/F-3 version. Not since 1963 had Airfix made a completely new miniature of this classic 1950s supersonic jet.

The year 1999 was selected as the date when Airfix would celebrate its half-century as a maker of kits, the reasoning being that it was 50 years since the Ferguson Tractor was first released. I wasn't the only writer who approached Humbrol for permission to tell the story of Airfix's momentous journey, which actually began in 1939, but I was determined to try to secure the opportunity, especially as I had always been disappointed by the lack of detail I'd been able to include in my 1984 paperback, *The Model World of Airfix*.

In order to sort out those who were particularly passionate about Airfix from operators keen to turn a fast buck with a commemorative book, and of course to help them check individual bone fides, Airfix employed a licensing agency to help them make a selection. Once I had negotiated this hurdle it was off to Marfleet to meet Trevor Snowden and managing director Frank Martin. I'm delighted to say that I passed muster – and *Airfix: Celebrating 50 years of the Greatest Kits in the World* was the result.

To be honest, Airfix's anniversary kit release was something of a disappointment to kit enthusiasts,

In 1992 if you couldn't afford a real one, or weren't old enough for a driving licence, an Airfix Maserati would do

many of whom were hoping for a version of the classic agricultural tractor which had kick-started everything. Nevertheless the Wallace & Gromit Aeroplane and Motorbike & Sidecar kits doubtless went down well with the legions of fans of Aardman's marvellous stop-motion animation series.

Marketing manager Darrell Burge told me that from 1999 the Aardman licence has proved to be a great success, with Hornby picking the licence up and continuing it. '*Shaun the Sheep* came along at just the right time to relaunch this great licence and develop it further,' said Darrell. 'The team at Aardman's office in Bristol are great to work with, and I believe it shows in the quality of the products we've managed to release.'

Batting for Airfix

I like to think that I might have had a tiny hand in the revitalisation of Airfix with the publication of my 1999 commemorative volume. Certainly, the reception it received when the book was launched at the IPMS (UK) National Show at Telford, Shropshire, in November 1999 seemed to confirm the brand's continued popularity. Shortly afterwards I was contacted by radio stations up and down the United Kingdom, each keen to discuss Airfix, a name with which many of their radio presenters and lots of their listeners too were extremely familiar.

Then, early in 2000, came an invitation to appear on a television programme that looked sympathetically at the wide variety of collecting passions occupying Britain's legions of enthusiasts. Channel Four television's *Collectors' Lot* programme was broadcast in November 2000. Recorded earlier that year at the home of Roy Cross, it featured yours truly and the master artist, he of so many stunning Airfix box tops, talking about Airfix. Roy's bit was probably of more value to the viewers because he took the time to explain his technique, talking about the procedure he employed to execute so many stunning artworks, and each so accurately.

CHAPTER 7

CHOCKS AWAY!

On the surface at least, Airfix entered the 21st century in pretty good shape, appearing to be stronger than ever. Their anniversary celebrations in 1999 had placed the brand front and centre with the British modelling fraternity and rekindled fond memories of 'making an Airfix' for the many who, as youngsters, had made their kits but had since put away such childish things.

But appearances can be deceptive. All was not well at Airfix. Its parent Humbrol was saddled with debt, and the relationship with the Heller brand in France, somewhat fractious at the best of times, was stretched to breaking point. Heller was an essential factor in Airfix's success, however. The French company manufactured all of Airfix's kits and possessed all of its mould tools.

As is generally the case when businesses are unhappy the root cause was lack of spare cash. Later in this chapter I feature interviews with Frank Martin and Trevor Snowden, who were at Airfix in 2000 and are back together again at the brand's new home at Hornby. These gentlemen know more than most about precisely what went on at Airfix at the turn of the new millennium and beyond and provide a unique insight into Airfix's 21st-century turmoil.

Airfix will forever be associated with model aircraft. Fittingly the company continues to produce some of the best in the business. So if modern multi role Tornados (above right) are your thing or you prefer piston engined WWII fighters or bombers... or even veteran delta wing V-Bombers like the Vulcan (sounds weird for such a modern looking thing, but design work began on it more than 60 years ago) you are sure to find the 'plane you like in the Airfix range

Despite problems, the dawn of the new century saw some new kit releases from Airfix. In 1999 and in association with the Oscar-winning animation house, Aardman, Airfix released two brand new 1/16th scale Wallace & Gromit kits. Being based on purely fictitious subjects, neither the Motorbike and Side Car or Wallace's Aeroplane were the kind of miniatures Airfix usually released and despite being anathema to aircraft and armoured fighting vehicle purists who made up the core constituency of die-hard Airfix fans, these new kits proved popular with their intended market, youngsters and novice modellers.

It has to be admitted, however, that real fans had hoped Airfix might produce a limited edition kit of the Ferguson Tractor, the plastic finished replica and later construction kit which had, almost by accident, propelled Airfix into the model kit business in 1949. There are a few mould tools that have been lost or damaged over the years, mostly for replicas for which it would be commercial suicide to re-tool. The Ferguson mould disappeared years ago, and starting all over again would be unfeasible – especially when Airfix could probably only be sure of selling a few thousand to fanatics. In these days of all singing all dancing farm machines and earth movers, the appeal of a tractor design dating back to the immediate post-Second World War years would be distinctly limited. The rest of 1999's kit production was limited to re-releases.

Neither the Motorbike and Side Car or Wallace's Aeroplane were the kind of miniatures Airfix usually released.

Apart from the modification of their 1970s 1/24th scale Harrier tool, turning it into a BAe Harrier GR3 or one of two US AV8 variants, there wasn't much new in the year 2000 either. Modifications were also the name of the game in 2001, with both of Airfix's veteran Lynx (helicopter) and Lancaster (bomber) kits being converted to Westland Navy Lynx HMA.8 and Lancaster B.I Special versions respectively.

In fact, throughout successive years modifications to existing tools or re-releases of old kits packaged in bright new boxes was the name of the game. An increasing number of moulds originating at Heller's factory in France also found their way into the Airfix range – an inexpensive way of making the British firm appear to be very active.

In 2002 Airfix's 1/48th scale Spitfire MkVB kit was converted to a Vc and even a Seafire IIIc version and the 1/24th scale Harrier was again tweaked, turning it into a BAe Sea Harrier FRS-1.

Airfix was quite busy in 2003. There were two new 1/48th scale kits, both BAe Hawks, one from the Red Arrows, the other the 100 series. Airfix's late 1970s 1/48th scale DH Mosquito tool was extensively modified including converting it to a night fighter version and a high speed photo reconnaissance variant. Airfix's mid-1970s 1/48th scale Panavia Tornado kit was upgraded to GR4 and GR4A versions.

England's qualification for the 2006 World Cup finals in Germany whipped up the usual frenzy of excited anticipation about the prospects for the English team, still living on the laurels of its first and only win in 1966. Like lots of others in England, Airfix were caught up in the excitement and decided that their new tools for 2004 should be not one, but three large and relatively expensive sets, each of four nine-inch tall players from the squad. Apart from the fact that buying all three sets required a pretty hefty investment, one of the problems with this release was that the most popular figure, David Beckham, was only in one of the boxes.

Another was down to Mr Beckham's penchant for changing his hairstyle with alarming regularity. The miniature Becks in the box didn't look like the player who strode out on to the pitch. Perhaps not surprisingly, these kits didn't do very well.

In 2005 Airfix at last set the modelling fraternity alight with the release of their 1/72nd scale BAC TSR-2 replica. Once again Airfix had cornered the market by releasing a replica of an aircraft which many enthusiasts had long hoped for and which no rival manufacturer had yet tackled. Although it was a kit of a particularly famous British design, a revolutionary but expensive aircraft sadly cancelled by the new Labour government in favour of the US General Dynamics F-111 in 1965, the appeal of TSR-2 amongst model and aviation fans is international. Upon its release as a limited edition kit, Airfix's new kit sold out. Like Trevor Snowden, I'm confident that Airfix's larger, 1/48th scale version of the same aircraft will sell even better.

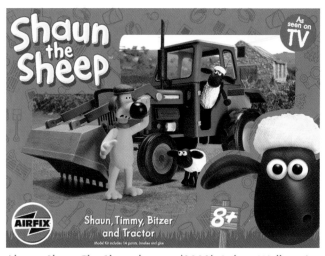

Above: Shaun The Sheep box art (2008). Below: Wallace & Gromit kits

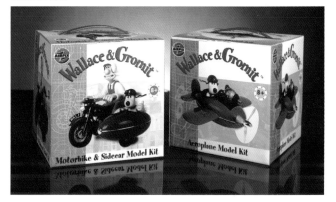

The year 2005 also saw Airfix release some exciting modifications of existing tools. Their 1/72nd Spitfire Vb becoming a Vc and their old Superkit Mustang evolving into a P-51K variant. Airfix's vintage US Sherman tank was modified to become a Second World War Crab mine flail version and its equally old British Churchill tank became a Crocodile flame-thrower.

Heller was sold off in 2005, but continued to manufacture kits for Humbrol.

In 2006 Airfix added another kit to their Wallace & Gromit range, a 1/12th scale replica of the duo's Anti-Pesto Van from *The Curse of the Were-Rabbit*, Aardman Animation's new film released the previous year. The only modification that year Airfix made to their 1/72nd scale Britten Norman Islander kit, the firm releasing a new Defender version of this versatile aircraft.

It's hardly surprising that Airfix's new offerings were even more limited than usual in 2006. In August of that year it went bust, and lay dormant in the hands of the receivers until November, when Hornby plucked it to safety.

The news that a cherished national institution such as Airfix had gone to the wall, for the second time in a quarter of a century, caused an enormous stir.

I first heard about the story in a Stop Press e-mail from the Airfix Collectors Club, timed at

7.30 p.m. on the evening of Wednesday 30 August, which read:

> 'As of 5.00 p.m. BST, Airfix has gone into administration, and all in Hull have lost their jobs. This has been confirmed by Andy Farmer at Airfix. Reason: Heller went into administration earlier and they are now reneging on their contract to supply kits to Airfix. They are also disputing ownership of the moulds. This process could take two years in the French courts and in the meantime the moulds cannot be accessed. Airfix went to Bank of Scotland and they took legal advice, deciding they cannot support Airfix (Humbrol) any longer so they have withdrawn finance.'

Because Airfix went into receivership relatively late in the evening, the story missed the Thursday morning editions, generally appearing in print on Friday, 1 September.

The piece in Britain's *Financial Times*, the august mouthpiece of London's financial community, was headlined: 'Airfix comes unstuck after sales plummet'. The report stated: 'Airfix, provider of plastic aircraft kits to generations of schoolboys, has been grounded by a combination of debt and supply chain failure. Grant Thornton has been appointed as administrators to the company, which is understood to have debts of more than twice the annual turnover of £10m.'

'Airfix, model maker to the nation, comes to a sticky end,' chimed Ben Fenton of the *Daily Telegraph*. 'The engine is on fire, the nose is pointing straight down and, wouldn't you know it, the canopy is covered in glue: after 54 years, Airfix was crashing and burning yesterday … The administrators say they are hopeful of selling the brand and the moulds. If they do, Airfix may pull out of its dive, but for the moment, the company seems doomed.'

Below: Anonymous and original F86D North American Sabre box-top rough (this kit was released in 1975 so it may or may not be the work of Roy Cross who stopped working for Airfix in 1974). Left: Original F86D North American Sabre box-top rough c/w with box top overlay showing the restricted area within which the artist was forced to work

F86S North American Sabre box-top rough with and without artwork overlay

There was a palpable sense of sadness throughout the British media. This is perhaps not surprising, because I'm sure almost every man aged between 35 and 65 in that industry would have certainly made at least one Airfix kit whilst growing up, and I'm sure a number of them sensibly continued to assemble said models well into adulthood.

'Buyer hunt as Airfix comes unstuck' was the headline in the Business & Media section of the *Observer* published on Sunday, 3 September. The article by Oliver Morgan said: 'The future of Airfix, purveyor of model Spitfires and Lancaster bombers to the baby boomer generation, rests on a scalpel-edge this weekend, as administrators work their way through 25 expressions of interest for the company … Hornby, the model train manufacturer, confirmed it was one of them, and it is thought US toy maker Hasbro might be interested.'

Hornby to the Rescue

In fact, Airfix wasn't dead and buried yet, merely in a coma from which many of us were sure it would be revived. For example, although an article in the industry journal *Trade News* had asked, 'Do children really want traditional toys, or are they the victims of their parents' fond memories?' the same paper also observed: 'Certainly, there can be sound business reasons for reintroducing once-successful toys.'

Airfix wasn't dead and buried yet, merely in a coma.

On the morning of 10 November 2006 *The Times* gave us the news we had all been hoping for. 'Hornby steams to the rescue of Airfix' was the headline. 'Hornby, the maker of toy trains and Scalextric cars, is to rescue Airfix from administration, adding the maker of model aircraft, tanks and ships to its stable of brands,' wrote Neelam Verjee. 'The deal, to be announced today, will unite some of the best known hobby brands after Hornby agreed a £2.6 million deal with the administrators, Grant Thornton, to buy the Airfix brand, as well as Humbrol, the paints and model accessories business, and Young Scientist, which makes chemistry sets. It is thought that Hornby, which saw off competition from rivals including Germany's Revell to secure the brands, is planning to restructure the business and transfer distribution and sales and marketing operations to its head office in Kent.'

The following day the *Guardian* newspaper ran a piece, headlined 'Hornby puts together deal for Airfix', in which journalist Benjamin Dierks wrote, 'The new owners will try to reinvigorate the Airfix business by investing in new products aimed at the younger market and also focusing on traditional products for older model fans.' Hornby CEO Frank Martin was quoted as saying, 'The strategic fit with Hornby is excellent and a detailed integration plan has already been put in place to ensure that we improve the profit performance rapidly.'

This was fabulous news. Upon learning the news of the sad tale of Airfix's collapse in the late summer, Collectingfriends.com, the toy and model collectors' online community I had co-founded with Peter Donaldson and a group of other good friends around the same time, immediately published a feature I wrote entitled 'It's happened to my favourite brand again!' In the article, which attracted huge attention, I had written:

'Blow me down. Twice in my admittedly not so young life Airfix has gone off the rails. What's happening with my favourite brand – the kit manufacturer whose products fill me with warm nostalgia whenever I see them? The first time Airfix was in trouble was in 1981 when, as a result of a range of complex problems, the great name ceased trading in January of that year. Cruel irony dictated that the announcement of this sudden misfortune was made whilst Airfix staff were exhibiting the company's latest products at the 1981 Earl's Court Toy Fair! Now we hear that another complex series of events have forced Airfix to cease trading again. Because of owner Humbrol's relationship with French company Heller, which hit the rails first, all the valuable Airfix mould tools are in France at Heller's factory at Trun near Falaise. ... Good luck Airfix!'

I was overjoyed to be able to break the news of Hornby's last-minute rescue on Collectingfriends. com the same morning as the national dailies carried the story – and especially to get a word from Frank Martin, the Hornby boss who, as it happened, had previously worked for Airfix. The new article was headlined 'Hornby Saves the Day'.

Here is a short section of the interview:

AW: 'After you left Airfix did you ever think you'd be involved with it again?'

FM: 'I always thought it was a possibility, especially because the move to Hornby meant that I worked within an allied industry sector and hadn't made a radical change of career. Over the years I had become increasingly distressed to learn of Humbrol's difficulties and was aware of the consequent problems at Airfix ... There was a lot of press speculation after Humbrol's collapse regarding its relationship with French kit firm Heller (owned by Humbrol since the early 1980s until it broke away as a result of a management buy out in 2005). Heller, also in trouble, had gone into administration before Airfix, a fact that exacerbated the latter's problems because Airfix kits were still manufactured in ... Heller's factory in Trun! Some commentators compared French and British corporate law and reckoned any purchaser of Airfix would have real difficulty getting its hands on Airfix's only long-term asset – its valuable mould tool bank.'

AW: 'What are your immediate priorities concerning Airfix?'

Frank Martin

FM: 'The key thing is to get product back into the market as soon as possible. Hopefully
        by Christmas. Our intention is to commence manufacture domestically with a UK
        contract moulding company. There are numerous injection moulding companies in
        Britain. Producing polystyrene kits is not a labour intensive business. Once the test
        shots have been approved it is a relatively straightforward process to get the parts
        packaged and ready for market. On the other hand Hornby trains and Scalextric
        cars, which need a great deal of manual work to assemble and detail them, demand
        a high labour content, which is why they are manufactured in China, where labour
        costs are lower than in the UK. However, it is perfectly conceivable that Airfix kits
        will be manufactured in the UK in the long term, thereby scotching suggestions that
        we would automatically choose to have them made in China. If some do go overseas,
        it is possible that only a very few tools will leave these shores again.'

AW: 'Any other plans?'

FM: 'I strongly believe that Airfix needs to attract new consumers. Airfix products must
        appeal to non-modellers. So, the products should be subject driven – not marketed
        as 'the latest Airfix kit' but as a new *Doctor Who* product from Airfix or a new
        Transformers one from Airfix. The fact that they require assembly from a kit of
        parts should be almost incidental. We are currently in discussion with the licence
        holders of properties like the ones mentioned and others too, and plan to release
        simpler kits aimed at attracting new entrants into the market and the hobby.'

Airfix Afloat

In 2007, with all the tools back from France where they had been stored at Heller's factory, the
plant from which for 20 years or so Airfix kits had been moulded and packaged, and with key
staff from Airfix's research, design and marketing department also firmly ensconced in their
Margate home, Hornby began to resume the flow of Airfix kits.

   The January 2007 issue of *Collectors Gazette* featured the good news on its front cover,
alongside a photograph of Trevor Snowden taken by Mat Irvine at UK IPMS National show,
previously mentioned by Ken Jones. The caption read: 'Trevor Snowden, long-time product

Above: Trevor Snowden. Below and opposite: Exciting Doctor Who packaging for *Daleks In Manhattan* set "Over 14cm tall!" (2008)

manager at Humbrol-Airfix, is part of the new division of Hornby. He is holding a test shot of the 1/72nd scale Lifeboat which was near release when the original company ceased trading.' Trevor was quoted as saying: 'This is by far and away the best outcome for Airfix and Humbrol. I am very pleased to be part of the new team and I am sure the old Airfix will be back on its feet in no time.'

Hornby pretty much began 2007 by releasing two kits that had been close to reaching the shops in the last days of Humbrol, a new lifeboat and the long-awaited Nimrod. Both were very well received.

Airfix's replica of an RNLI Severn Class Lifeboat was moulded in 1/72nd scale. An unusual subject, the kit proved very popular. A small proportion had in fact found their way on to the market and commanded healthy returns for speculators selling them during the months before Hornby's rescue, when Airfix lay dormant.

The other kit, like the 1/48th scale late version Spitfires and the various 1/48th scale English Electric Lightning jet fighter versions released in the 1990s, is another Trevor Snowden signature kit and one for which modellers seemed to have been waiting for ever – the massive 1/72nd scale HS Nimrod MR-2P. The Nimrod had been an on-

off project at Airfix since the 1970s. Enthusiasts had supposed that if Airfix did manufacture a version of this maritime reconnaissance aircraft they would do so using the 1/144th scale tool from their veteran DH Comet jet liner. Well, Trevor had other ideas and Hornby supported him. The Nimrod version was realised in the much larger and far more costly 1/72nd scale. Fortunately, its arrival was met with wide acclaim.

Airfix also further modified their versatile 1/48th scale Spitfire tool, releasing a Battle of Britain period Mk1 version of this classic airframe in 2007.

Enter the Doctor

Hornby demonstrated that they meant business by signing an agreement with BBC TV for the *Doctor Who* franchise, securing the licence to produce new Airfix kits associated with the resurgent series, which had captured an entirely new audience whilst thrilling old fans because of its higher production values and big budget presentation. In June 2007 Times Online published a feature under the startling heading 'Airfix cements deal with Dr Who' – don't worry, soon all the puns will be exhausted – which went on to say: 'The new range completes a remarkable turn around for Airfix, which faced collapse last August after parent company Humbrol fell into administration.'

A television crew from Britain's public service broadcaster captured the excitement surrounding Airfix's rebirth under the Hornby flag and the news that it had secured a licence from the BBC and would be releasing kits from the *Doctor Who* series.

In fact the team effectively shadowed Airfix throughout most of 2007, recording the trials and tribulations of getting a new product to market, a situation exacerbated somewhat by the fact that the firm intended making a replica of a British institution which has numerous fans, each of whom knew precisely how the Doctor, his assistant Martha and his spaceship, the Tardis, all the intended subjects of a new 1/12th scale kit, Welcome Aboard, should look. The other factor that made it a somewhat more complex feat for the crew, as well as the staff of Airfix who were shadowed there, was the fact that a lot of the recording took place at Airfix's manufacturer in China. Certainly Trevor Snowden, the star of the show, spent many an anxious moment after he returned to his hotel bed following visits to the Chinese injection moulding plant and later might visit the hotel lounge bar – both venues into which the BBC and its cameras enjoyed unlimited access.

Moving Forward

He needn't have worried. *The Money Programme* special: 'Airfix – Britain's Next Top Model?' broadcast on BBC2 on Friday, 7 December was a success. Produced by Maria David from BBC Wales and featuring actor Craig Cash (in character as Malcolm from the hit British TV comedy series *Mrs Merton*) painting an Airfix plane, the programme was great promotion, on prime-time TV – at Christmas – for a brand which little more than 12 months previously had been knocked to the floor and seemed unlikely ever to get up again.

'One of the most famous names in toys is back, after going bust. Airfix has been bought by model train giant Hornby, which plans to rebuild the brand. Will today's youth fall for Airfix's retro appeal, and will today's Playstation generation even notice?' the programme asked. It attempted to answer this question by discussing the conundrum of how you get youngsters inspired by a hobby some might consider old-fashioned or rather too militaristic.

'If we can apply the same lessons that we've learnt with Hornby to the Airfix business, really focus on what the needs of the enthusiasts are, but also to make the product more relevant to a new generation of collectors, then I think we'll succeed,' answered chief executive Frank Martin. He acknowledged that 'the Airfix product range has a fairly military focus,' but went on to say, 'We'll keep that, but also recognise that kids are interested in lots of other things.'

The BBC team also recorded Jeremy Brook, Secretary of the Airfix Collectors Club and publisher, editor and general factotum whose efforts produce for its members, on an amazingly regular basis, the excellent newsletter *Constant Scale*. He and other Airfix enthusiasts were recorded at the RAF Fairford air show. Luminaries such as top record producer Pete Waterman, the man who along with Mike Stock and Matt Aitken propelled the likes of Kylie Minogue and Rick Astley to the top of the charts, also featured heavily. Waterman has a passion for steam trains and owns many full-sized examples – and he also appreciates the lure of model railways, the core business of Airfix's new owner Hornby.

As those who watched the show will know, in its race to get its new *Doctor Who* kit into the shops by Christmas, Airfix struggled to meet its deadline. It wasn't as easy getting approvals for the likeness of a familiar TV star to whom, partly at least, his face is his fortune as perhaps it is to get an aircraft manufacturer to OK the design of a model of their new aircraft, a kit possibly produced from the aid of their original plans in the first place. 'It has only partially succeeded,' the commentary conceded. 'The toy has made it to a leading London store, but the bulk of the 25,000 run will not be available until the New Year.'

Although it was a difficult birth, when modellers got their sweaty hands on Welcome Aboard they were generally very happy.

Jim James of Starship Modeler, an American website dedicated to the sci-fi buff, thought the new kit was 'well thought out' and that the breakdown of parts 'produced great figure poses – the likenesses for the figures are the best I've ever seen in a mass produced kit, it really looks like David Tennant!' – which was praise indeed. In a typically American manner, the reviewer concluded by saying: 'This is a cool model.'

At the time of writing, Airfix are close to the release of the follow-up to Welcome Aboard with another 1/12th scale *Doctor Who* kit, Dalek Encounter. Like its predecessor, this model will be an all singing, all dancing affair, complete with sound chips and other gizmos. The enormous appeal of the Doctor's metal-clad nemesis from the planet Skaro is guaranteed to result in high sales and acclaim equal to that for the inaugural Airfix release from the popular sci-fi series which, amazingly, was first broadcast on British television in 1963.

'The *Doctor Who* licence was brilliant for raising the awareness of Airfix as a brand.'

One person who is especially delighted with the *Doctor Who* deal is Airfix marketing manager Darrell Burge, who said to me: 'the *Doctor Who* licence was brilliant for raising the awareness of Airfix as a brand,' he told me. 'This licence is more difficult to work with just because there are more people involved outside of Hornby, many of whom haven't worked with products such as ours before. The whole process has improved, though, and the second *Doctor Who* set, Daleks in Manhattan, has been much more straightforward to implement because we've benefited from the steep learning curve of the first set. At the end of the day we have finished up with two absolutely fabulous products that are amongst the best Airfix models ever.'

Darrell, who had been with Airfix at Humbrol since the 1980s, recalled for me what it was like during the time of the 2006 problems and the build-up to the Hornby rescue: 'It was difficult to accept that the terrific team of people that we had built up both in and out of Marfleet, who had given a large chunk of their working and in many cases personal lives to the business, were all likely to lose their jobs through circumstances beyond their control. Even though it was recognised by everyone that the business was in great difficulties, it was a real shock once the redundancies started and friends departed. It was also frustrating that the outside world was unaware of the problems and just believed that the stock issues and very few new kits launched were down to inefficiencies of individuals, which wasn't the case at all.

'Hornby coming in and acquiring the brand and all its assets was a real godsend for Airfix (and Humbrol). With its huge number of loyal fans and enthusiasts and the position in the hobby market generally the future looks very good. All markets need a strong, recognisable brand to continually bring new people in and sustain it for the future.'

Other new Airfix releases in 2008 included new moulds in 1/72nd scale of a variety of English Electric Canberras, a new Mk.IXc Spifire, 1/48th scale versions of the aforementioned Canberra, including a US Martin B-57B version and, most exciting of all a potentially stunning 1/48th scale version of BAC's TSR-2. I saw a pre-production example of this great kit and was immediately sure it will prove even more popular than its 1/72nd scale counterpart. That, after all, sold out the moment it first became available.

There are 1/12th scale additions to Airfix's growing Aardman Animation range, *Shaun the Sheep* with either a Landrover or a Tractor, joining various existing Wallace & Gromit kits.

Various modifications took place in 2008. Airfix's vintage Gloster Gladiator biplane, HS Buccaneer, Westland Sea King helicopter and Fokker F.27 Friendship twin-engined monoplane, all in 1/72nd scale, were the subject of extensive work to either bring the tools up to date or produce conversions to other marks in each production series.

An Airfix Club Special of the Supermarine Spitfire Mk.XVIe, in the useful 1/48th scale, has already proved a big success. Part of its appeal doubtless being the exclusivity of the offer – only members of Airfix's own modellers club being able to get hold of one.

In 2008 Airfix modified some of their 1/76th scale tanks once more. The trusty old Sherman being converted to a Calliope, the T34 verion of this ubiquitous US tank that was fitted with 60 4.5-inch rocket launchers welded to its turret. The British Matilda tank was converted into the Hedgehog, an Australian version with seven spigot mortars fitted to the rear of the hull and providing, literally, a sting in the armoured vehicle's tail. The trusty old Airfix Churchill tank has been adapted to provide a Bridge Layer design, the version of the tank that in one simple movement could lay a 10-metre span capable of supporting up to 60 tons.

As always, numerous re-releases were added to the 2008 range, and I was particularly pleased to see the return of an old favourite of mine, the Boulton Paul Defiant turret fighter, this time in its correct NF.1 (night fighter) guise.

The year 2008 also saw the addition of a range of exciting 1/76th scale models from the former JB Models range, Airfix having recently purchased the manufacturer. Consequently, we now have miniatures of such unusual vehicles as the US M113 ACAV of the Vietnam War period, a pre-war British Vickers Light Tank, a Bedford Tactical Aircraft Refueller along with a variety of Landrover variants and, at last, a replica of the Saladin, a British armoured car from the days of the Cold War, which Airfix had promised, but never delivered, as long ago as 1968.

On 31 March 2008 London's *Evening Standard* carried the headline: 'Deliveries delayed but Hornby on right lines'. The article stated: 'Hornby issued a profits warning today, but insists it is still steaming ahead. The model railways-to-Scalextric business has enjoyed a turnaround in its fortunes in the last few years but said product shipment delays from suppliers in the Far East will hold back results. Sales for the year to the end of March are expected to reach £56 million, 19 per cent up on the previous year but behind previous expectations. Profits will now be £9 million at best, a disappointment to investors.'

The article, having noted that Hornby shares had fallen 10¼p to 195¼p, then quoted Hornby chairman Neil Johnson as saying: 'We are pleased with the overall health of our business in this increasingly difficult economic environment. We are confident that our strategy of building a broadly based hobby business will continue to enhance shareholder value. Whilst we expect the economic environment to remain challenging, we are confident that we enter the new financial year with the right platform to continue growing.'

With prescience that somewhat contradicted the negative tone of the introduction, the article concluded: 'Hornby has acquired several brands in recent years and says it has enough cash to make further deals if opportunities arise.'

The morning editions of Britain's *Guardian* and *Financial Times* newspapers dated Friday 2 May both carried stories about just such a deal – Hornby's sudden acquisition of the famous British die-cast toy manufacturer Corgi.

'All Aboard. After Scalextric and Airfix, Hornby adds Corgi to its toy collection' was the headline in the *Guardian* that day. 'It is the biggest happening in Toytown for a long time,' wrote Richard Wray. 'Hornby, the venerable maker of model railways, moved into the car business yesterday when it added Corgi to its burgeoning box of British toy brands in the hope of once again making the die-cast metal models as sought after as they were in their heyday … Over the past few years Hornby, based in Margate, Kent, has been single-handedly revitalising the British heritage toy industry, gathering up companies which in the 1960s and 70s would have accounted for the entire contents of most boys' bedroom cupboards … Two years ago, Hornby added Airfix, the plastic model firm that can trace its origins back to the start of World War II, to its collection.'

I was even elevated from Airfix expert to toy historian and quoted as saying: 'Before the war, Dinky had the market but post-war had Matchbox and Corgi to contend with. Corgi was famous by the early 1960s because they had windows whilst Dinky and Matchbox didn't – they were more simple metal castings. Dinky was always a little bit more expensive because their models were often larger, whilst Matchbox was famous for its smaller pocket-money type toys.'

Following Hornby's surprise acquisition of Corgi, barely 18 months after it purchased Airfix, Britain's *Independent* newspaper ran a special, two-page illustrated feature headed 'Toy Story – Whatever happened to the old favourites?' In the article, complete with colour photographs of each brand in the Hornby family, journalist Jonathan Brown wrote: 'Hornby's acquisition of Corgi is a courageous attempt to prove that traditional toys can compete with computer games for the attention of 21st-century children.' The feature detailed Corgi's origins as Mettoy, a manufacturer based in South Wales, many of whose employees were former miners grateful for the opportunity to make die-cast toy cars as their traditional jobs in the pits

Original artwork for new 1/72nd scale Nimrod MR2P, John D Jones

disappeared. It told of Corgi's purchase in 1999 by Zindhart Holdings, a Hong Kong-based company. 'Yesterday, in a move that would have been warmly welcomed by its founders, the company was back in British hands after it was effectively swallowed up by rival toymaker Hornby as part of a £7.5 million deal, plus £800,000 for existing stock.'

Frank Martin found the time to provide some words about his purchase of Corgi for inclusion on my collectors' website Collectingfriends.com. 'I wouldn't say I had a deprived childhood, but most of my die-casts were second-hand,' he told me. 'However, I particularly remember two toy cars. One was a Dinky 1949 model short-wheelbase Land Rover, and the other, a Corgi die-cast, was a superb Studebaker Golden Hawk.'

Frank also said he did remember that the Corgi model was quite sophisticated, featuring working suspension and Mettoy's famous transparent windows. Indeed mint and boxed versions of this 'gold-plated' model (Corgi 211S) still turn up at auction for relatively modest sums, so who knows, maybe Mr Martin will treat himself to a nostalgic dose of retail therapy!

I have been fortunate to enjoy the privilege of being close to Airfix and some of those who have worked for the company for more than 25 years now. During that period I have visited the kit company's HQ, first when it was owned by Palitoy in Leicestershire and later in Kingston upon Hull during Humbrol's hegemony. Sadly, I never visited Airfix when they were based in their long-time home at Garrett Lane in Wandsworth. To be honest, however, I have never known a period of optimism to compare

Despite the best efforts of various management teams, it never seemed likely that Airfix could ever again reach the lofty heights it enjoyed in the 1960s and 1970s.

with that at Airfix in current times. Previously, despite the best efforts of various management teams, it never seemed likely that Airfix could ever again reach the lofty heights it enjoyed in the 1960s and 1970s. It probably never will in pure turnover terms – the business has contracted violently and the buying habits of youngsters have changed for ever – but I reckon that under Hornby's auspices, Airfix will thrive and do as well as any construction kit company can hope to in today's volatile global economy.

Certainly, Airfix's future looks distinctly rosy, as confirmed by the dramatic announcement of its big hitter for 2009, its anniversary year – the fantastic 1/24th scale De Havilland Mosquito NF.II / FB.VI. I've seen the kit in its CAD (computer aided design) form and I can confirm that Trevor and his team have left no stone unturned as regards the amount of detail, including internal details, on this kit.

Indeed, as can be seen by reading the interviews from Trevor Snowden and Frank Martin with which I conclude this chapter, all those at Airfix, not least Frank and Trevor, have high hopes for the success of this kit. It will doubtless signal Hornby's arrival as a major player in the world of plastic construction kits.

Trevor Snowden

I think it fitting therefore that we begin with Trevor Snowden, whose passionate commitment gave flight to the Mosquito in the first place. Although we have kept closely in touch, and indeed Trevor Snowden helped me greatly whilst I was writing *Classic Kits* in 2004, the last time I had sat down properly with him and thrust my trusty Pearcorder under his chin was in 1998, whilst finalising my 50th anniversary history of Airfix.

'Mr Snowden, for the second time in precisely a decade I'm sitting before you to ask questions about your involvement with Airfix. Have things changed much since Hornby took over a couple of years ago?'

Clearing his throat and with a gleam in his eyes, Trevor's reply was immediate.

> 'Absolutely massively. For the Airfix brand you have to say the changes have only been for the better, especially because of the amount of money Hornby has put in to it. For me, really the only sad part concerns the fact that so many people at Humbrol lost their jobs and, that the Humber Oil Company (hence Humb-rol), founded in 1919 by the Barton family, no longer exists. But certainly for the Airfix brand and for its fans, it's probably the best thing that could have ever happened.'

Under Hornby's auspices Trevor has also noticed that his daily job as Airfix's senior product development engineer has also improved greatly, allowing him the scope and freedom to explore new territory denied him during the latter years under Humbrol.

> 'Basically Hornby have far more money to invest. Another important factor is the attitude of the management here – it is far more positive than it was at Humbrol. Here, they've more of an appreciation of what is needed because they've discovered that such an approach – putting in more detail and scale accuracy, for example – has worked so well with Hornby model trains and Scalextric cars. All this effort has been proved to pay dividends. Hornby have aimed for the connoisseur of the product, someone who appreciates fine quality and haven't been content with attracting children, a market Humbrol were always chasing.'

Trevor recalled some pretty tough times after Frank Martin left Humbrol and Airfix in 2000.

> 'After Frank left, the new CEO was Stephen Luddington. He was there during the period of the changeover when Allen & McGuire started to take a back seat and the Royal Bank of Scotland became more and more involved. When A&M re-financed Airfix, borrowing a lot of money from the bank, this was the era when it started to change from management running the company to the bank running it.

> 'Business Development Group, or BDG, were the team of business people put in by the bank who further restructured the company. Then, Stephen Lord, a partner from this team left BDG and became a full-time managing director of Airfix, taken on at the bank's request. Finally came the ex-Corgi management. Taken on because

Above: Left, Trevor Snowden, Product Development Engineer, seated at his over crowded desk and right with Carl Hart, Product Engineer, scrutinise the CAD (computer aided design) files of the forthcoming 1/24th scale De Havilland Mosquito

Stephen Lord had moved to France to assume a new role at Heller, which had moved apart from Airfix, becoming its subcontractor rather than sister company.

'We at first thought that it would only be Chris Guest, but soon we found out that several others from Corgi would be accompanying him, joining Airfix as directors. They were the management team in control when Airfix went in to receivership in August 2006.'

It's little wonder that in his last years at Marfleet, Hull, Trevor and his colleagues faced an uncertain future. Certainly, if even a team with such experience as those who had joined from one of the strongest brands in the British toy industry, Corgi, were unable to turn things around, the future for Airfix was clearly very bleak. 'It was a strange situation then,' Trevor reflected. 'You could see the end of the road looming ahead but you hoped that it wouldn't arrive. I didn't think the inevitable would happen because of my age – or rather that I had done a specialist job steadily for more than 20 years.

'This period was obviously a worrying time. We knew that Hornby was hovering in the background and might be interested in Airfix, which was reassuring, but realised that any rescue couldn't happen until Humbrol/Airfix went into receivership.'

When I interviewed Trevor at Hornby's Margate HQ, he had only recently turned 65 – retirement age. Like many of his colleagues he had assumed that he would be packing his bags and returning to his Yorkshire home full-time (Trevor works long hours Monday to Thursday, but spends Friday through Sunday in Hull). He is recognised by Frank Martin and others in management as too important an asset to lose, and I'm pleased to report that 'Our Trevor' has been asked to stay on and happily remains the guardian of the Airfix brand – a role he has enjoyed and so admirably discharged for years.

Trevor, who has boundless enthusiasm for the possibilities of plastic construction kit manufacture, is admirably equipped to provide Airfix with authoritative advice and hands-on knowledge gained from years in the industry. As he says, he began his career by serving his time as a tool maker and draughtsman with BTH (British Thompson Houston), a British engineering and heavy industrial company, based in Warwickshire, who were known primarily for their electrical systems and steam turbines. The Wikipedia entry for BTH says: 'In the 1960s and around BTH apprenticeships were highly thought of because its apprentices were exposed to production of a wide range of industrial products; and each year in Rugby there was a big parade of floats run by its apprentices.' Clearly Trevor was amongst the best in his field.

'Lucy Houston donated the £100,000 to the Schneider Trophy in 1931, so from the start of my career there's always been a link with aviation, a passion of mine,' beamed Trevor.

During the 1970s Trevor was employed as technical manager for Hollis Brothers, a timber company based in Hull. 'We made sort of associated wood products, like coat hangers and chairs, but out of plastic,' he told me.

Immediately before he joined Humbrol in the early 1980s, Trevor had 'a small job in plastic moulding', joining the famous paint manufacturer well before they finally acquired Airfix in 1986. Legend has it that having been outbid by the huge General Mills Corporation who bought Airfix in 1981, after it went bust for the first time, in a fit of pique Humbrol purchased French construction kit company Heller instead. Certainly that year, as part of Hobby Products Group, the two kit manufacturers became a subsidiary of the US Borden Corporation.

A keen modeller – he is now a lifetime member of the International Plastic Modeller's Society (IPMS) and the creator of numerous stunning replicas – Trevor was delighted when Humbrol clinched the deal with General Mills and their British subsidiary Palitoy, who divested themselves of their ownership of Airfix in 1986.

I asked Trevor what he thought of Airfix's future.

'At the moment I think it looks very rosy,' he said. 'Obviously Hornby will look after it. There's no question of that. So long as there's not a massive downturn in the UK economy, then they will put money into it and it will in fact prosper.'

For me and many other baby-boomers, part of the charm of Airfix is the fact that although the range is being continuously improved and updated, you can still find old favourites in the catalogue. These have a kind of totemic power capable of raising the spirits and whisking the older purchaser back to the innocent days of youth.

I realised that these venerable old tools are regularly subjected to refurbishment, and being Airfix's principal asset are treated with kid gloves. 'Didn't they wear out?' I asked Trevor.

'Well it all depends, of course, on the people who are moulding from them and how much care they take,' he answered. 'As long as they are not damaged these tools go on and on. High impact polystyrene isn't abrasive, so therefore there isn't the wear you might expect. In fact the only wear is caused by the injection moulding machine closing, and then not too much. We do refurbish our moulds, but if you consider that the small-scale *Golden Hind* in the Classic Ships range, our first real kit released in 1952, is produced from the original tool, made all those years ago, you can get some idea of the robust nature of the mould tools. Provided they are looked after, the tools can continue working virtually indefinitely.'

The Great Mosquito?

I was keen to hear about the most exciting Airfix kit for years, Hornby's signature model and one which will be the talk of the industry and the envy of Airfix's rivals. I mean of course the super 1/24th scale De Havilland Mosquito – the famous Wooden Wonder – scheduled for release in 2009. Hadn't this kit been on the drawing board at Airfix for years and, like the recently released 1/72nd scale Nimrod kit, been one of the most eagerly awaited Airfix releases, talked about with excited anticipation by modellers for generations? Trevor knew the whole story:

> **AIRFIX** 'The late Pat Transfield, the pattern maker and designer of the 1/24th scale Superkits, first started to seriously explore the possibilities of a 1/24th scale Mosquito as long ago as 1973. Then they were done rather differently, made as wooden patterns rather than CAD designs. Anyway, during a meeting here shortly after it acquired Airfix, Hornby decided to commit to a kit that would stamp its name firmly on Airfix. In the meeting I was asked what I thought would make a suitable kit. So I thought, "Well, it's worth chucking it in to see what happens" – and suggested a 1/24th scale Mosquito. I said, "Let's do the kit that Airfix could never do. Let's make the large-scale Mosquito." To their great credit, Hornby said, "Yes. Do it!" One could have fallen off a chair or been knocked over by a feather!'

Trevor told me that the Mosquito never made it to market because it was simply too expensive to tool. These days manufacturers like Airfix realise it is cheaper to include duplicate parts manufactured from the same tool – two of the same moulds for twin-engined aircraft like the Mosquito, for example – rather than laboriously cutting steel for each engine: 'If you look at all the original 24th scale kits, they were totally complete and Airfix would have tooled two engines and everything else for the proposed Mosquito, resulting in well over 600 parts. Nowadays we look at the problem and say "Well, parts that are duplicated can be moulded twice" – consequently you can reduce that figure down to around 400 new parts. Only two-thirds of the parts Airfix would have looked at originally, and consequently the tooling costs are reduced enormously.'

Roy Cross art for German WWII Reconnaissance Set (1974)

During my interview with him in August 2008 I asked Trevor to let me know what stage the fabled 1/24th scale Mosquito had reached, to which he replied: 'At this moment of time, as of today's date, we are about to begin cutting steel. The design is virtually completed, we've only a few things to check and then it will begin to be made into a mould! In its first instance the kit will come out as an Fb VI and an NF II, so a fighter-bomber Mark VI and a night fighter Mark II. There will be scope, however, to release bomber and two-stage versions at a later date. So, therefore, the engine in particular will be versatile enough to produce a two-stage Merlin and then of course the wing has been designed so that a new fuselage can be added to it for the bomber.'

Box-Tops

'The job's a hobby and the hobby's a job.'

Another thing which greatly appealed to me, like Airfix's return to the manufacture of giant 1/24th scale kits, a development it pioneered in 1969 with the release of the classic Spitfire Mk 1a Superkit, was the use of paintings on box tops rather than photographs of often badly constructed kits. Trevor explained why photography had taken over: 'Photos were included on Airfix boxes, first by Palitoy and subsequently by Humbrol, as a response to American consumer laws, which stipulated that what was shown on the lid had to be precisely what was within. Obviously an illustration was only an impression of the contents. The only way to get around this ruling and sell kits in America was to use a photograph of the model. Over the years this stipulation was relaxed as people realised that it really didn't matter that there was a painting on the box front, and then the Americans relaxed their laws and all manufacturers resumed featuring paintings rather than photos on their box tops. It was the same with depictions of violence. Any suggestion of bombs dropping or machine guns firing was removed from Airfix artwork in the mid-1970s, and everything became a bit bland. But eventually people realised that these box tops weren't glorifying war as such – in some respects it's just a representation of history. These things were fighters. They were bombers. They shot at each other or dropped bombs. This is what you expected to see.'

Soviet Cold War bomber Ilyushin IL-28 1970s reissue of 1968 kit featuring Ron Jobson's artwork, with roughs

As my tape appeared to be nearing its end, I asked Trevor to finish by telling me what he thought was the best thing about his job. 'Oh, well … the job's a hobby and the hobby's a job. To me it's a way of life and has been since I was given the job in research and development at Airfix when Humbrol bought the company in 1986. It became so much of a responsibility. A massive responsibility, because I knew that there was all those thousands of hours' effort expended by all those who did a similar job at Airfix before me. I felt like the custodian of the brand, and I have always tried as best I could to look after Airfix. It is a great name and I never, ever thought that I would have ever been instrumental in any company that was a nationally known company. To me one of the great things in my life has been to look after Airfix.'

Frank Martin

Frank Martin became reacquainted with Airfix as a major toy and hobby company when he attended his first Toy Fair at Brighton in 1976 (the last year the fair was held there).

> 'At that time I was a very young assistant product manager in the toy division of The Raleigh Cycle Company. The UK toy industry at the time was indeed still a UK business, with hardly any overseas manufacturers showing at the fair. How things have changed! The period 1979–83 saw the decimation of the UK industry. The combination of an outrageously strong pound, high UK inflation and suicidal interest rates made life virtually impossible for UK manufacturers. By this time I was marketing director of the recently formed Hasbro UK and observed the carnage from the relative safety of a non-UK manufacturing base.
>
> 'I left Hasbro in 1986 to develop my career in general management outside the toy industry, but not long before I left I was driving through South London, took a wrong turn and came face to face with the Airfix Industries building in Haldane Place, Garrett Lane.'

As he turned the corner Frank was confronted by a huge demolition crane about to swing its mighty jib. Instantly, the facade of the building, complete with Airfix name and logo, collapsed into a pile of dust and rubble. 'It was one of the saddest sights I've ever seen. Little did I think that ten years later I would be privileged to lead the company that owns Airfix.'

I noted the above when I last interviewed Frank Martin in Hull in 1998, when he was managing director of Humbrol, the owners of Airfix. Since that time an awful lot has happened in Frank's career. In January 2001 he became CEO of Hornby plc, the legendary British company, branded using the surname of another Frank, its founder, whose patent number GB190100587A, filed in 1901, evolved into Meccano and turned its creator into a multimillionaire.

When I next interviewed Frank Martin in spring 2008, at my request he brought me up to date with all the exciting changes that had taken place since we last spoke.

> 'Shortly after the publication of the Airfix 50th anniversary book the venture capital investors in the Humbrol business re-financed it, which resulted in a significant amount of additional debt being taken on. At the time I felt the amount was too great, but it was agreed upon – a decision taken out

of my hands. Then in 2000 Hornby, which was at that stage and still is a public company, was actually put up for sale.

'The reason for this offer was that Hornby had been going through some difficult times. They were in the middle of moving production out of the UK to China but, despite this, a few of the institutional shareholders couldn't really see a future for the business. It was therefore prevailed upon the board to put the business up for sale.'

On behalf of Humbrol Frank Martin obtained the prospectus detailing what was on offer at Hornby and how much the owners wanted for the famous brand and its assets.

'I felt that there was such a perfect, logical fit between Humbrol and Hornby that its purchase would make the perfect acquisition. Unfortunately Allen & McGuire, the owners of Humbrol at the time, had committed themselves to another large acquisition and they didn't have the necessary funds required to purchase Hornby.

'Consequently, during the course of 2000 the process went on for about six months or so, and during this time I investigated the possibility of buying both Humbrol and Hornby and combining the two businesses. In the event, for various reasons it wasn't possible to engineer that deal, but in the meantime I had got to know the directors of Hornby reasonably well, particularly the non-executive ones. However, towards the end of 2000 it seemed that there were no other credible offers for their business in order to take it private, and therefore the board was left with no alternative but to continue running Hornby as a public company.

'During this process, however, the major shareholders and non-executive directors had decided that they wanted a change of chief executive and they approached me. After a fairly short series of meetings, given the fact that we had got to know each other reasonably well over the course of the previous months, they offered me the job.

'I joined Hornby in January 2001 and for the next couple of years I really concentrated on building the core Hornby (UK) business as well as its international operations and sales via distributors.'

Hornby's Growing Stable

Frank told me that the business became very profitable, very quickly and the share price rose significantly. 'Then, as with all public companies, you are expected to propose strategies for continuing the growth of the business and developing plans for its longer-term future growth. I could see that because of the different international track gauges in the marketplace, our overseas opportunities with the Hornby model railway brand were limited – the scale used in the UK being different from the rest of the world – consequently we really had no opportunities

Me 109 E box top rough c/w with overlay (1976)
probably the work of Ken McDonough

internationally. Therefore we began a process of acquiring well-known brands, those against which competitively we would have got into difficulties around Europe.'

And so between March 2004 and April 2008 Hornby acquired Electrotren (a leading Spanish model railway company established in 1951); Lima Group, which comprised the French model railway company Jouef, a direct competitor to Hornby but which had ironically distributed Scalextric in Europe; and the Italian company, Rivarossi, founded in 1946, producer of the largest selection of American steam locomotives available in HO and N Scales. Over the last few years, Rivarossi had also acquired such famous brands as Arnold (a well-known German N gauge model railway manufacturer) and Pocher (famous for their luxurious large-scale model car kits), and these naturally joined Hornby's growing stable. In November 2006 Hornby purchased Airfix, and in May 2008 British die-cast model car manufacturer Corgi joined the team.

'We made all these acquisitions over the course of only four years, so it's been a period of fairly rapid growth,' added Frank. This dramatic but well-planned expansion reaped almost immediate commercial benefits, which were soon revealed on Hornby's bottom line. 'In the year I arrived at Hornby we had sales of £24 million and a profit of £1.4 million. In our most recent financial year ended March 2008 we reported sales of £56 million and profits of £9 million. So it's been a fantastic period. One of the high spots, amongst many, during this time was the opportunity to purchase Airfix and put our businesses together in the logical way I had first envisaged in 1999.'

Immediately after Frank Martin left Airfix, the owners, Allen & McGuire, brought in a new CEO, Stephen Luddington, who came from outside the toy industry. 'This is not necessarily a bad thing, but looking from the outside I was staggered by the changes I saw taking place,' said Frank. 'I felt that, at the time I left, although the kit business was stable it was certainly

Above: The new model Harrier (1974)

not capable of any significant growth. This expansion required a lot of capital investment, and Allen & McGuire didn't have the funds then to invest in further capital projects. In fact, whilst I was at Humbrol we had been steadily investing in and expanding the arts and crafts division, but after I left it seemed that within a year all this stopped, and indeed this business with its annual £4 million sales had been effectively written off with no replacement strategy in place. This seemed decidedly the wrong course of action.'

Frank's pessimism was obviously well founded.

'Of course what happened then was that the first CEO who had arrived left because things were going badly. The banks grew increasingly restless because various covenants were being breached. A corporate recovery firm was brought in to try and start restructuring the business, eventually one of their employees becoming the new managing director. Next both Humbrol and Airfix were split from the Heller business in France, each becoming separate entities. The industrial paints division was sold off and all manufacturing in Hull terminated, which I thought was a great shame because it was always a very profitable business. It was then decided that Humbrol should become more of a virtual business, with everything sub-contracted. All of these changes took place against a background of falling sales and no investment. It was really heading one way, especially factoring in the debt burden they were carrying.'

With any business, numerous competing factors operate on it and once things start to go wrong a series of inexorable events often conspire towards its downfall. The next thing that happened was that Heller, who held most of Airfix's assets in the shape of its tool bank and who were in any case the manufacturers of its kits, was sold to a management buy-out.

'The banks immediately stepped in, effectively taking control of the Humbrol business, with Allen & McGuire being moved to one side. Subsequently a new management team was brought in. Actually this group had previously run Corgi. It's a small world indeed!'

It seemed that this latest management team might crack things and raise Humbrol to the lofty position that such a well-established company deserves to occupy. A 6 February press release from Humbrol/Airfix said that they had just received a welcome boost to their futures with the arrival of a new top management team: 'Len Kalkun has taken over as Chief Operating Officer, while Colin Summerbell heads up Sales and Marketing and Peter Johns is the new Supply Director. This team, of ex-Corgi fame, is led by Chris Guest as Chairman.'

Although there were several others interested in securing Airfix, very few had the experience of the scale model industry, and particularly of Airfix of course, that I had gained whilst actually there in the 1990s.

'This team was given the opportunity of turning the business around,' said Frank. 'I think they had a good chance of doing so, because the debt was written down by a significant amount and they were consequently in a much better position financially.' He continued: 'Unfortunately, however, the Heller business in France went into receivership. Heller was Airfix's primary supplier, and the French receiver insisted on cash upfront, but as there was insufficient working capital in the Humbrol business this was not possible. In late August 2006 Humbrol too fell into the hands of the receiver.

'We immediately contacted the receivers and asked to be put on the list of those who might be interested in purchasing it. The result was that we ended up buying Humbrol, along with Airfix, of course, from the receiver early in November 2006.'

I asked Frank if there were many other suitors, for Airfix especially, and what, apart from financial muscle, enabled Hornby to propose the winning bid.

'Although there were several others interested in securing Airfix, very few had the experience of the scale model industry, and particularly of Airfix of course, that I had gained whilst actually there in the 1990s. Naturally, this lack of first-hand knowledge made other potential investors nervous,' he told me.

Few of the other interested parties possessed a candidate like Frank, who had such an intimate knowledge of the business in which they were about to invest. A huge factor vexing anyone who might potentially stump up the cash to purchase Humbrol was the fact that the key ingredients to the future success of its star brand Airfix – the kit company's precious mould tools – were under lock and key at Heller's factory at Trun, near Falaise, in deepest France. Even Frank Martin was troubled by the scenario of purchasing an impotent brand, in name alone.

'How were we going to get those tools out once we had acquired the assets?' This was the question that occupied much of Frank's thinking as he weighed up the pros and cons of making a bid for Humbrol. However, he was perhaps better placed than any other potential investor to figure out a solution that was equitable to all parties with a vested interest in the myriad chunks of Airfix machine steel in the Gallic warehouses – and, of course, he was familiar with the Heller business in France from his time with Airfix in the past decade. 'It is all very well acquiring title to the assets, but actually physically getting control of them can be a very different matter.' However, Frank Martin never gave up trying to suggest a method acceptable to everyone. 'What I was able to do was to strike a deal with the general manager

Top: HO-OO German Panther tank
Main image: HO-OO Forward Command Post

of the Heller business who was in fact also trying to buy it out of receivership. If he ensured that the receiver in France honoured the ownership of all the tools as being Humbrol's possessions, and subsequently ours if we bought it, then in return I would grant him a unique distribution agreement in France. This would confer on Heller the distribution rights for paint in France for an agreed period of time. 'So, we were able to have a totally above-board, but separate and contingent deal in place which gave us the confidence to sign a cheque for the receivers.'

Within ten days of Frank Martin signing the contract, all the valuable mould tools, some of them over 50 years old, were safely back in the UK, a fleet of lorries having transported the consignment of some twelve hundred heavy tools. It was no mean feat. 'All these tools were returned without a hitch or any damage,' Frank beamed. 'Ironically the one tool we can't yet find is a pretty crucial one – the 1/32nd scale Second World War British Tommies. We've got the Germans, we've got the Japanese and the Americans, but we haven't got the Brits! So we may have to lay down a replacement. However, if that's the only one missing, it's a small price to pay.'

Taking the longer view

I asked Frank how he thought Airfix had changed since he was last at the helm.

> **AIRFIX** 'I think the overriding thing is that when I was running the business there was always a sense that we were desperately short of cash – all the time. We never had enough money to invest properly in new product development or bring in new tools from outside.
>
> 'The difference now is that under Hornby ownership we are very cash generative as a business. Hornby has an immensely strong and very widespread distribution

network around the world. We are not quite so prone to the ups and downs within a particular product sector or in a specific market and can therefore afford to take a longer view as to how we nurture the Airfix brand. I think an example of this is our ability to lay down the tooling required for the forthcoming 1/24th scale Mosquito, which is destined to be a spectacular kit and has been on the drawing board since Airfix was an independent company in the 1970s. So from a legacy point of view it will give me, and especially Trevor Snowden, a big kick.'

Now that Hornby has evolved into the residence of iconic British brands including Scalextric, Airfix and now Corgi, I asked Frank Martin how much time he can afford to spend with each brand.

'From my point of view it's frustrating because I actually don't have any time to spend on individual brands. Fortunately, we've got very good people who each know a lot more about the individual brands than I do. I only tend to get involved if there's some sort of logjam – for example, if someone's trying to get a product to meet a price point and there's a difference of opinion between the sales, marketing or product development department about what goes in and what's left out. That's when I tend to get involved in the detail of product decisions. The rest of the time we have to run it very much on a financial basis – there's a pot of money and a certain amount of it goes towards capital expenditure, some on marketing and an amount allocated for investment in stock. We have got to allocate these funds, not necessarily with the largest short-term gain in mind, but where we think the strength of the business will be enhanced for the long term by any investment.

'I think the biggest change in my role is focusing on the longer view. My job increasingly involves liaising with the City, and with shareholders, plus keeping an eye out for possible acquisitions and future strategic moves. I also have to ensure that the subsidiaries are all performing as well as they should. It's very much the responsibility of the various brand heads in marketing or product development to determine the strategies for individual brands.'

I asked Frank if he was bullish about Airfix's future prospects as a construction kit brand. 'I'm very bullish about it. For all the reasons I've just described. If you are trying to manage a construction kit brand in what is a reduced market compared to what it was 50 years ago and even 25 years ago, unless you are part of a large group in the position of benefiting from a broadly spread business portfolio, you are probably always going to need to keep an eye on the short term. The strength of Airfix as a brand is that it is as widely known now as it ever was, and the response we get from modellers about even some of our old moulds being manufactured under licence by third parties confirms this.'

As I neared the end of my time with Frank (I was always conscious that because of his responsibility for so many brands, my taking him away from the Hornby tiller, even for 40 minutes, might be detrimental to business), I started to wind up my interview by asking him a very simple question.

'Frank, what's the best part of your job?' I enquired. He replied without any hesitation:

> 'There's no doubt doing deals is great fun. It really gets the adrenalin going. I suppose being able to take a business in 2000, the Hornby business, old economy stock in the midst of the dot com revolution and a business considered long past its sell-by date – "Who needs Hornby?" – to be able to take it and prove that brands like Hornby and Scalextric still had relevance in today's world, that's enormously satisfying. That and funding what's necessary to take us into digital and cutting-edge technology, which will ensure that each brand continues to have relevance. And then actually to build a broadly based business with iconic brands which actually should ensure a much more stable business for the employees, the modellers and the collectors – all stake-holders and interested parties – all of whom can look at Hornby and the brands within it as much more stable and more confident of a prosperous long-term future, with more ongoing potential than each would have had under individual ownership.'

Finally I asked Frank if he saw the possibility of Hornby acquiring more construction kit brands to sit alongside Airfix. Perhaps even a famous North American kit manufacturer?

'You never say "never" in this business, but I think our current brand portfolio serves as the basis for development over the next three to five years. We don't actually need to add more but should focus on building the brands we've got!'

Nevertheless, given all the dramatic developments during this early phase of the 21st century, and given Mr Martin's propensity to surprise and impress both kit enthusiasts and City analysts, I would say we ain't seen nothing yet.

APPENDICES

APPENDIX 1
KIT CATALOGUE

* 1st Mould / ** 2nd Mould

1952

Golden Hind

1953

Spitfire Mk I (BTK)

1954

Santa Maria
Shannon Frigate

1955

Cutty Sark
Southern Cross
1911 Rolls-Royce
Spitfire Mk IX

1956

Gladiator Mk I
Bristol Fighter
Me BF109
Hurricane IV RP
Golden Hind
HMS *Victory*
Lysander
Westland S55
1911 Rolls-Royce
1904 Darracq
1930 Bentley
1910 Model T Ford
1905 Rolls-Royce

1957

S.E. 6 B
Fokker DR1
Sopwith Camel
Albatros DV
Stuka JU.87B

D.H. Comet
D.H. Tiger Moth
R.E.8
Hawker Hart
Great Western
Santa Maria
Shannon
Cutty Sark
Mayflower
Mosquito FB VI
Walrus Mk II
1907 Lanchester
Signal Box
Country Inn
Bungalow
General Store
Detached House

1958

MiG 15
Mustang P51D*
FW 190D*
Sky Hawk
Auster Antartic
Grumman Gosling
Revenge
Bristol Beaufighter
P38J Lightning
Saunders Roe SR53
Kiosk & Platform Steps
Booking Hall
D.H. Heron
Platform Fittings
Station Accessories
Thatched Cottage
Station Platform
Footbridge
Shop & Flat
Village Church
Windmill
Platform Figures
Wellington B111
Avro Lancaster B1

1959

Sea Hawk

Fiat G91
Mitsubishi Zero
Hawker Typhoon
Jet Provost
HMS *Cossack*
Me 110D
Coldstream Guardsman
Lifeguard Trumpeter
Yeoman of the Guard
Napoleon
Bristol Belvedere
Signal Gantry
Platform Canopy
Trackside Accessories
Level Crossing
Fencing & Gates
Black Prince
Dornier 217
Fairey Rotodyne
1926 Morris Cowley
Telephone Poles
Girder Bridge
Travelling Crane
HMS *Victorious*
Bristol Superfreighter
Sunderland

1960

Spitfire Mk IX**
Me 262
Boulton Paul Defiant
Hovercraft SR-NI
Hawker Hunter
Bristol Bloodhound
Henry VIII
Black Prince
Joan of Arc
Esso Tank Wagon
Buccaneer
HMS *Tiger*
Water Tower
Engine Shed
Railbus
Douglas Dakota
HMS *Hood*
Fokker Friendship

1961

Turntable
Vickers Vanguard
HMS *Daring*
HMS *Campbeltown*
Panther Tank
Sherman Tank
Churchill Tank
Sunbeam Rapier
Austin Healy Sprite Mk I
Renault Dauphine
Morris Minor
Richard I
Oliver Cromwell
Charles I
Mineral Wagon
Brake Van
Cattle Wagon
Cement Wagon
Sud Aviation Caravelle
HMS *Nelson*
H.P. Halifax
SS *Canberra*
D.H. Comet 4B

1962

75mm Assault Gun
Stalin 3 Tank
Avro Anson
N.A. Harvard II
Scammel Tank Transporter
1904 Mercedes
Meat Van
Refrigerated Van
Heinkel He III H-20
Hawker P.1127
Bismarck
Boeing B17G
RMS Queen Elizabeth
Omnibus B Type

1963

YAk 9D
E.E. Lightning
Starfighter

26-Pounder Gun
E-Type Jaguar
Ariel Arrow Motorcycle
Julius Caesar
Douglas Boston
Lockheed Hudson III
HMS *Devonshire*
Lowmac
Scammel Scarab
Boeing Sea Knight
HMS *Warspite*
B24J Liberator
SS *France*
Endeavour
Royal Sovereign

1964

Folland Gnat
Grumman Wildcat
Curtiss Kitty Hawk
15-ton Diesel Crane
Aichi D3 A1 'Val'
HMS *Hotspur*
Tiger Tank
Bren Gun Carrier
German Armoured Car
Mirage 3C
Stormovik
Vought F4U Corsair
Centurion Tank
Volkswagen Beetle
MG 1100
J.U. 88
HMS *Suffolk*
Prestwin Silo Wagon
VC10
Scharnhorst
Mauretania
Catalina PBY 5A
1914 Dennis Fire Engine
Revenge

1965

Me 109 G
Airacobra
Roland CII
Boomerang
DUKW
Aichi Val
Vertol 107-11
BAC III
Dinah
Fairey Firefly
Buffalo & Jeep
Boy Scout
Avenger TBM 3
HP42 Heracles
Boeing 727
HMS *Ajax*
L.C.M. 3 & Sherman

B25 Mitchell
Junkers Ju52/3M
HMS *Victory*
James Bond and Odd Job

1966

Freedom Fighter
Westland Scout
Half Track Personnel
Carrier
Matador & Gun
Arado
Thunderbolt
Westland H.A.R. MkI
Triumph TR4A
M.G.B
H.S. Trident
HMS *Ark Royal*
Concorde*
Old Bill Type Bus
Beam Engine
Short Stirling
Queen's Scout (1/12th)
B-29 Superfortress
Trevithick Loco

1967

Fiat G50
Fiesler Storch
Avro 504K
Spad VII
Hannover CLIII
WWI Tank (Mother)
Vought Kingfisher
Douglas Dauntless
MiG 21 C
  D.H.4
Free Enterprise II
88mm Gun & Tractor
Aston Martin DB5
Porsche Carrera 6
1902 De Deitrich
Triumph Herald
Black Widow
Savoia-Marchetti SM79
Boeing 314 Clipper
Heinkel HE177
1804 Steam Loco
Cutty Sark
Wallis Autogyro

1968

Hawker Demon*
(Conversion)
T.34 Tank
Hellcat
Beagle Bassett
Angel Interceptor
Skyraider

Bristol Blenheim
Helldiver
Henschel 129
Mercedes 280SL
Model T Ford 1912
Honda CB450
H.S. 125 Dominie
Grumman Duck
Fairey Battle
P.E.2.
HMS *Fearless*
Ferrari 250LM
Ford Trimotor
Ilyshin IL28
H.P. Hampden
Tirpitz
Handley Page 0/400
Queen Elizabeth II
James Bond Toyota
The Prince
F IIIA

1969

Cessna
Lee Grant Tank
Bronco OV-10A
Harrier
Focke Wulf FW189
Douglas Devastator TBD-1
RAF Emergency Set
Ford Escort
Alpha Romeo 1933
Sikorsky Sea King
H.P. Jetstream
Lunar Module
Boeing 737
Jaguar 420
Ford 3-litre GT
B.S.A. C15
B.M.W. R69
Orion Space Craft
Paddle Engine
Boeing 747
Lockheed Hercules
Apollo Saturn V
Discovery
Hawker Harrier
SR-N4 Hovercraft

1970

D.H. Chipmunk
Bristol Bulldog
HMS *Leander*
Glostor Meteor
Henschel Hs 123 A-I
Leopard Tank
B.A.C. Jaguar
Blohm & Voss BV 141
RAF Refuelling Set
Ford Capri

HMS *Iron Duke*
Russian Vostok
B.H.C. SRN4
Supermarine Spitfire MkI

1971

British Guardsman (54mm)
Saab Draken
Rommel (Ship)
HMS *Manxman*
Chieftain Tank
Panzer IV
Crusader Tank
Bond Bug 700E
British Hussar 1815 (54mm)
Saab Viggen
D.H.C. Beaver
Maxi B.M.C.
Porsche 917
Vauxhall Prince Henry 1911
N. American Vigilante
F4 Phantom
Douglas Invader
Lockheed Tristar
Saturn IB
Me BF109 (1/24th)
1930 4½-litre Bentley (1/12th)

1972

Britten Norman Islander
2nd Dragoons (54mm)
Super Mystere B2
Morris Marina
Dornier Do.17
Monty's Humber
The Wasa
P51D Mustang (1/24th)
HMS *Amazon*
42nd Highlander

1973

Cessna Bird Dog
Gazelle S.A. 341
French Imperial Guard (54mm)
HMS *Hood*
Bismarck
Puma S.A. 330
DC 9
Sam Guideline Missile
RAF Recovery Set
B26 Martin Marauder
HMS *Belfast*
Moskva
St Louis
Hurricane MkI (1/24th)
Polish Lancer 1815 (54mm)
Dakota Gunship (Conversion)
Vosper M.T.B.

Matilda Tank
Hurricane MkIIB

1974

Cherokee Arrow II
Sopwith Pup
HMS *Cossack*
Chi Ha Tank
Scorpion Light Tank
95th Rifleman (54mm)
1776 American Soldier
Lockheed Shooting Star
B.A.C. Strike Master
P51D Mustang
Spitfire V6
German Reconn. Set
French Cuirassier (54mm)
George Washington (54mm)
Republic Thunderstreak
Anne Boleyn
Queen Elizabeth I
B.A.C. Canberra
Prinz Eugen
Harrier GRI

1975

S.A. Bulldog
French Line Infantryman (54mm)
British Grenadier 1776 (54mm)
N.A. Sabre
Narvik Class Destroyer
HMS *Ark Royal*
Bugatti 35B
Short Skyvan
Panavia Tornado
Forward Command Post
Multipose 8th Army
Multipose Afrika Corps
A300B Airbus
Rommel's Half-track
Show Jumper
Crusader III Tank
German E-boat

1976

HMS *Suffolk*
French Legionnaire
Pikeman 1642
Fouga Magister
Me BF 109E
H.A. 5 22 Westland
Britten Norman Defender
    (conversion)
Lifeguard 1815 (54mm)
Bengal Lancer (54mm)
Army Lynx Helicopter
MG Magnette 1933
    French Grenadier (1/12th)
    Tyrannosaurus Rex
Triceratops

Bullfinches
FIII E (conversion)
Multipose US Marines
Multipose German Infantry
F14-A Tommcat
Concorde (update)
Junkers 87B Stuka (1/24th)

1977

Me 163
Musketeer
Prinz Eugen (1/200)
40mm Bofors Gun & Tractor
Cavalier/Roundhead
Sepecat Jaguar
Navy Lynx Helicopter
Douglas Skyray
Henschel Hs. 126
Multipose Japanese Infantry
Lee Tank (1/32nd)
Grant Tank (1/32nd)
Golden Hind
FW190 A8/F8

1978

Whirlwind Mk I
N.A. Mustang P51B
Ankylosaurus
Stegosaurus
Blue Titmouse
Multipose British Infantry
Multipose US Infantry
Star Cruiser
US Army Cargo Truck
Space Shuttle
USS Forrestal

1979

FW 190D*
Spitfire MkIA
M.B.B. 105 Helicopter
Auster A.O.P.6 (conversion)
Stuka*
Boeing Sea Knight
Hawker Hurricane
Opel Blitz & Pak 40
Dimetrodon
Corythosaurus
Spitfire VB (1/48th)
Me BF109F (1/48th)
Hurricane (1/48th)
Mirage FIC
Robins
Fokker Troopship (conversion)
S-3A Viking
F-15 Eagle
RAF Rescue Launch
Bengal Lancer (1/12th)
HMS *Bounty*
Norton Motorcycle

1980

Douglas DC10
FW190 A5 (1/24th)
MIG 23 Flogger
Alpha Jet
Pteranodon
Hawker Fury (1/48th)
Banshee F2
Cortina
Zodiac
Capri
Kingfisher
Starcruiser
17PD Anti-Tank Gun
Mosquito (1/48th)
Lancaster B.III (new kit)
Ford C900
Countach LP500s
BMW MI
BMW Motorcycle

1981

Sikorsky H.H. 53C
Focke Wulf FW 190A
Little Owl
Robins
Tyrannosaurus Rex
Triceratops
Pteranodon
Corythosaurus
The General (1/25th)
Christie Fire Engine (1/12th)
Shelby Cobra (1/16th)

1982

F-18A Hornet
F-16A Falcon
Sikorsky CH 53G Helicopter
Stuka (1/48th)
HMS *George V*
HMS *Repulse*
Ford Express
Wild Breed Mustang
Blackbird
Burnout Firebird
Squad Rod Nova
Dragster
Black Belt Firebird
Night Stalker
Ford Mark VI
Ford Express
Firebird
Cavalier
Sidewinder
Rolling Thunder
Saddle Tramp
Ground Shaker
Swamp Rat Jeep
Freedom Rider
Mount'n'Goat Jeep

Class Act
Sabre Vette
McLaren Mk 8D
Dust Devil
Bad Company
Thunder's Truck
Duke's Digger
Boss Hogg's Hauler
Cooter's Cruiser
General Lee Charger
Cooter's Tow Truck
Woodpecker
Brontosaurus
Millenium Falcon™
Snow Speeder™
Battle on Hoth™
Encounter with Yoda™
AT-AT™
Star Destroyer™
Flying Saucer

1983

X-Wing Fighter™
Slave 1™
Rebel Base™
Hunter FGA.9 (conversion)
VC10 Refuelling (conversion)
Vulcan B2
Kaman Seasprite
F 5-E Tiger
A10 Thunderbolt
F 105 Thunderchief
Grumman Prowler
OV-10D Bronco (conversion)
Sea Harrier (1/48th)
Porsche 935
Ford Escort
Supercharged Dragster
Indy Pace Car
1983 Corvette
Toyota Supra
Fall Guy Truck™
Fall Guy Camaro™

1984

Kamov Hormone A/C
Boeing 727-200 (Iberia
    conversion)
Rockwell B-1B
Lockheed U2B/D
Tornado GR1 (conversion)
Tie Interceptor™
Hughes AH-64 Apache
A-Wing Fighter™
B-Wing Fighter™
Hercules Gunship (conversion)
Tornado F2
Mil 24 Hind
Sikorsky Sea King
Westland Sea King (conversion)
HP 0/400

Knight Rider™
Martin B-57B (conversion)

1985

Tornado F2 ADV
Hardcastle & McCormick Pick-up™
Hardcastle & McCormick Coyote™
Streethawk Car™
Streethawk Bike™
C3PO™
AT-AT™
Scout Walker™
R2-D2™

1986

No new toolings

1987

No new toolings

1988

BAe T45 Goshawk (tooled but
   never released)
Harrier GR-3 (1/48th)
Lightning F3 (conversion from
   F1A)

1989

Hawker-Siddeley Buccaneer S-2B
Tornado F-3

1990

Shorts Tucano
Super Etendard
Mirage 2000
MiG 29 Fulcrum two seater
   (single-seater mould shared
   with Heller)
Su 27A Flanker two seater
   (two-seater mould shared with
   Heller)
Hughes Apache (1/48th)

1991

Harrier GR5
Harrier GR7
Boeing AWACS E-3D Sentry
   (conversion) Heller mould
Etendard (1/48th mould shared
   with Heller)

The following automobile kits are
all to 1/24th scale and though
listed they are not original Airfix
toolings:
   Ferrari 250 GTO
   Triumph TR2
   Austin-Healey Sprite

Jaguar XK-E
Jaguar E-Type
Mercedes 170
Mercedes 500K
Alfa Romeo
Bugatti T50

1992

YF-22 Lightning II
   (mould shared with Heller)
F-117A Stealth (mould shared
   with Heller)
Eurofighter EFA
Etendard IVP (1/48th)
Mirage 2000 (1/48th mould
   shared with Heller)
Hi-Tech Weapons mould
Tornado GR-1A (1/48th)
MiG 17 (1/48th ex SMER)

The following automobile kits are
all to 1/24th scale and are
Airfix/Heller shared toolings:
   Scania Eurotruck
   Refrigerated Trailer
   Semi Trailer
   Triumph TR-7
   Mercedes 300 SL
   Bugatti EB110
   Citroen 2CV
   BMW M1
   3.5 CSL
   Maserati Bora
   Boomerang
   Merak
   Ferrari Rainbow
   Ferrari Dino
   Daytona
   Lotus Esprit
   Lamborghini Jota
   Lamborghini Countach
   Lamborghini Countach LP500S
   De Tomaso Pantera
   Corvette
   Renault Alpine
   Porsche 928 S4
   Peugeot 905

1993

Avro Lancaster BIII Special
   'Dambuster' (conversion)
HMS Amazon, Leander and
   Devonshire (all 'Exocet'
   conversions of existing tools)
F-15E Strike Eagle (conversion)

1994

Gloster Javelin FAW 9/9R
   (conversion of Heller's T3)
Sepecat Jaguar GR1A
   (Heller 1/48th)

H.S. Buccaneer S2B (1/48th)

1995

H.S. Buccaneer S2, S2C, S2D,
   SMK50 (1/48th)
Tornado GR1B
   (1/48th conversion)
D.H. Mosquito NF. XIX/J.30
   (conversion)

1996

Supermarine Spitfire F22/24
   (1/48th)
Supermarine Seafire FR46/47
   (1/48th)

1997

'Battle Zone'
('Airfix Junior'):
   Night Owl
   Black Widow
   Phantom
   Eclipse
   Crusader
   Liberator
   Gladiator
   Vigilante

1998

Mayflower – 'Ships in Bottles'
   (ex-MB)
Cutty Sark – 'Ships in Bottles'
   (ex-MB)
Charles Morgan Whaler 'Ships in
   Bottles' (ex-MB)
Gulf Porsche 917 (1/32nd)
Ferrari 250 LM (1/32nd)
Vampire FB5 (ex Heller)
English Electric Lightning F-2A/F6
   (1/48th)
English Electric Lightning F-1/F-
   1A/F-2/F-3 (1/48th)

1999

Wallace & Gromit Aeroplane
Wallace & Gromit Motorbike &
   Sidecar
B-17 G Flying Fortress
Corsair F4U-1A (1/48th)
Focke Wulf 190A-8 (1/48th)
P51-D Mustang (1/48th)
MiG 23 (1/144th)
F-20 Tiger Shark (1/144th)
General Dynamics F-16 XL
   (1/144th)
F-4E Phantom II (1/144th)
MiG 21 (1/144th)
Fiat G91 Frecce Tricolori
Boeing 747-400 (1/300th)

Boeing 777 (1/300th)
Boeing AWACS Sentry
Eurofighter Typhoon

2000

BAE Harrier GR3 / AV-8A / AV-8S
   (1/24th)

POLYBAGGED KITS
Saab Viggen (1/144th)
F-104 Starfighter (1/144th)
Supermarine Spitfire Mk.VIIIc
   (1/48th)
Grumman F6F-3 Hellcat (1/48th)
Curtiss Kittyhawk Mk.Ia (1/48th)

2001

MODIFICATIONS
Westland Navy Lynx HMA.8
Lancaster B.I Special
Supermarine Spitfire Mk.Vb
   (1/24th)

HELLER MOULDS
McLaren F.1 (1/43rd)
Williams F.1 (1/43rd)
Citroen Xsara T4 WRC (1/43rd)
Subaru Impreza (1/43rd)
Peugeot 206 WRC
Citroen Xsara T4 WRC (1/24th)
Peugeot 206 WRC (1/24th)

POLYBAGGED KITS
Dornier do217 Mistel
Chinook
Douglas DC3 Dakota
C130 Hercules
Rav 4 (1/24th)
MGB (1/24th)
Aston Martin DB5 (1/24th)

2002

MODIFICATIONS
Spitfire Mk.Vc / Seafire IIIc
   (1/48th)
BAE Sea Harrier FRS-1 (1/24th)

HELLER MOULDS
Sepecat Jaguar GR3 (1/48th)
Dassault Super Etendard (1/48th)
Ford Focus (1/43rd)
Mitsubishi WRC (1/43rd)
Mitsubishi WRC (1/24th)
Subaru Impreza WRC (1/24th)
Honda 500cc (1/24th)
Suzuki 500cc (1/24th)
Yamaha 500cc (1/24th)

POLYBAGGED KITS
Saab JA-37 Viggen (1/48th0

2003

NEW MOULDS
BAE Red Arrows Hawk (1/48th)
BAE Hawk 100 Series (1/48th)

MODIFICATIONS
D.H. Mosquito NF.30 (1/48th)
D.H. Mosquito B Mk.XVI/PR.XVI
  (1/48th)

HELLER MOULDS
N.A. F-86F Sabre
Subaru Ev2 Asphalt (1/43rd)
Ford Focus WRC (1/24th)
Peugeot 206 WRC Safari (1/24th)
Honda 4 Stroke (1/24th)
Honda 500cc NSR500 (1/12th)
Yamaha 500cc Y2RM1 (1/12th)

2004

NEW MOULDS
England Football Stars Set 1
  (1/12th)
England Football Stars Set 2
  (1/12th)
England Football Stars Set 3
  (1/12th)

MODIFICATIONS
Panavia Tornado GR4 / 4A
  (1/72nd)
Panavia Tornado F.3 / EF.3
  (1/48th)

HELLER MOULDS
Sukhoi Su-27 Flanker B (1/72nd)
Concorde (1/72nd)
LCVP Landing Craft (1/72nd)
Willys Jeep (1/72nd)
GMC Truck (1/72nd)

POLYBAGGED KITS
Boeing AH-64D Apache Longbow
  (1/72nd)
Bell AH-1T Sea Cobra (1/72nd)
Challenger II Tank (1/35th)
Abrams M1A2 Tank (1/35th)
GMC DUKW (1/35th)

2005

NEW MOULDS
BAC TSR-2 (1/72nd)
Supermarine Spitfire Mk.IX /
  Mk.XVIe(1/48th)

MODIFICATIONS
Supermarine Spitfire Mk.Vc
  (1/72nd)
N.A. P-51K Mustang (1/24th)
Sherman 'Crab' Tank (1/76th)
Churchill 'Crocodile' Tank (1/76th)

HELLER MOULDS
Saab S/J-29 Tunnan (1/72nd)
Kriegsmarine Set (1/400th)

POLYBAGGED KITS
N.A. T-6G Texan (1/72nd)

2006

NEW MOULDS
Wallace & Gromit Anti-Pesto Van
  (1/12th scale)

MODIFICATION
Britten Norman Islander (1/72nd)

HELLER MOULDS
D.H. Dragon Rapide (1/72nd)
Lockheed Super Constellation
  (1/72nd)
HMS *Hood* (1/400th)
HMS *King George V* (1/400th)
Scharnhorst & *Gneisenau*
  (1/400th)
Bismarck & *Tirpitz* (1/400th)

2007

NEW MOULDS
H.S. Nimrod MR-2P (1/72nd)
RNLI Severn Class Lifeboat
  (1/72nd)
Doctor Who 'Welcome Aboard'
  (1/12th)

MODIFICATIONS
Supermarine Spitfire Mk.I
  (1/48th)

2008

NEW MOULDS
BAE Red Arrows Hawk (1/72nd)
Supermarine Spitfire Mk.IXc
  (1/72nd)
BAE Hawk 128 / 132 (1/72nd)
English Electric Canberra B (I) 8
  (1/72nd)
English Electric Canberra PR.9
  (1/72nd)
English Electric Canberra B.2 /
  B.20 (1/48th)
English Electric Canberra B (I) 8
  (1/48th)
English Electric Canberra PR.9
  (1/48th)
Martin B-57B Canberra (1/48th)
BAC TSR-2 (1/48th)
Shaun the Sheep with Landrover
  (1/12th)
Shaun the Sheep with Tractor
  (1/12th)
Doctor Who 'Dalek Encounter'
  (1/12th)

Above: Multipose WWII German Infantry
Below: Airfix 1/32 Desert Combat Pack from 1976
Bottom: Airfix Enamel tin 1970s

MODIFICATIONS
Gloster Gladiator
H.S. Buccaneer RAF + Navy
Westland Sea King HAS.5
Fokker F.27 Friendship
Supermarine Spitfire Mk.XVIe
  (1/48th)
(Airfix Club Special)
Sherman 'Calliope' Tank (1/76th)
Matilda 'Hedgehog' (1/76th)
Churchill Bridge Layer (1/76th)

Ex JB Models (all 1/76th):
  LWB Landrover (Soft Top)
  M113 U.S. ACAV
  LWB Landrover (Hard Top)
  Saladin Mk.II Armoured Car
  Bedford Mk.4 Tonne Truck
  M113 Fire Support Version
  Saracen APC Mk.1/2/3

Bedford MK Tactical Aircraft
  Refueller
Vickers Light Tank
Landrover 1 Tonne FC Truck
  G.S. Body
British M119 105mm Light
  Field Gun
Landrover 1 Tonne FC
  Ambulance

POLYBAGGED KITS
Fairey Fulmar Mk.I / II (1/72nd)
Hawker Sea Fury (1/72nd)
Hawker Tempest V (1/72nd)
Gloster Meteor F.8 (1/72nd)
Boeing AH-64 Apache Longbow
  (1/72nd)
Boeing Chinook (1/72nd)
Horsa Glider (1/72nd)
Vickers Wellington Mk.IA / IC
  (1/72nd)
Focke Wulf Mistel (1/72nd)
HMS *Montgomery* (1/400th)
HMNoS *St Albans* (1/400th)
WWII British Infantry (1/72nd)

2009

NEW MOULDS
De Havilland Mosquito NF.II /
  FB.VI (1/24th)

Above: Roy Cross original art for 1968 Captain Scarlet Angel Interceptor. Below: Airfix studio shot of assembled Angel Interceptor kits

APPENDIX 2

Airfix – What's hot and what's not

It's an old but true adage that the true value of something depends on what someone is prepared to pay for it. This is certainly true for those collecting Airfix kits, because despite regular reissues of models produced in exactly the same way as their predecessors, true fans are prepared to pay top-dollar for an original kit, even if it's in a tatty box. A case in point is Airfix's 1/24th scale James Bond Autogyro model. Although it was re-released in the 1990s for under £10, collectors were still prepared to pay £350 for a 1967 original. There are some truly rare kits, however, models for which the original mould tool has either been lost or damaged. These include Airfix's very first replica, the 1949 Ferguson Tractor. Other especially collectable kits include the original Spitfire (BTK), SS *France*, the 1/72nd SAM Guideline Missile set and another James Bond kit, the 1/24th scale Aston Martin DB5.

APPENDIX 3

Top tips for a better kit

This book is not just aimed at collectors. I know many modellers, the famous Mat Irvine amongst them, who buy models to construct, not covet. To be honest, though, I would think carefully about building a very rare kit. After all, there are plenty of old models which are still around in their thousands and can be constructed without any fears that you might be destroying an heirloom.

Before you do construct a kit, to get the most out of it, there are one or two preparations that will help result in a better replica:

Remove items from the sprue or runner to which they are attached by cutting them with a craft knife not by snapping them off. Use a file and some wet and dry paper to remove any mould lines or ejector-pin marks and use liquid adhesive, which can be applied more sparingly than the more viscous tube variety. Then let everything dry for at least a day. When painting, start with the lighter colours first (don't forget to paint visible interior details before you assemble fuselages or attach a car's body work to the chassis. Leave to dry for at least a day.

Original Roy Cross art for Airfix's Beach Buggy (1972) – a replica of Ronald Sharman's Bugle Buggy

Decals, or transfers, stick best to gloss surfaces. You can spray a matt-finished kit with a thin coat of gloss varnish, apply the markings and then finish with a topcoat of matt varnish, or you can use one of the proprietary decal softeners available.

When complete, kits are best kept free from dust, in a glass cabinet or under a transparent plastic display case.

APPENDIX 4

Personal favourites – Airfix classics

And now some real personal indulgence: A short list of some of my all-time Airfix favourites. Because I made it so many times in my youth, the classic 1/72nd scale Spitfire Mk IX which first appeared in 1955 is a particular favourite. To be honest, though, I probably only ever made the 1960 version of this kit – designer John Edwards improved it five years after its first release as soon as he had better learnt the intricacies of plastic injection moulding.

I'm also very fond of 1964's 1/72nd scale PBY-5A Catalina, the Angel Interceptor from 1968, 1974's 54mm French Cuirassier and the marvellously large 1/24th scale Junkers JU-87B Stuka from 1976.

More recently, I am a great fan of Trevor Snowden's 1/48th scale E.E. Lightnings (1998) and his 1/72nd scale TSR 2 (2006).

INDEX